Deliverance
of the Gleanings

---

fills the expectations and needs of all who seek honest Biblical answers for the future of a world in rebellion.

D. G. BELL

Printed in Victoria, Canada

Cover: an original oil painting by Colin Pringle, Master Artist

All Bible verses quoted are from the King James Version of the Bible

National Library of Canada Cataloguing in Publication

Bell, D. G. (Donald G.)
 Deliverance of the gleanings / D.G. Bell.
 ISBN 1-55369-546-1
 1. Tribulation (Christian eschatology) I. Title.
BT888.B44 2002   236'.9   C2002-902139-1

TRAFFORD

This book was published *on-demand* **in cooperation with Trafford Publishing.**
On-demand publishing is a unique process and service of making a book available for retail sale to the public taking advantage of on-demand manufacturing and Internet marketing.
On-demand publishing includes promotions, retail sales, manufacturing, order fulfilment, accounting and collecting royalties on behalf of the author.

Suite 6E, 2333 Government St., Victoria, B.C. V8T 4P4, CANADA
Phone   250-383-6864   Toll-free   1-888-232-4444 (Canada & US)
Fax   250-383-6804   E-mail   sales@trafford.com
Web site   www.trafford.com   TRAFFORD PUBLISHING IS A DIVISION OF TRAFFORD HOLDINGS LTD.
Trafford Catalogue #02-0359   www.trafford.com/robots/02-0359.html

10   9   8   7   6   5   4

DEDICATION

I first want to dedicate this work to my Gracious Lord and to my faithful and patient revealer, the Holy Spirit, who led me though those seven years of the tribulation, and without whose perspicacity and perspicuity this book would never have been written. And secondly, to my loving and patient wife Nadine, who graciously shared me with the computer through the years it took to develop this book.

Deliverance of the Gleanings

TABLE OF CONTENTS

With the waning use of prophets to disseminate His Holy word, the Lord commissions the prophet Daniel to record in a book the certainty of the judgments and their future location in time   Now it might have been the Lord's intention in the beginning to limit the information given to Daniel to just one revelation, but years later He gave Daniel four additional revelations and added more weighty information about the tribulation period.

This chapter deals with the first three of the five revelations, and brings to light the Lord's unbelievable plans for extraditing Satan from the heavens and sending him to earth on a dual mission. We are also introduced to the Anti-Christ who becomes involved in the Devil's mission. So it is no wonder that the two were destined to finally meet in Jerusalem on the final day of the Jewish tribulation period.

With this added bounty of sensitive information, the fourth and fifth visions became considerably more complex in nature and in fact, nearly overwhelmed Daniel.

In this chapter, we pool the information from all five of the revelations, just as the Lord had done with Daniel, in order to portray one panoramic view of the whole Jewish judgment period of three and a half years, encompassing it's beginning and its ending with the surprise desolation of Israel. Also included is a complete dozier on a man whom we assume is the Anti-Christ, however he is seen through the writings of Daniel as being the leader of a ten-nation alliance in the end-times.

This chapter continues the saga of this man who not only initiates the judgment period but remains the moving force through the whole period. Only at the last moment do we discover that he has a co-conspirator in his operations who is none other than Satan. But the true feature of these revelations to Daniel is the capability of recognizing, not only the definite signs of this rapidly approaching judgment period, but also the predetermined pattern that it will follow as well as the man in charge.

Chapter 4. **The Divided Tribulation Period**.............Page 76

God has always planned for the Jews to be punished apart from the rest of the world and in their own place and time. And He reveals the secret of the partitioning in the fourth revelation to Daniel. This incredible division determines the set-up and adjudication of the judgments that is realized in the book of Revelation by the different names given to the two groups of punishments. This is an extremely important feature of the tribulation and must be recognized as such by the reader.

Chapter 5. **The Heir Apparent**.................................Page 84

Daniel's lengthy biography of the Anti-Christ reveals the surprising evidence of this man's ancestry that traces his lineage back to an ancient line of relatively unknown Syrian Kings, which tends to legitimize his claim to the present Syrian throne. But rather than accept that inheritance he goes to Jerusalem in search of his destiny. Ultimately, the road leads him to his real inheritance, which lies in the kingship of the world.

Chapter 6. **The Fourth Trumpet Judgment**............Page 105

Because of an incident that happened in Israel during the judgment period, the Arabs became incensed over a rumored Jewish proposal to build their new Temple on the site of the destroyed Mosque, and decided to go to war with Israel. As a result of this rumor, a third of the population of Israel will be destroyed.

In this chapter we investigate what really happened in that fourth judgment that not only brought about the shortening of the days and nights but brought a sudden increase in the earth's rotational speed, which in turn caused world-wide catastrophes through earthquakes, volcanic eruptions, tidal wave formations and terrible storms. All of this tremendous destruction around the earth also included the demolition of the Muslim Mosque on Mt. Zion.

Chapter 7. **The Pretender**...Page 112

With this man having such an important role in the Tribulation, we look at Daniel's record of the background of the European Union President, a.k.a the Anti-Christ. In delving into historical records concerning his ancestral heritage, and find out that his ancestors descended from the Jewish tribe of Dan, who was the fifth son of the twelve sons of Jacob. And it's interesting to learn how his destiny as the leader of the European Union fulfilled the ancient prophetic 'blessing' of his father. We also get a glimpse of why he was chosen by the Lord to perform this task, just as Judas was selected for his task of betrayal.

Chapter 8. The Harvest..Page 118

On the very day that the judgment period begins, the 'harvesting' process of the believers, which has been going on for the past several months, comes to a dramatic conclusion in the wonderful event called the Rapture, when in a moment of time the believers are taken out of the way of the punishments that will follow on the earth.

In this harvesting process there are four actions that must precede the Rapture event, all of which can only begin after the European Union President has been installed. This chapter delineates those actions and explains their the function and purpose in the harvesting process of the believers. Here the European leader and the Lord have dual roles in the program to separate the believers from the non-believers in the great apostasy in the months prior to the Rapture.

Chapter 9. The Seals on the Scroll.......................... Page 132

Because the seven 'Seal Opening' events happened to be recorded just prior to the judgments in the book of Revelation, they are considered by many Christians to be in conjunction with the actual judgments. Here this fallacy is investigated, and it seems that the first four of these 'Seal openings,' often referred to as the 'four horsemen' are actually witnessing spirits of the Lord, while two other three serve as information repositories.

Chapter 10. The Seventh Seal....................................Page 143

This seal opening is dealt with separately because its removal from the scroll allows the scroll to be opened and the judgment period to commence. However, in investigating the 'silence' surrounding this opening, it becomes apparent that its opening puts into operation other startling events, including the Rapture.

Chapter 11 The Beginning.......................................Page 149

Now the actual Tribulation begins and this chapter picks up on the opening round of punishments to be adjudged upon the land of Israel. The scene begins with the Peace covenant signing in Jerusalem, with the Union President presiding over the ceremonies, and follows through the progression of the first four punishments disposed upon the land of Israel for sustaining the rebellious people. There are relatively few casualties from these plagues but tremendous property damage is sustained. This is a tremendously informative chapter that explains in detail the successive judgments of two volcanic eruptions, a wayward meteor which strikes the earth in upper Israel, and concludes with the terribly destructive earth shaking of the fourth judgment.

Chapter 12. **The Plague of Demons**

Following the four plagues upon the land, it is now time for the punishment of the people, and they are forewarned by angelic messengers that their punishments are imminent. The fifth judgment, which is defined as the first of three 'woes,' is a demonic plague that will be put upon the Jews, and when it progresses the way that it has been prophesied by the Lord and yields the deaths that have been predestined, one third of the Jewish population in Israel will perish from starvation before the plague runs its five month course. Here we follow the course of that plague in Israel and learn the true facts about it and its degradation of the people.

Chapter 13 **Falling by the Sword**

Following the demonic plague, there was little respite for the weary Jews before enemy Arab forces disregarded the peace covenant and invaded Israel. This was destined to be the sixth Trumpet judgment upon the Jews, and like the previous plague of the demons it was prophesied to further punish the Jews by diminishing their population by another third. It's a terrible situation for both the Jews and the Arabs who also suffer in equal numbers to the Jews. Here the author traces the history of the Arab's 'perpetual' hatred against the Jews, and how that unique feature was the determining factor in the Lord's choice of the Arabs as His instruments of punishment in the sixth judgment war.

Chapter 14. **The Burden Bearer**

Before the seventh judgment is brought to bear upon the Jews, there is a short interlude in which the Lord makes a change in the conveyance of the judgments. From here on in, as it is explained, John will take on the responsibility of discharging the remaining punishments rather than just being a recorder of them. His first assignment is to call forth Satan from the pit where he had been confined since his removal from heaven. Now the union between the deceased Anti-Christ and the Devil takes place which initiates the seventh Trumpet judgment on the Jews.

This chapter follows the saga of the 'Beast' of Revelation, from Satan's emergence from the pit, through his moment of incarnation into the body of the slain President, and to his enforcement of the desolation process against the Jews. All of these things happen on the last day of the Indignation. According to John, the seventh king's dominion was destined to be short, but he will be given a new life as the eighth king.

The period of the judgments on the Jews is over and the 'great tribulation' has entered its first day. From this point we again pick up on the odyssey of the Beast. With his mission in Israel accomplished, he moves on to greener and greater pastures to become the leader of the western world and effectively of the whole world.

At this juncture the Vial judgments are being held up for two years while the Beast makes his attempts to drive the new believers into his camp. The Beast has been given wide latitude in his choice of methods for his campaign against the new believers in Christ, as well as the Jews around the world, to pressure them into making a choice between submission to him or accepting death. These pressure tactics include the familiar edicts of 'worshipping his image' and taking his 'personal mark' upon their bodies. This two-year period is the time allotted for these new 'believers of the second chance' to gain their Deliverance in the 'gleanings of the harvest.'

In previous chapters there was one area of this man's life that wasn't brought out, and that was the period of his relatively short career from his installation as the European Union President until he enters into Israel following the Union's expeditionary intervention into the Arab-Israeli war. This covers a period of roughly four years and it's during the first several months of this time that he endeavors to drive a wedge between the believers in the Christian fellowships. But the Church is given a break when he assumes the responsibility of developing a viable peace covenant between the Arab factions and Israel. Peace comes into being but it is short lived. The Arab forces invade Israel and the Union is forced to send in troops to quell the fighting. Following that action the President goes to Israel to ensure the peace and is slain a month later.

        This chapter gives complete coverage and understanding of the first
six Vial judgments laid upon the Gentile nations of the world during a
time which is commonly referred to as 'the great tribulation.' Each
punishment is examined for its purpose, along with the preparations
being made by the Beast for the coming battle of Armageddon. There
are many surprises in this section for the reader who has normally
witnessed a dearth of information about these plagues.

        John was forestalled in finalizing his tribulation record to add an
account dealing with a certain noble city that had been singled out for
annihilation. It wasn't because of her architectural beauty or the
particular sagaciousness of the inhabitants that she was selected for
notoriety, but for the distinction of allowing herself to become the
earthly stronghold of the enemy of God. Two full chapters of the book
of Revelation deal with the rise and fall of this great city of Rome, and
this chapter explores the reasoning behind the total destruction of this
city and just how God accomplishes it.

        John closes his record on the judgments just as I do with the
seventh Vial judgment which is that now famous battle of Armageddon
that takes place on the last day of the judgment period. This day has
been called 'the Day of the Lord.' It has been an incredible journey
that must have an end, but meanwhile we have explored all of the
avenues of the end-time prophecies, and have ended on this blue note
of the vengeance of God. From this battle, the Lord emerges a victor
over Satan, the Anti-Christ, and the millions of weary followers of the
Beast. Hopefully, the reader is left with an indelible panorama of what
the Bible called a 'time of trouble, such as never was since there was a
nation even to that same time.'

DELIVERANCE
of the Gleanings

INTRODUCTION

This author sits in the shadow of the works of two mighty men of God whose noble and faithful efforts reproduced the two most masterful books on the subject of the end-times. Without question, the writings of Daniel and the Apostle John are brilliant, resourceful, extremely informative, and executed exactly as the Lord wanted them, but for one reason or another, most of His communications with these men have continued to elude many readers. And it is my hope that this book will bring more insight into the awesome visions and revelations that were delivered to these men.

As you would expect, the subject of this book is the judgment period of the end-times, commonly referred to as the tribulation period, which typically both Biblical authors have hypothesized will occur in the present era. Our responsibility is to evaluate the veracity of that premise, and make adjustments in our lives accordingly

In conjunction with that, let me say that the Lord has promised that blessings and deliverance would be bestowed upon all those who choose to follow Him, but He has also promised that punishments will be poured upon all those who fail to choose wisely, and it is those punishments that are being defined and explained in this book.

But tucked away in the middle of all of these wonderments, is a little recognized revelation that sets forth the one extenuating factor in the adjudication of the punishments. It tells of a surprising second opportunity for an individual to obtain salvation and deliverance which will be offered by our Merciful God immediately prior to the feared great tribulation. This second opportunity for redemption is referred to as the Deliverance of the Gleanings, but you should be warned, that unlike the olive branch of forgiveness and redemption that is presently being offered without any sacrifice on your part, other than that of your will, the deliverance that takes place down the road will carry the very heavy price tag of a personal life sacrifice.

The story of the tribulation begins with God's first announcement to Moses of a future time of judgment that would come upon His people, the Jews.

"When your people are in tribulation, and all these things are come upon you, even in the latter days, if you will turn to the Lord your God,... He will not forsake you nor destroy you, nor forsake the covenant of your fathers." (Deut. 4:30,31)

This warning of a future judgment was a continuing theme of the ancient prophets from the time of the Exodus until the Babylonian captivity, with the presumption that as long as this verbal sword of punishment was left hanging over the heads of His people they were more prone to being kept in line. But with their excursion into servitude in Babylon, which came about because of the people's rebellion against God's leadership, changes were about to be made.

God made the determination that henceforth the people would be held accountable for examining their lives through the written word rather than through the voices of the prophets, and with that in mind He commissioned Daniel to put the promise of the judgment period down in writing along with its parameters of the time and place in the future. When it came to defining the judgments' future location however, the Lord chose to correlate its presence with certain other definable happenings on earth, rather than just picking out some random year in the future, which He certainly could have done, but it would have defeated the purpose of the judgments, which was to corral the behavior of His people toward Him.

With Daniel's book completed, further communication about the judgment period ended, until Jesus brought up the subject in a conversation with His Disciples, at a time when He was answering their specific questions about the end-times. There is no question that Jesus knew Daniel's writings were sufficient in themselves to pinpoint the exact location of the future judgment period, that is, relative to certain events which would come to pass, but He also knew the impatience and vicissitudes of men, so He added a few of His own signs concerning world situations that would arise prior to

12

the judgment period. Unfortunately, those signs have more often than not, been taken for the judgments themselves, possibly because of His remarks about the scourge of 'wars and rumors of wars,' and upheavals within nations that would become increasingly prevalent in the Middle Eastern and European regions just before the dawn of the judgment period. Which signs have already become quite obvious and have inadvertently raised concerns among all peoples that if we are not already in the end-times embattlement, then surely we must be standing on the doorstep.

And in these uncertain days the writings of Daniel, more so than any other book on the subject, can supply the reader with definitive answers as to what must come next in the Near East and the European regions. However, because his writings relate almost exclusively to events within the nation of Israel and in the lives of the Jewish people during that period, they are constrained to exposing situations that will arise in the Near East after a formal peace agreement has been negotiated between the Arab nations and Israel.

Of the many vision and revelations given to Daniel over his lifetime, only five have been recorded that actually deal with the tribulation period and propound the future era when that period would occur. The first of these five revelations is the familiar vision of a great statue or image, in which different areas of the body were intended to represent the four great Gentile empires that would reign successively on the earth and hold dominion over the Jews. This so-called period of the 'times of the Gentiles' began in the contemporary era of Daniel, which would be circa BC 600, and will continue until the second coming of Christ and the setting up of His Kingdom.

The second of his five revelations took a different approach in its identification of these same four Empires. They would be depicted by four totally different beasts, with special cognizance given to the fourth beast which is said to have ten horns on its head. These ten horns were intended to represent a rather loosely unified 'multinational empire' that evolve out of the ashes of the fourth empire. This alliance of ten nations is not being depicted as an Empire, however Daniel portrays it as the predominant world power in the era in which the tribulation period occurs, as well as when

Christ returns at the close of that period. There are also signs in this second revelation which tend to pinpoint a specific year within the era of that alliance when the tribulation will begin.

But in this second and succeeding revelations, the Lord has made a major shift in His purpose for giving the revelations. Where His prior objective was to outline the future position of the tribulation period, that objective now becomes secondary to what will be an amazing exposure of God's secret plan to cleanse the heavens of all vestiges of sin, by removing Satan and his myriad of angels from their ageless heavenly abode and casting them all into the bowels of the earth. So the outline of this incredible plan now becomes dominant feature of the revelations.

But don't be misled into believing that this plan just proposes an aggravated imposition of the **spirit** of Satan on the peoples of the earth. This will be the actual transfer of Satan to the earth for a three and a half year period, where he will abide in bodily form among the people, similar to the conditions that the Lord experienced when He dwelt on the earth centuries ago.

This inconceivable extradition, which is intended to take place at the mid-point of the tribulation period, is the first time such a Divine edict has been announced in scripture since the Messiah's coming was prophesied by Isaiah some three millennia ago. But what makes this announcement about Satan so astonishing, is that subsequent to his incarceration in the depths of the earth, he will be called forth from the pit to perform a mighty work for the Lord on the earth.

For those who may not be aware of it, the Lord's original plan was to have Daniel write a proclamation for the posterity of the Jews, informing them of His intended future Divine judgment in reparation for their rebellion against Him. That part of the plan hasn't changed. The Lord will still furnish information on the judgments' future location, but with the added feature of Satan's extradition to earth, the focus of the revelations will be on that element rather than on the positioning factor.

For some reason the Lord withheld the purpose for Satan's earthly incursion from Daniel, choosing instead to reveal it to the Prophet Ezekiel, who would go on to describe the process of the judgments during the tribulation period, when two-thirds of the Jewish population in Israel will suffer death through plagues, famines, and war, with the remaining third of the population being expelled from their homeland in 'the great desolation of Israel.'

This desolation takes place literally on the last day of the Jewish tribulation, and for reasons of His own the Lord has determined that the success of the desolation depends upon the unique capabilities of Satan, who must somehow be transferred to the earth and embodied within a human frame. This is where Daniel comes into the picture.

Through the last four of the five visions and revelations Daniel will be given the basic outline of the plan for bringing Satan down to earth and incorporating him into an accommodating human frame, or 'human assistant' as the case may be. This person must be a man who is willing to arrive on the scene well ahead of time and prepare the stage for the Devil's entry, which in this case means he will be the one who will forfeit his body at the proper time for the Devil's needs

Because of this individual's importance to the whole operation, a major portion of Daniel's visions and revelations are given over to supplying information about this volunteer, in preparation for that fateful day when the inevitable happens. Thus we find Daniel's journal tracing the course of this man from the time of his inauguration as President of the European Union until he makes that fateful trip to Jerusalem where he and the Devil cross paths. When the meeting between the two takes place, their individual personalities suddenly merge into a single entity, and from that point on, Daniel's journal projects only the sinister offerings of this single 'personage,' whose mission is to persecute and force the hapless Jews from their homeland. Incidentally, this creature later becomes known to us as the Beast,

However, well before that historic meeting in Jerusalem takes place you can sense in Daniel's writings the heightening suspense of this coming meeting, as each revelation focuses more distinctly on that climactic moment when Satan arrives.

The story really begins with the President's flight to Jerusalem

15

where he stayed for nearly a month before his untimely death by an assassin's blade that brutally cut short a gifted political career. This happened just three days before Satan was to due to make his appearance.

But our story doesn't end there. The Apostle John follows up on Daniel's fascinating stories of Satan and the slain President, who by this time is being recognized as the Anti-Christ, and he continues with his own story featuring this unique creature that evolved from the melding of the two.

John is the one who actually tagged the name 'Beast' on the creature, and in recounting the story of this 'Beast' from Daniel's journal he harks back to the President's assassination, intimating that it was his death that triggered the chain of events that brought Hell down to earth.

He goes on to describe an awesome battle that takes place in heaven around the same time, when the 'turn-coat' angelic forces of Satan were so far out numbered by the loyal angelic armies of the Lord that Satan was defeated, and he and his angelic band were cast unceremoniously into the earth to await a future judgment. Moreover, John wrote, on the third day following the President's death an equally amazing thing happened before the eyes of an unsuspecting world.

In the midst of his own funeral service, the former President's life was miraculously returned to him through the successful transfer of Satan into the lifeless shell, which gave living proof that the plans for the transfer had succeeded

John continues to pursue the terrible actions of this Beast, who, within hours of his investiture turns his wrath upon the two witnesses who had previously been sent down from God to warn the Jews of Satan's coming. He had the two witnesses murdered on the street in front of his headquarters for all to see, and almost immediately after the slaying he went to the plaza beneath the Western Wall in Jerusalem, where he loosed a fiery tirade of epithets against the Lord God and His anointed. Before his anger subsided he also spit forth the command for the Jews to be expelled from their homeland in the awesome third Diaspora.

The issuance of these terrible words and Beast's actions that

16

day in the desecration of the Holy place, were in the back of Jesus' mind when He said;

"When you see the 'abomination of desolation standing in the Holy place,,, flee into the mountains." (Matt. 24:15)

Three days later, with his mission in Israel accomplished; the odyssey of the Beast takes him back to Brussels where he picks up the mantle of world authority. With that power in his hands he sets his sights on his second task of ridding the earth of all believers in the Lord and followers of the Creator. His insatiable and relentless lust for worship and power continues to drive him until he ultimately brings a holocaust upon all mankind before he too is destroyed by his own wickedness.

However, in this maelstrom of terror and devastation, there is one solitary break in the storm clouds, which occurs when our Merciful God shines a bright ray of hope on the earth. He comes down with an offer of a reprieve from the tragedies of the coming great tribulation and one more golden opportunity for redemption and deliverance for all those who have not taken the mark of the Beast nor worshipped his image.

Woven into this awesome account of the Beast, is a vivid description of seven judgments that will be put on the Jews and the land of Israel. These are uniquely missing from Daniel's journal. There is also a detailed account of the judgments that will be put on the Gentiles during the great tribulation, so that ultimately, what we find being revealed in the journals of both of these faithful prophets, is not two disjointed accounts of the tribulation period, but one astonishing continuous diary of the almost daily events that will take place during those seven years. And all of it set in relationship to the wicked deeds of the Beast, whose most important tasks for the Lord during this period will be to deliver the Jewish remnant into their earthly sanctuary and the believers of the second chance into their heavenly sanctuary.

While reviewing the book of Daniel, I became aware of interpretative compromises that have been made in some end-time prophecies by otherwise well meaning translators. Some of these irregular interpretations originate with Christian educators who

17

strongly believe that God's over-riding attribute is Love, and they express anxiety if He is associated with any concept of revengefulness or retaliation. To these folks, it becomes less intimidating to their faith if they remove God from the picture and paint the tribulation in broad terms as being a spiritual test of faith that Christians, and Christianity as a whole, must go through before the Lord returns.

But there may be another more perplexing reason for the many diverse interpretations, which strangely enough, looks at the possibility of the end-time prophecies having been sealed from man's understanding. In this aspect, the scriptures tell us that one of the Lord's commissions was to "seal-up the visions and the prophecies of the end-times," and if indeed this sealing has been accomplished by Him, it may be that in an indirect way the Lord is responsible for the wide discrepancies of interpretations. (Dan. 9:24)

It's entirely possible that sometime in the past, and in some distinct way, the Lord took the initiative of clouding mankind's interpretive abilities through some incomprehensive infringement on the mind, whereby all of the vital aspects of the visions and prophecies of the end-times have been effectively sealed from understanding. Thus, an individual can assuredly read the prophecies but be totally oblivious to their meaning.

While I admit that this is a provocative idea, there is a legitimate scriptural basis for this supposition. His own Chosen people experienced the same type of obliteration of their understanding of the scriptures. It happened at a time when the spiritual condition of the people had deteriorated so badly that God finally decided to do something about it. He performed what is described in the scriptures as 'a marvelous and wonderful work among His people.' And because of it, 'their wisdom of the scriptures suddenly perished 'and their 'understanding was hidden as the words of a book that is sealed.' It was as though 'He had poured upon them the spirit of deep sleep, and the closing of their eyes.' Isaiah tells us. (Isa. 29:10-16)

How the Lord accomplished this feat is not explained, but its effect on the people was catastrophic. It reduced their rational capability to the point where they could neither read nor understand their own scriptures, nor could they comprehend the oral recitation by the prophets. This total "blindness" to their scriptures came over all of the Jews at the same time. (Rom.11: 25-27)

This "sealing" of the scriptures is also mentioned in Rev. 22:10, which speaks of the Lord requesting John, to; **"Seal not the sayings"** of the prophecy of the book, which would indicate that the *reading* of the book was not to be hindered. However, the *" sayings "* does not necessarily mean *"understanding,"* as the two capabilities are as different in their meaning as 'knowledge' and 'wisdom.' But because the Lord introduced "sealing" into His request, it seems to indicate that John must have intended to seal the book in some fashion, which he did by the way, when he used some rather abstruse terms. But it is quite possible that the Lord was waiting for John to complete his work so that He could fulfill the specific task that was required of Him, which was to **"seal up the vision and the prophecy."** (Dan.9: 24)

It is interesting to note that the word "vision" was included with the prophecy, for it was through the visions of Daniel and John that the bulk of the end-time prophecies were carried.

There are other scriptures that postulate the "sealing" of all of the end-time prophecies, such as in Dan 12:4, where Daniel is told to, *"Shut up the words, and seal the book, even to the time of the end,"* and in Rev. 10:4, where John is told to *" Seal up those things which the seven thunders uttered, and write them not. "*

It's obvious that the prophetic words in Daniel and other diverse places are there for anyone to **read,** and if the existing canon of scripture is accepted as being complete, with no inference that more "sealed" scriptures are waiting to be discovered in the latter days, then the "sealing" process that is being spoken of here, must apply to our existing prophetic scriptures. And lacking any logical answers for the extreme diversity of interpretations enjoyed by normal people, all of whom view the same words and arrive at their own interpretation, while not denying the disposition and accuracy of another's interpretation, it can reasonably be assumed that such a myriad of interpretations could be the result of yet another 'marvelous work done by the Lord within the minds of men.'

CHAPTER 1

The Tribulation

God's double-edged sword of vengeance has been menacing humanity ever since the first rains in the Garden of Eden. Our early parents were rocked by the pronouncement of the fateful consequences that awaited them for the aggravation they brought upon their Creator. Because of one overt act of disobedience on their part, the whole atmosphere of the once perfect environment became charged with the wickedness of the Devil, whose pernicious ways eventually permeated the whole of creation. And it was in the wake of these evil workings of the Devil that the Lord vented His tide of vengeance, which in time infiltrated the oracles of His prophets with such words as 'retribution, indignation, and recompense,' and the all too familiar 'tribulation.' All of which spoke of a future time when God would punish mankind for their willful rebellion and disobedience of His statutes.

For generations the mere declaration of these words by the prophets induced fear and trembling into the hearts of the people because they conjured up visions of terrible plagues and slaughtering. However, as time wore on the promise of a future chastisement for their sins lost its power over the people, and the words of the prophets no longer seared the hearts with terror. As a consequence, their slide into debauchery and idol worship worsened, until the patience of the Lord had finally been stretched to its limit. It was then that He decided that if His written Word and the prophets' warnings of their rebelliousness were going to be ignored, then He would simply remove them both from the scene.

Such extreme measures were destined to bring disastrous repercussions on the Jews, and according to the Apostle Paul, it was the first step in His 'casting aside' of the Chosen people, but on the other hand it cracked the door ever so slightly for the eventual entry of the Gentile peoples into His Mercy and Grace. (Romans 11:7,8)

At the time of this incident, the Prophets Isaiah and Elisha were ministering in Samaria and the northern lands of Israel. But now they were enjoined to move to the south, so that the Lord could go ahead with the next step of removing His Word from the peoples' understanding. At the same time He apparently removed the teaching of His Word in the Temple, which for all intents and purposes closed all access to the scriptures. (Isaiah 29: 10-14)

There is no indication that this sealing of the scriptures was ever rescinded, and the scriptures themselves give evidence that the Word was being read and apparently understood at a later time when future prophets witnessed of the Lord to the people.

However, it was not long after He had imposed this 'sealing' of the scriptures, that the Lord allowed the ten northern tribes of Israel to be taken from their homeland by the King of Assyria, who summarily dispersed them throughout his foreign land. And as it turned out, one hundred and twenty-five years later, and for the same rebellious attitude as their kinsmen in the north, the 'goodly' or 'upper class' of the remaining southern tribes were removed from their land in the first of three such evacuations, and deposed as slaves in Babylon.

By now the Jews had realized their mistake. They had stretched their relationship with the Lord to its breaking point, and they were suffering the consequences. They were exiled from their land, their Temple, the Ark of the Covenant and the Holy Word, and now they were cut-off from all contact with the Lord whatsoever. And save for a young prophet named Ezekiel, who was suffering the same exile in Babylon, the Lord had completely turned His back upon them.

That should have been the end of the story, but for some reason God relented from His hard stance and decided to turn things around between them and renew the old relationship with His people. He first opened a door of communication through His prophet Jeremiah, who was still living in Jerusalem at the time. He enjoined him to send a letter to the exiles in Babylon, informing them that the Lord was going to reduce the time of their exile to seventy years and make their existence there a little easier.

Around this time the Lord also decided to communicate with a young Hebrew exile by the name of Daniel, to whom He would reveal the plans for the future judgments. He would lay out on the table as it were, those erstwhile plans for retribution that the prophets had so often foretold but which now would be put in writing so that His people would have a permanent record and a constant reminder of the retribution to come.

The Lord began revealing His tribulation secrets to Daniel on the day that he was called into the presence of the Babylonian King Nebuchadnezzar, to hopefully reveal for the King a certain dream that had been given to him in his sleep, but which he had promptly forgotten upon wakening. The court astrologers had been queried earlier by the King to see if they could relate the dream and it's interpretation, but unfortunately they could neither recall the dream or interpret it, and for this they were all sentenced to death.

Now Daniel faced the same challenge, and he was painfully aware that should he fail to answer the King correctly, he too would follow in the footsteps of the court seers. But with God's help in giving him the same dream along with its interpretation, he was able to go before the King on the following day and relate the dream in its entirety along with its interpretation. (Dan. chap. 4)

Whether or not this dream sequence was intended to be the lone revelation of the future judgment period is debatable. And though it provided Daniel with a prophetical view of the Jews' destiny under Gentile dominion from the contemporary Babylonian enslavement until the Lord sets up His Kingdom on earth, it revealed nothing about the time of the judgment. But that changed with the second revelation that was given to Daniel some forty years later. The same four Gentile Empires that were portrayed in the dream sequence are again described, but several new features that dealt specifically with the tribulation period were added. One of these was the announcement of the precise timing of the judgment period.

Once the door to the judgments was cracked with this news, other elements of the Lord's plans for the judgment period began to emerge. The first of which is our introduction to a mysterious individual who enters the tribulation picture via the European political scene, where he is seen sitting pompously in the President's chair of a ten-nation alliance. This by the way, is the same alliance that was brought to our attention in the first revelation through the symbolism of the ten toes on the feet of a great image. Only now we learn that this alliance has selected a veritable unknown to preside over them as their President. But it's not the election process that summons our attention, it's the timing of the election in the course of other European events.

If you recall in the previous vision of the image, the tribulation period was intended to occur sometime during the era of this alliance, but there was no discernable evidence of it happening at any specific time within that era, which by the way has already stretched for nearly half a century.

But in this second revelation we are made aware of a presidential election that will take place within the ruling Council of an alliance that is defined as having a membership of ten nations. And if we are to consider Daniel's prophetical 'ten-member' alliance is representative of the present day European Union, whose present membership exceeds ten, it's obvious that before this particular election can take place its membership will have to be reduced to ten.

And until that reduction is made, the election will not go forward and the plans for the tribulation period will continue to be put on hold. For it is this President's ignominious privilege to initiate the tribulation.

From this it would appear that the membership reduction issue and the election of its President are the key issues preventing the end-time plans from beginning. When these obstacles have been removed, the next step in the plans of the Lord calls for the newly-elected President to mediate an ever-elusive peace covenant between the Arab nations and Israel. When that covenant is ratified by both parties, peace will be restored to the Near-East region. However, this peace covenant and the tribulation period are irrevocably linked together, and the moment that the President signs the treaty into existence he inadvertently signs the tribulation into existence.

Daniel records the signing of the covenant but he gives only dim references to any role that the President has in the tribulation until we read of a sudden trip that he makes to Israel, which seemed incongruous because it comes so soon after the deployment of a Union Expeditionary force to the same region.

Though Daniel gives no mention of the events that were

transpiring in Israel there were tremendous things going on.

As soon as the borders were secured from any overt intrusion the Lord began administering the Trumpet judgments in Israel. All of the judgments could be considered serious but it was the fourth judgment in the series that began the downward spiral of the nation. In short, it was a world-wide earthshaking that caused terrible destruction in virtually every country in the world, including Israel, where the main edifice of the Muslim world was totally destroyed. News of its destruction spread quickly and it was ill-received by the Arabs, who thought the Israelites had a hand in its destruction. Their anger over the incident triggered a re-mobilization of the Arab coalition's armies which a year later culminated in a war of reprisal against the Jews. The war continued unabated for nearly a year before the European Union forces were called into the fray, and right behind them came the Union President.

Daniel doesn't mention that the President's hurried trip to Israel was also tied to an extremely important assignment from the Lord, that called for him to go to Jerusalem at a certain time and wait there until a second mysterious individual appeared, whose mission was to finalize the seventh Trumpet judgment on the Jews.

But according to Daniel, there was at least one other reason for the President's sudden trip to Israel, and that was to fulfill an ancient ancestral prophecy which foretold of his gaining lordship over his Jewish brethren. Yes, the President is a Jew, but he is also descended from Syrian royalty and strangely enough, his royal estate also lies in Jerusalem where he must go to inherit it.

As it turned out, the President arrived in Jerusalem close on the heals of the Union troops, who were in the mopping-up stage of operations after the battle. They had driven the last of the marauding Arabs from the region and instituted marshal law in Israel

Ironically, this war is not defined in Daniel's journal, even though it was probably the most crucial factor in the events of the end-times. It had been brought on by the Lord as the sixth Trumpet judgment upon the Jews, with the purpose of diminishing the Jewish population of Israel by one third, according to a prophecy in Ezekiel, and in the eleven months since the war began, it had done just that by claiming the lives of nearly two million Jews and an untold number of Arabs.

Diplomatic efforts had been frequently made to try and de-fuse the tense situation over the Mosques' destruction and prevent any overt action on the part of the Arabs, but without warning their armies invaded Israel and began to engage in what they claimed was a 'Jihad' or 'holy war' of extermination of the Jews.

The fierce conflict in Israel continued to escalate as thousands of Arab troops poured into the embattled nation and exacted their terrible toll on the Jews, until finally, eleven months into the war, the European Union was pressured into sending troops in to quell the fighting. We have to realize that during this time the out-side world was also submerged in its own insurmountable problems of reconstruction following the terrible round of earthquakes, and there was little incentive to intervene in the Near-East conflict.

It was at this critical juncture, when the Union Expeditionary forces were coming ashore on the Gaza coast of the Mediterranean Sea, that the narrator to Daniel began again with his saga of the President. And the intensity of his story seems to mount from the moment the Union troops' began wading ashore and dispersing up and down the coast. All enemy resistance fell before them. The Egyptian forces that had been hurriedly dispatched and sent up from the south were ill prepared for the attack and out-maneuvered by the night invasion tactic. They were subsequently put down. Meanwhile, the troops making their rapid assault northward met weak resistance in their advance. At a pre-arranged location the troops headed inland toward Jerusalem where they ran into stiffer resistance from the Arab armies. But we have to presume at this point that the Lord had already predicated the early collapse of the Arab resistance, because three days into the operation the Arab's will to continue caved in and the war ground to a halt..

With the hostilities ended, the President was able to come into Jerusalem, where, for no apparent reason, he decided to remain and establish a permanent command headquarters for the peacekeeping operation. This was rather an unusual stance for the President to take, but he was adamant about it, and admittedly for a short while everything seemed to go well in the war-torn nation. The days remained calm and quiet, and recovery from the plagues and the recent war was promising, which made the next event in his occupation a total surprise. He was found slain in his apartment one morning.

This surprising tragedy would seem to bring the saga of the President to a climactic ending, possibly because his death came unexpectedly in the closing scene of Daniel's last revelation. But there was still a mystery surrounding his death that hadn't been satisfactorily explained by Daniel, such as why he was killed, and was his mission ever accomplished? And there were the other startling developments in Jerusalem that seemed to begin happening the moment the President was murdered.

With these developments, the veil over the President's life and death begins to recede and the picture of the President's mission to Israel becomes clear. It was planned by the Lord that three days after the man's assassination, the Devil would take up residence in the frame of the dead President and restore it to life. But what evolves from that union will be neither human or celestial. It will be a new creature that would later be referred to by the Apostle John as 'the Beast.' And in those few remaining hours of the Jewish tribulation period, this Beast, will have just enough time to destroy the two witnesses that were sent down from God and issue those devastating commands from the Holy place in Israel, which called for the complete expulsion of the Jews from their homeland.

So, as it turned out, the assassination wasn't to be the climax of the President's incredible saga, it was merely a necessary precursor to his further work in the tribulation.

The Apostle John picks up on Daniel's account of the President's death and reveals some rather vivid details of the events following the assassination. In his book of the Revelation, John describes the turmoil and uproar in Israel that followed the President's death, and of a war that was being waged in heaven which had its own brace of tragic circumstances. In the wake of that battle, John states, Satan and his myriad of angels were cast out of heaven and sent into the bowels of the earth where they were to await further judgment. But their expulsion from heaven had already set in motion a wide range of incredible happenings in Jerusalem, the first

26

of which was the incarnation of the President, which came about so suddenly during his funeral service, that it caught everyone off guard.

None of those attending his funeral were remotely aware of what was happening at that instant when Satan was suddenly extricated from his temporary confinement in the earth and in a breath of time deposited into the lifeless body of the President. Immediately, new life soared through the body, and amazingly, in full view of a surprised audience and the televised world, a revived President rose up out of his coffin and walked among the astonished mourners. But the shocking truth was that this personage who walked among them was neither a human nor a celestial being, but a unique combination of both.

Now Satan becomes the motivating factor in the awesome events of the days ahead, a fact which Daniel could only intimate in his writings because he wasn't privy to all of the details. Had he been given all of the facts surrounding the Devil's extradition and subsequent incarnation, he undoubtedly would have written them up in his journal. As it was, with the limited information that he was provided, Daniel could only record the terrible tragedies that befell the Jews immediately following the incarnation.

Needless to say, the world community was shocked by the death of the President, as well they should be, but their sorrow was turned to joy and relief when the news of the revived President filled the media. Their first reaction was to promise this 'new President' leadership over the whole western world, but before that would happen, this 'Beast' would bring his revengeful persecution and suffering on the children of God in Israel and the dreaded expulsion from their homeland.

This expulsion, which the Jews had sworn would never happen again, becomes their third Diaspora which also culminates the seventh Trumpet judgment and completes the cycle of the Lord's punishments on the Jews.

This suspense-filled story in Daniel's journal might have ended on this depressing note if were not for his insistence on knowing what would be the end of his people. He pleaded with the Lord about this, saying, " *O my Lord, what shall be the end of these things?*"

And the Lord, sensing the desperation in Daniel's voice answered him;
"Go thy way Daniel: for the words are closed up and sealed until the time of the end. But many shall be purified, and made white, and tried, and thy people shall be delivered, everyone that shall be found written in the book." (Dan. 12: 1,8,9)

So Daniel's story really ends on somewhat of a conciliatory note, if not a victorious one, for it seems that what was intended to be a holocaust by the Beast was turned into a glorious Deliverance of the remnant by the Lord.

Incorporated into this gripping story of the President and Satan, are a number of side issues and other salient features of that remarkable period in time. Some of these features are very detailed, such as the invasion plans of the European Union forces after they make their landing at Gaza and the trek north along the coast of the Mediterranean Sea before heading inland to Jerusalem. This was done so that no destruction would come upon the ancient city of Petra and the surrounding area of the Dead Sea, which will become the destination of the fleeing Israelites in the coming Diaspora.

On the other hand, some other pertinent information about the tribulation period, such as its duration and it's division, were delivered in a more covert manner and hidden away in the fourth revelation. In that same revelation, we come across the angel Gabriel's brief overview of the judgment period, which, in his typical foreshortened style of exposition, revealed that the peace covenant between the Arabs and the Jews was designated to last for seven years, which strangely enough coincided with the number of years allotted for the tribulation period.

And the Lord illustrated a division of this seven year time period into two equal portions. This was done through the President's sudden departure for Israel in *"the midst of the week "* or in the middle of those seven years. The first three-and-a-half year portion of the tribulation was allotted for the Jewish judgment period, that was defined in an earlier revelation as the "Indignation" of the Jews.

The narrator's explanation for this sudden trip was, to *'cause the sacrifice and oblation to cease'* in Israel, which the President eventually did along with other intrusive acts into the affairs of the Jews, but his primary reason for going there was at the behest of the Lord. He was abiding the Lord's leading when he followed on the heels of the Union troops when they interceded into what was purported to be a Holy war of the Muslim Arabs against the Jews. Other than that incentive from the Lord, there was absolutely no reason for him to make the trip, and certainly no other high-ranking official would have done such a thing unless he was drawn into it.

Unfortunately, this bloody war had stemmed from an unsubstantiated rumor that the Jews' intended to build their new Jewish Temple on the site where the Muslim Mosque once stood. But to understand that connection, you will have to know about other events that were going on in Israel during that time.

It happened just eighteen months after the peace covenant had been initiated and the tribulation punishments were still in progress in Israel. Without warning the whole earth was suddenly shaken by a whole series of deadly earthquakes that evidently came as a result of the 'day-shortening' event of the fourth Trumpet judgment. (Rev. 8:12) And Israel, along with the rest of the world, was being tortured by the earthshaking. And it's reasonable to assume that the Muslim Mosque in Jerusalem was also demolished at that time. But a fear arose among the neighboring states, that this destruction of the Mosque was exactly what the Jews had been waiting for so that they could build their Temple on that site. This would be all the excuse the Arabs needed to instigate a war of reprisal on the Jews.

In fact, in John's book of the Revelation, where he gives an account of the Arab invasion and the war that followed, John makes the point that the Arabs had actually been preparing for this war for over a year but were held back from making their attack on Israel until the Lord had determined the proper time for their invasion. This timing of their preparations closely tallies with the earthquake's occurrence. (Rev 9:14,15)

THE PARTITIONING OF THE JUDGMENTS

One of the most significant pieces of information to come out of Daniel's revelations, and the one that is invariably overlooked, is the Lord's partitioning of the seven-year period. As you well know, it has always been the Lord's plan to punish all of the people remaining on the earth after the Rapture of the believers has taken place, but for reasons of His own He intends to punish the Jews separately from the Gentiles, and this would only be feasible if the Jews were set apart in some distinct way from the rest of the world. To accomplish that separation, He has set aside the first three and a half-years of the judgment period as a time that would be used strictly for punishing the Jews. And it follows that the second three and a half-year period will then be used for the punishment of all of the rest of the worlds peoples.

Daniel recognized that there would be this separation but much to his despair, he was given no information on the use of the second three and a half years. In fact, there is only one inference in his journal that relates to a second punishment period, with only a hint of the 'other peoples' that would be involved in any judgment. And as significant as this division of the time period is to the application of the respective judgments, on both the Jews and the Gentiles, this is the only piece of information in the book of Daniel that even remotely points to any 'Gentile involvement.' And presumably, the only reason for its inclusion was to establish its existence here in Daniel's journal, so that John would be able to correctly distinguish the punishments between the Jews and the Gentiles.

There again, John never made an issue of this separation because he likely assumed that his readers would be familiar with Daniel's account of it. So when he assigned the group names of 'Trumpet' and 'Vial' to the various judgments, he was simply reaffirming Daniel's theme of the separated punishments. And by the time he got around to writing the second section of his journal dealing with the application of the Vial judgments, the Lord had revealed to him just who those other recipients were, and as you may have already suspected, they were the rest of the worlds' populace who would be considered Gentiles.

As we unfold Daniel's revelations one after the other, and slowly peel away all of the mystifying figurative language and turn our thinking over to the idioms of that period, what lays before us is an astounding, if not incredible account of the Lord's ingenious plan to send Satan down to earth on the closing day of the Jewish judgment period. Missing of course from his journal are the individual punishments, for the Lord's deliberations to Daniel were directed toward the tribulation's beginning, which came about with the signature of the Anti-Christ on a peace document, then, leaving behind all of the intermediate punishments which would be revealed later in John's book of Revelation, He hustled Daniel to the fearful ending of the Jewish tribulation, wherein is revealed the awesome persecutions by the Beast that ultimately brought about the drastic sweeping desolation of the land of Israel.   And when we couple the information garnered from Daniel's revelations with that of the Apostle John, what appears before our eyes is an amazingly detailed panorama of those whole seven frightful years of the tribulation, which is what I shall endeavor to portray in this book.

CHAPTER 2

The Plan Revealed

Daniel's story begins with the first vision that came to him some ten years after he had been taken as a captive slave to Babylon along with hundreds of his fellow Hebrews.   This first Diaspora, or exile, followed a siege against Jerusalem in BC 605 by the Chaldean King apparent, named Nebuchadnezzar.   The siege and the following enslavement of the Jews was a last ditch effort by the Lord to obtain retaliation against His people for their constant disobedience and rebellion against His Lordship.   But the Lord evidently relented from His anger, at least sufficiently to begin communicating with His people again through the Prophets Ezekiel and Jeremiah, and eventually through young Daniel, which happened in a rather auspicious way through a dream sequence.

It seems that in the pagan society of Babylonia, a person's dreams were considered to be omens from their gods and as such they had a real impact on the people. Many of whom guided their lives by their content. King Nebuchadnezzar was no exception to those traditions; in fact, he kept a number of astrologers in his court for the sole purpose of divinations and dream interpretations.

THE FIRST REVELATION - THE KING'S DREAM

On one particular night, the King had an especially troubling dream that he was unable to recall after being awakened.   This frustrated him greatly, and he inquired of his court astrologers if they could describe the dream and it's meaning.   But they were just as baffled as he, and couldn't answer him, and for this they were sentenced to death, with Daniel being included.   Fortunately, their death sentences were later commuted, when, through a series of events young Daniel was able to define the dream and its interpretation for the King.

In this particular instance though, it was more than likely that the King was given his dream sequence by the Lord in order to initiate the end-time revelations, and if this was so, the experience also became Daniel's initiation into what would eventually be a series of revelations and visions that would define the future judgment period. In fact, this first dream sequence with its interpretation would become the backdrop, so to speak, for the rest of the series, for in it, Daniel's mind would be catapulted from his own contemporary age over an indeterminate future period of time and a plethora of events, unto the second coming of the Lord and the setting up of His Kingdom.

Daniel's dream came on the night following his initial appearance before the King. He relates how the Lord gave him the identical dream to the King, along with its interpretation, so that on the following morning, when he again appeared before the King, he was able to relate the entire dream and its interpretation, and in the process saved the lives of the court astrologers as well as his own.

Before giving his exposition on the dream however, he made sure that he first gave homage to the Lord, by informing the King that the secrets of the dream were given to him by his Lord, and that the knowledge of it was not of his own ability. He then gave homage to the King lest he become distressed over the interpretation, for Daniel was wise enough to know that should the King be displeased with the interpretation he could still lose his head over the ordeal. So he chose his words carefully and began his description of the dream;

"O King," he said, "You saw a great image that was perfect in form but was oddly constructed of different types of metals for each section of the body. The head was of made of fine gold, the breast and arms were of silver, the belly and the thighs were of brass, and the legs were made of iron, but the feet with the ten toes were made of a mixture of iron and clay. (Dan 2: 28-29)

Daniel noticed that the dream so far had not been particularly disturbing to the King so he continued,

"You also saw a great stone cut out of a mountain without hands, and it was dashed against the feet of the image and broke them into pieces, and the pieces were ground into dust, which was then carried away with the wind. And then you saw that stone grow *into a mountain that filled the whole earth."*   (Dan 2: 34-35)

This finished his recount of the dream, but he was still aware that the interpretation could have a more deleterious effect on the King, so he proceeded more cautiously with this part, after again giving the King due respect for his exalted position.

" Thou, O king art a king of kings: for the God of Heaven hath given thee a kingdom, power, and strength and glory. And wherever the children of men dwell, the beasts of the fields and the fowls of the heaven hath he given into your hand, and hath made thee ruler over them all. Thou art this head of gold."

Then, looking at the King to see if the expression on his face indicated that it was safe to continue, he ventured:

"Your kingdom will be supplanted by another inferior one, as was represented by the breast and two arms made of silver, and that kingdom in turn will be displaced by still another. The fourth kingdom will very powerful and strong, as depicted by the legs being made of iron, but as the adjoining feet and toes of the image were composed of both iron and clay, in the latter end of that kingdom the authority will be assumed by a council of common men."

"Then sire, after the days of those kings, the God of heaven shall set up a kingdom that shall never be destroyed nor will any other kingdom supplant it, but it shall instead destroy them, and last forever. And inasmuch as you have seen this great stone destroy the image completely, so will this kingdom remain after all of the other nations have passed away."   (Dan. 2:37-45)

Although the image pictured various world Empires that would successively come into power over the ages, in its completed form, it represented an extended period during which the so-called 'Gentile powers' would hold dominion over the Jewish nation.

In this aspect, each of the image's successive Gentile Empires would take over its predecessor's power and status as indicated by their respective placement in the image, beginning with the head, or the Babylonian Empire. The second in line was the Medo-Persian Empire, as represented by the arms and shoulders of the image, and the third, the Grecian Empire, followed by the fourth and last, the powerful Roman Empire.

We know from historical records that those four so-called

world empires did reign supreme and in succession, as was foretold, but while the might of Imperial Rome disappeared in the third century, its presence and authority has been revived in these latter days, so to speak, through the recent federation of the former provinces of the old Roman Empire. And when this union of present day nations was signed into existence several years ago, it was the intention of the signers to have it identified with the former Roman Empire.

Thus far, however, the governing council of this Union has been unsuccessful in limiting its membership of nations to the required ten, but in God's timing, that too will be accomplished and Daniel's prophecies concerning the image will be fulfilled and the tribulation period can begin. (Dan. 2: 45) (Luke 21:24)

The second portion of the King's dream takes us beyond the formation stage of the Union to preview its demise along with all of the other governing authorities of the world. This final stage of man's dominion was depicted in the dream sequence by the ultimate destruction of the great image by a 'great stone that was cut out of a mountain without hands.' This 'great stone' portrays the Lord Himself returning to the earth in great Power and Glory, at which time Satan's dominion over humanity will be eliminated, and the Lord's Kingdom and authority will reign over all of the earth.

THE SECOND REVELATION - THE FOUR BEASTS

In many respects Daniel's second revelation could be considered as an 'expanded version' of the dream sequence that was given to mollify the King's curiosity. That vision was given under rather unusual circumstances, when Daniel's life was at stake if he could not satisfy the King with a truthful answer. But forty years have passed and many things had changed, not the least of which was Daniel's mental capacity for discerning the revelations, which may be one reason why the Lord began again with the revelations. But the over-riding reason, I believe, was due to a shift in the Lord's plans as to what He wanted to reveal in those visions.

Where the emphasis in the former revelation had been on the expectancy of the future judgments and their placement in the future, which incidentally will continue to be stressed through the follow-on revelations, the agenda of this second revelation will be the feasibility of extricating Satan from the heavens and depositing him onto the earth and into a situation here where he can do a useful work for the Lord in the tribulation.

What is noticeably missing from all of the revelations is a record of the punishments that will be put upon the Jews during the judgment period. Those punishments are all part of an extremely intricate operation in which the angels will be playing a prominent role, but in the last judgment on the Jews, which involves the desolation of Israel, Satan will become the featured player. To accomplish this role however, Satan must be put on the earth and into a human body. This extradition of Satan from heaven to the earth will not only be the most delicate procedure of the whole operation, but the most vulnerable to disruption.

It follows suit that the transfer of Satan into an earthly body would not be feasible without the complement of a human being who would be ready and willing to offer up his life so that the Devil might take over his body. This will take an exceptional individual with all of the right characteristics for the job, but most of all, he must be handpicked by the Lord. That man is made known to Daniel in this second revelation, when he suddenly appears on the European scene in the prestigious position of the Presidency of the ten-nation alliance.

Through this revelation Daniel will follow the career of this individual from his inauguration to his incarnation three and a half years later. However the projection of this man's life through the vision comes too fast for Daniel to assimilate. Couple that with the man's sudden 'makeover' from a human into a superhuman and the terror that this individual would bestow on his fellow Jews after his incarnation was more than Daniel could absorb in one vision.

The Lord recognized Daniel's dilemma, so rather than heaping coals on the fire by telling him about the desolation of his countrymen, He backed off and diverted the remainder of the vision to scenes of heavenly affairs. However, before the vision ended the Lord would have the vision switch back to a scene which displayed the penalty that would be extracted from this individual for allowing

Satan to take over. This scene did little to ease the heartsick feeling that Daniel had for the plight of his countrymen, but he lived with it.

Like the first vision of the dream sequence, this vision was probably intended to be an 'all-purpose' revelation, meaning that it supplied all of the information necessary to both pin-point the tribulation's future location and introduce the man who would have authority over the Jews during the tribulation period. Included also, was an overwhelming display of events surrounding the conclusion of the tribulation period, including the ultimate demise of this mystery man, along with his worldly dominion.

To begin with, this second revelation reviews the same four great Empires that would rule over the Jews from the time of Daniel's enslavement in Babylon until the second coming of the Lord. This information was supplied in the former revelation through the use of an image that depicted a human whose different body areas exemplified the different Empires. Those four empires are now being typified by four radically different beasts that come into Daniel's view one after the other, and as each beast passes before him he described its characteristic features that best typified the Empire it was intended to represent.

Daniel was particularly taken aback by the awesomeness of the fourth beast. Compared to the others it was more dreadful and terrible looking with its great iron teeth and awesome ten horns that protruded from the top of its head. This beast was intended to represent the great Roman Empire, with the great iron teeth depicting the invincible Roman armies and the ten horns exemplifying a resurgence of that Empire in the latter days. That resurgence would come in the form of ten independent European nations that would unite as one and become a powerful European alliance with a ruling Council.

The Lord probably supplied this detailed information about the alliance to hopefully allay Daniel's fears that the punishments were waiting in Jerusalem for the exile's return at the close of their present enslavement. And it assured Daniel that the judgments would come far in the future, in an era when the ruling power over the Jews would be in the hands of an elected leader rather than an absolute monarch such as Nebuchadnezzar.

Daniel might have been aware from the information that was given him, that the judgment period was destined to occur sometime within the era of this ten-nation alliance, and just lost sight of the fact, so the Lord furnished him with additional information. And included in that information was a sign that virtually indicated the specific year within the era of the alliance when the judgments would occur. Surprisingly enough, that sign is given through an analogy of a small horn that grows up amid the ten existing horns on the beast. Metaphorically, this small horn depicts the mystery man who is put into the enviable position of leadership of the ten-nation alliance. Notice if you will how the revelation portrays this.

Daniel is peering closely at the head of the beast with the ten horns, where he sees a small horn growing amid the horns. It appears to be growing at an alarming rate as well as altering in shape until it takes on the shape of a man's head with discernable human facial features. This peculiar development of the 'little horn' set it apart from the others, which, in itself was significant to Daniel, for he recognized that this was the Lord's way of introducing him to this 'mystery man' who would become the leader of the alliance. But it's the timing of this man's rise to leadership that furnishes the sign of the tribulation. It will only happen when there are specifically ten alliance members. And because it is this new President's prerogative to initiate the tribulation period, it will soon follow.

With the future timing of the tribulation affirmed, the Lord immediately fast-forwarded the vision three and a half years into the future of the mystery man. In this one brief verse the man's career development has vaulted from the Presidency to the incarnation, and Daniel is now picturing him only moments after that incarnation happens. The only conspicuous difference in the man over that three and a half year period was the obvious change in his character, and Daniel chose to deliberate on that change and describe it for us in his journal. There is, of course, the possibility that Daniel knew what had happened to the man to bring about that change of character, but was cautioned by the Lord against reproducing it in his writings. In which case he could only amplify on the change that came over the

President. He was however, permitted to describe the super powers that were given to the man through the exchange, and he boldly intimates that these powers bordered on the celestial.

His description of the man's character change is expressed in phrases like;

"He shall speak great words against the most High, and shall wear out the saints of the most High, and think to change times and laws..." which translates into the wrath and blaspheme that spewed from the mouth of this 'new creature' only moments after Satan had found himself deposited in the body of the President. Satan's intense wrath as well as his need to slander and blaspheme the Creator welled up in his newfound heart, and as Daniel relates, the man's initial reaction to the situation he found himself in was to blaspheme the Creator and attempt to persecute the Jews by cutting them off from worshipping the Creator. This extreme wrath of his continues to drive him throughout the final hours of the judgment period.

We can assume that when Daniel found out about Satan's involvement in the judgments, and particularly the persecution of his brethren, that information greatly dispirited Daniel. In fact, he became so heartsick over the matter that the Lord had to hold off relaying any more information about this particular episode. Instead, He switched the remainder of the vision to multiple scenes of heavenly situations that seemed irrelevant to the affairs on earth, however, before the vision concludes it will again display the events that take place in the closing hours of the seven year tribulation, including the scenes showing the final demise of the President.

We know that Daniel maintained a close relationship with the Lord throughout his life, and received many visions and revelations over the years that were not of the judgment period, but those that were, he usually referenced to a particular year in the life of the then reigning monarch in Babylon, where he lived in exile. Thus his second revelation on the judgments is dated in the first year of Belshazzar, the grandson of Nebuchadnezzar. His father, Nabulis, assumed the throne after King Nebuchadnezzar's death in BC 562, and was the actual reigning monarch, with Belshazzar as his crown prince, but at some point they had formed a co-regency, as is indicated by his being able to offer Daniel the position of 'third ruler' in the kingdom, behind Belshazzar and his father. This would date the second revelation around BC 555 or some forty years after the first one. By this time, Daniel would be in his early sixties, bowed and slightly overwhelmed by the mound of information he was about to be given. (Dan. 5:29-30)

In the previous vision we saw how the four Gentile Empires were depicted by different types of metals used in the make-up of the image, with each type of metal reflecting that particular Empire's affinity to God and how He in turn considered each of them. Now these same Empires are being characterized by vastly dissimilar beasts, which appear one after the other in Daniel's vision. He sees each of them as some sort of monstrosity that was meant to portray the characteristics of the individual Empires and their rulers.

Some readers may be wondering at this time, how there are only four Empires listed out of the many hundreds that have existed throughout the ages. The reason is, that in the book of Daniel the Lord is dealing only with the affairs of the Jewish nation, and these four are the only ones that have held absolute dominion over the Jewish nation since the time of Daniel. However there was a break in that authoritative power following the Diaspora in AD 135, when the Jewish nation was, for all intents and purposes defunct until 1948 when it was reborn. Today no country holds dominion over the nation of Israel, however, the Lord has predicated that during the tribulation period the 'resurgent Roman Empire' will again pick up the mantle of authority over the Jews through an individual, who is the Anti-Christ.

The first of these representative beasts to come forward resembled a lion with eagle's wings on its back, but it also had some of the human faculties which allowed it to stand upright and walk as a man. This beast was evidently earmarked to represent Nebuchadnezzar, the first king of the Babylonian Empire, of whom the scriptures says:

'Thou art a king of kings, and the God of heaven has given thee a kingdom, power, strength, and glory over all that dwell on the earth, of the children of men, of the beasts and the fowls of the air.'
(Dan. 2:38)

Certainly a lion, as the king of the beasts, and the eagle as the master of the air, along with the faculties of a human portrayed the noble characteristics of this King and his kingdom, at least in comparison to the others.

Following that beast came one that resembled a bear, a great beast that was intended to depict the dual kingship of Cyrus over the vast Persian empire and Darius the Mede, who would be made prince over the Babylonian Empire, following the defeat of its present King Belshazzar.

The bear was shown with three ribs in its mouth, which spoke of three powerful Persian Kings, namely Xerxes I, Artexerxes I, his son, and Artexerxes II, who would succeed Cyrus on the throne of Persia. The last of these kings would go on to extend the Persian Empire over virtually all the Middle-East area, even unto Greece. These three kings, the prophecy states, 'rose up and ate much flesh,' giving reference to the expansion of the empire through battles. (Dan.7: 5)

The Lord evidently held no ill will toward these Gentile rulers and allowed them to remain in power through the duration of the captivity of the Jews and beyond. He also gave Cyrus the unction to free the captives and provide them with the resources and the protection they needed to return to their homeland.

The third beast, which we will see more of in the next vision, remotely resembled a leopard, but it had four heads and upon its back four wings like a fowl. This beast was intended to represent the Macedonian Empire, whose swiftly moving and conquering armies extended its domain all across Asia Minor even unto India, usurping all of the former possessions of the Medes and Persians along the way.

That Empire was broken up after the death of Alexander, and divided among his four top generals, who are herein depicted by the four heads on the beast. In the next revelation, the legions of Alexander are represented by a goat, whose single horn on its head represents Alexander himself. His death would be typified by this single horn being broken off, and the four horns that would grow in its place represented the four generals who would divide the kingdom among themselves.

But at this point our attention is drawn to the emergence of a non-descript fourth beast with great iron teeth and ten horns protruding from its head. This beast was intended to represent the powerful Roman Empire, whose massive legions devoured all of the nations before it, with the ten horns representing a ten-nation alliance that would rise out of the ashes of the Roman Empire in the end times. Incidentally, the Apostle John will later envision this same beast, except his picture of the beast is even more ugly with seven heads displayed instead of one, but it still features the ten horns.

The vision now hovers on these ten horns, where a nubbin of a horn is beginning to grow out. Daniel writes that this 'little horn' grew quickly before his eyes and soon became larger and more robust than any of the others, so large in fact, that it crowded out three of the other horns. But while continuing to grow it also began changing in shape and configuration until, what had been a horn had now evolved into a man's head with readily discernable facial features, including a mouth that opened suddenly and blared out a tirade of blasphemous profanity in some indiscernible language.

This scene of the 'little horn' that grew amid the ten other horns, was Daniel's first meeting with the man who would become the leader of the ten-nation alliance. Incidentally, the idea of referencing an individual to a 'horn,' is commonplace in the Bible. The same idiom was used in Psalms 18:2 where the Lord is called 'my rock' and the 'horn of my salvation,' and Daniel uses the word quite liberally in his identification of various notable personages and kings such as Alexander and Darius. And as for depicting the leader of the alliance as a "horn,' we shall find out later that it was a legitimate application because his ancestral background was from ancient Syrian royalty.

But it was the vision's portrayal of the horn's growth pattern, from a nubbin to a human-like monstrosity, that was most significant. For what it depicted was the emergence and the ensuing political career development of a man who would be a 'king,' as Daniel puts it, over a relatively short span of three and a half years.

Politically, you could say, he comes from a virtual non-entity into 'instant' leadership of a ten-nation alliance. At which point the man has reached a plateau in his life that entitled him to be called a *"little horn."* The word 'little' was used here because his Presidency could not be compared to the absolute power of the Caesars of the old Roman Empire. Nonetheless, this was only the first step in his career development, but it was an important step, for in this position he will be able to do wide-spread harm to the Jews in Israel as well as the Church, which incidentally, is on the earth at this time and will be for the next several months.

Very quickly though, Daniel reviews the next plateau in this man's life, which is reached some three and a half years later when he becomes incarnated by the Devil. This was the event that bought the radical change in the behavior of the man, and as Daniel writes:

"It was like "putting a face on the real enemy." (Dan.7: 20) In another place he makes the remark;

"I witnessed the diverseness of character that came over this 'new horn.' (Dan.7: 24)

Both of these description illustrate the fact that the incarnation had indeed happened in the man without its ever been mentioned.

Daniel's explicit notation of the vociferous blaspheme that exuded from the mouth of the creature, was another way of expressing the completion of the incarnation process and that the final stage of this mystery man's career had been reached.

Let me emphasize here, that at the time this revelation was given the extradition of Satan to the earth was considered to be a covert operation. The Lord had His reasons for it keeping it that way, which we will get into later, however the plans for the extradition had to be conveyed to Daniel and the only way to do it securely was to encrypt the information. The need for that security envelope has long since disappeared so the plans can be unfolded in their true form.

Still I continue to refer to the man in this fashion because the Lord had never chosen to reveal him to Daniel, who had problems of his own in trying to identify the new 'personage' that evolved from the incarnation. He finally introduces him in a different way, but not as a "horn" or even as a human, but as an "It," (Dan.8: 12)

The Apostle John had similar problems naming the creature, and he ended up referring to the creature as the "Beast," a name which has stuck with him ever since.

In case you haven't recognized it, this adroit exposition of the transition from human to superhuman gave Daniel an encapsulation of both the mystery man and his mission, and apparently it was this man's mission that greatly unnerved Daniel and caused the Lord to temporarily abandon His effort to pass along a full exposure of the Beast and his mission. Instead, He diverted the rest of the vision to other topics, which to some extent duplicated the closing scenes in the former vision of the King.

The scenes in the vision now shift from one subject to another like a motion picture projector panning a variety of topics from the coronation of the Lord in Heaven to the setting up of the Kingdom of God on the earth. One such scene portrayed the Great White Throne judgment in heaven, where the Father was shown seated on His Throne, and circling overhead were a myriad of beings. Some of the scenes had little to do with the tribulation period, while others informed Daniel that the Jews' indignation was not the end of all things, and that well beyond the temporal judgments there wouuld be an eternal judgment for everyone. All of these scenes were like a kaleidoscope of the Kingdom age and beyond, and though they may have settled Daniel's mind as to the distant future, they had little bearing on the end-times.

Then, just as suddenly, as though He had forgotten to tell Daniel something, the Lord turned the vision back to the scene of the 'ten horned beast' and the transformed 'little horn' who was still blasting the air with derogatory words. This scene continued to bother Daniel, but as he watched and listened to the wrath coming from the Beast, he saw the man being taken away and slain, and his body being tossed into some flames to be destroyed. Then he was allowed to see other beasts, which apparently represented other national entities of the world, also being destroyed, but amazingly enough, the people who made up those nations were allowed to live a while longer under the dominion of God's Kingdom on earth. (Dan.7: 11,12,14)

What Daniel has been allowed to witness was a plethora of events that will transpire at the conclusion of the seven-year tribulation period, which includes the death throes of the Beast and the False Prophet, the cessation of the Beast's kingdom on earth, and the demise of all worldly authority.

Finally he saw the setting up of the Kingdom of God on the earth, which was a scene that closely paralleled that portion of Nebuchadnezzar's dream where the great stone from heaven was seen smashing the feet of the image and turning the image into dust.

A scene very similar to this was given to John, who described it as a portrayal of the ultimate physical death of the Anti-Christ and the false prophet, where they are thrown into the lake of fire, while the ethereal Satan was cast back into the pit for another thousand years. (Rev. 19:19,20)

Unexpectedly, the vision continued, and for a third time Daniel was afforded another, though somewhat different, view of the Throne of the Father in Heaven. It happened to be a glorious picture of the Lord's Coronation in Heaven, wherein Christ is seen approaching the Throne of the Father who has extended His right hand which held a scroll. The Lord steps forward and receives the scroll as the scepter of His regency as the King of Kings and Lord of Lords. (Dan: 7:3-14)

This same Coronation scene is pictured by John in the fourth and fifth chapters of his book, and the scepter that is offered is in reality the seven-sealed scroll of the judgments, which conveys the message that the actual control of the tribulation is in the Lord's hands. But to Daniel this was the most unforgettable scene of the whole vision, for in it he has seen the Son of God and the Father together. The Prophet Isaiah had mentioned some time earlier of the existence of the Son of God and His coming to earth, and now Daniel is allowed to see him in all of His Glory and Majesty. With that memorable scene Daniel's long and extremely complex version came to an end, but his memories of it lingered on.

There were portions of the vision however which troubled him greatly, so it was no wonder that while he was still in the Spirit, he requested an explanation of these difficult portions from an Angel who was standing near. And the Angel, assuming that Daniel was referring to the opening scene of the four beasts, offered him this brief explanation:

"Those four great beasts are four kings which shall have world dominion, but then God's people will take the dominion from them and keep it for ever." (Dan.7: 17,18)

Now Daniel was mindful of that part from his previous vision of the image, but at the moment he was more concerned about the fourth beast and the identity of that little horn. From what he understood of the vision, the little horn symbolized some dispirited angry individual who would be able to exert tremendous authority over his people, and he was anxious to know more about him, so he re-phrased his question to the Angel;

"Tell me all about the fourth beast and the ten horns, and the other little horn that grew amid the ten horns, that turned into the likeness of a man who blasphemed God."

Then, for a moment Daniel hesitated. There was something else in the vision that he just remembered. It was the actions that this evil king takes against his people, so he asked of that also;

"Explain to me also about this 'horn' gaining authority over the people of God and the coming of the Lord of Heaven who will gain victory over the horn and return the kingdom to His people."

Either Daniel didn't want to believe what he had seen in the vision, because of the terrible oppression it exhibited on his people, or he was just seeking confirmation of what he had seen, in either case, he wanted to have the Angel explain the whole episode about the little horn again. And so the Angel, who seemed to be very knowledgeable of the vision and being pressed for more definitive answers, replied;

"The fourth beast of the vision depicts the fourth kingdom, which will be more powerful than those before it, and will subdue them and take dominion over the earth. The ten horns on its head represent ten kings that will arise from the ashes of that kingdom, and unite to form a new empire out of the old. Out of their midst, another king will arise who has no kingdom of his own but shall assume authority over the ten. Three of the ten kings will rebuke his authority and because of it they will be dismissed from the union. He will take authority over God's people, and persecute them, and bring derision on God by thinking to change the sacred laws and sacrifices. He shall hold that power over the people for three and a half years."

"But his end will come and his dominion will be taken away, and when that is done, the kingdom over all of the earth will be given to the saints of the most High forever." (Dan. 7:23-27)

The Angel's explanation of the vision still left unanswered

questions in Daniel's mind which still troubled him, probably because he wasn't given a reason for the terrible wrath, or 'the great words' against God that were being shouted aloud by the *'little horn.'* He knew that this blaspheme could only have come from a man who had a deep resentment against God, and he wanted to know the reason.

He wasn't told, but we know now that this blasphemous outburst originated with Satan, who was imprisoned within the man. But the Angel either wouldn't or couldn't go further down that path, because he would be exposing the direct involvement of Satan in the tribulation. He did say however, that as a direct result of this overwhelming change in the man, he would seek to destroy any and all worship of the Creator on earth and furthermore he would destroy the Jews, which is what the term *'wear out the saints of the Most High,'* implies. (Dan. 7:25)

THE THIRD REVELATION - THE EIGHTH KING

Another two years went by before the Lord attempted to continue His awesome story of the President, and there's a distinct possibility that He waited that long because He wasn't sure if Daniel was ready to hear more of the shattering story of the Devil and the humiliation he would bring on his countrymen. Mindful of this, the Lord opened His third revelation on a less disconcerting subject, by giving Daniel an allegorical description of what would be the last battle fought between the armies of King Alexander of Macedonia and King Darius of Persia, wherein Darius would be defeated and his vast Empire given over to Alexander. Certainly there was nothing intimidating about this disclosure, and it served a dual purpose, both in the recording of this future battle and Alexander's later death in the annuls of history. And it would serve as a time marker from which the tribulation's beginning could later be calculated.

It also set forth what might be called a 'heritage marker' of the Union President, whose ancestors would be derived from the loins of one of the kings who would supersede Alexander. And of course, it provided the Lord with a gentle way of easing into the President's saga again.

In a few brief scenes that followed in the vision, Daniel was taken from the death of Alexander through the parceling-out of his kingdom to the four generals, and from thence he was taken through the era of just one of these generals. Incidentally, all of these generals would become powerful national leaders in their own right, though Daniel deals with only one of them at this point, and that was the one whose province was provisionally located in the northern area of the Empire. (Dan.8: 9)

More will be spoken about this 'king of the north,' as he is referred to in the fifth revelation, but he is mentioned here because it will be from his loins that our future mystery man would ascend.

That one verse (Dan.8:9) will be the only 're-introduction' of the *little horn'* or the President, that the Lord will give to Daniel before catapulting him as He did before over the three-and a-half year span of the Jewish judgment period to its closing day, and depositing him on the doorstep of what will be the seventh and last judgment. Only this time the Lord is going to finish the story about the mysterious incarnation and the uproar that followed in the wake of this tragic event and caused the terrible bedlam in Israel in those last hours before the final desolation. The Devil would come down to Jerusalem and total chaos would follow.

Again, Daniel was aware, that in taking this monstrous leap from the beginning of the tribulation to its very end, that all of the in-between punishments to be dispersed on Israel were being passed over. And he may have wondered why, but he didn't question the Lord about them. We know from reading the book of Revelation that these punishments included the two devastating volcanic eruptions that seared half of the nation, followed by a destructive meteor that exploded on impact in Israel and poisoned the whole region's precious water resources, and then came that terrible earthshaking that destroyed many of Jerusalem's structures along with the Mosque of Omar on the Temple Mount. Following those four punishments on the land, the remaining three were destined for the people, with the first of these being the terrible plague of demon spirits that ended up destroying a third of the population in Israel. And following hard on the heels of that plague came the terrifying sixth judgment war that had just ended, in which another third of the Jewish people were killed.

Also left behind was the account of the President's foray into Israel at the close of that war and the many extraordinary incidents that shadowed him and eventually caused his assassination in Jerusalem. Instead, Daniel is being rushed over all of this to the waning hours of the indignation.

Once there however, he watches aghast at the awe-inspiring emergence of the 'new' President, or the 'IT' as he later calls him, this creature who springs to life in the body of the President and immediately begins his terrible persecution.

It would seem, that except for maintaining the continuity of the President's career story, this revelation could easily have been the concluding one in the series instead of being third in line, because it deals almost exclusively with the suspenseful conclusion of the President's brief career as a mortal and even briefer career with immortality. In effect, we have skipped over Daniel's last two revelations with the many startling things that happened immediately prior to this frightening moment, and we have ended up reading the last page of the book, which focuses on the events that happen during those last critical hours of the Jewish judgment period when the seventh Trumpet Judgment suddenly exploded on the Jewish people with all of the attendant fierceness and persecutions of the Devil.

To the exclusion of all else, it seems, this revelation about the loosening of Satan upon His people was the consummate message that the Lord has wanted to get across to Daniel, and yet He feared telling him.

Surprisingly, in the closing scene of this revelation, we find the Lord taking one more opportunity to reveal for those who will be living in the end-times, just when the dark clouds of the judgments should be expected to appear. He does this by having us listen-in on a conversation between two saints, who happen to be in the closing scene of the vision and who at that moment were discussing the time factor between the era of Alexander the Great and the recent events in Jerusalem. And it is their conclusion that these latest events will occur in what has been translated as ' *twenty-three hundred days*' from the time of Alexander's demise. Rightly, the time element should be recognized as being twenty-three hundred years instead of days, which tallies closely with the number of years from BC 323 to the present.

Understanding this vision, and the events surrounding those last three days of the indignation can be a difficult process for a reader who hasn't been given sufficient background information leading up to this moment, however, much of this needed information can be derived directly from the book of Revelation, thus making it possible to piece together all of the events of those last fateful days.

If, for a moment you would imagine yourself in downtown Jerusalem and not far from the building where, for the past several weeks the President had made his headquarters. The President has just been murdered, presumably by zealots, and the authorities have already instituted a frantic search for his killers in a futile effort to muffle the rising global furor of resentment against the Jews. Many suspects were rounded up and jailed in the process, including the two witnesses from God, who could have easily escaped, but allowed themselves to be taken with the others, knowing that their mission was completed and that they must put themselves in God's hands to somehow make their return to heaven.

While all this is happening, the President's funeral service was being delayed to allow time for the turmoil in Jerusalem to subside and for the arrival of the expected high-ranking international representatives who would be attending the funeral. Finally, three days after his death and on the morning of the final day of the judgment period, the funeral service of the President got under way. But midway through the service an amazing thing happened. The former President was miraculously restored to life. The world watched in silence as the man stepped forth out of the coffin, and what followed next was a tumultuous celebration.

From his outward appearance you would have sworn that this was the same man who had been slain, and he was physically, but this revived man who now walked through the midst of the attendees and accepted their accolades was a vastly different person from the former one, and surprisingly, it was this difference between his 'before and after' the incarnation experience that Daniel noticed and recorded in his journal.

Unfortunately, because of his coverage of what you might call the 'side effects' rather than the event itself, what had transpired from the time of the President's death until this 'new man' arose from the coffin is uniquely missing from his account. From this omission, we can only assume that he was not wholly informed about the incarnation event. And likely for good reason, for had he known, it's almost certain that he would have faithfully recorded the incarnation event in his journal, including the names of the participants, and Satan would have surely been informed as a consequence. Again his journal only records the radical change of character that came over the man, but even with that limited description, it is clear that the incarnation had taken place. He further records that the former mild mannered President, had suddenly changed into a monster, which is what his phrase *'a king of fierce countenance who understands dark sentences,'* implies. (Dan.8: 23)

John, on the other hand, was totally aware of the incarnation, yet he too faced the same dilemma in trying to describe the transition that took place. His sorely abbreviated description of the event went like this:

"There are seven kings: five are fallen, and one is, and the other is not yet come; and when he cometh, he must continue a short space. (11) And the beast that was, and is not, even he is the eighth, and is of the seven, and goeth into perdition." (Rev. 17:10,11))

Here, he's using an analogy of a certain 'seventh king' in a dynasty of kings, who had his reign cut short by his tragic death, but somehow was miraculously restored to life to finish out his career as the eighth king.

From the context of the chapter, we understand that this 'foreshortening' of the President's life was obviously due to his assassination, and when that happened, as the above verse suggests, Satan, who was not in any 'royal line of kings' per se, became a king by his incarnation into the body of the President, who, before his death was the legitimate heir and seventh in the royal line of Antigonus, the first king of Syria. Now, with the union of the President's body and the soul and spirit of Satan, the 'eighth' king emerges from death. However, to the world populace who knows nothing of the incarnation, he is simply the revived President. But however it turns out, the world still rejoices over their 'President' being snatched from the jaws of death.

In going over Daniel's account, we find that by his reckoning this third revelation came in the third year of the reign of King Belshazzar of Babylon, which would be circa BC 552.   He describes in his journal the strange situation of seeing himself within the vision, standing on the grounds of the royal palace in Shushan, which was the home of Cyrus, the extant reigning king of the Persian Empire.

This city was located in the province of Elam in the ancient land of Persia and several hundred miles from Babylon. Today, a city in that same location is called Shusqtar, in what is now the nation of Iran. There is a river called Ulai that still runs through the city as it did in those days below the palace of the King, and near which Daniel received his third vision which projected him some 220 years into the future.

The opening scene of the vision shows Daniel standing on the castle grounds of the Persian King who at the moment is being pictured as a large ram with two magnificent curled horns, dashing thither and yon over the landscape, but always distancing himself further and further away from where Daniel stood. And it seemed that wherever the ram traveled, he laid claim to that portion of land for his possession.

However, there came a time when the ram realized that he would be challenged for his possessions, and those expectations were soon fulfilled when a noble male goat with a single great horn (depicting Alexander) came swiftly from the west and marched boldly across the ram's territory. The two were destined to meet, and when they did there was a fierce conflict between them that continued for some time, but in the end the ram was mortally wounded and the goat became the proud possessor of the ram's vast domain. And as we are told, it was not long after the goat had settled in to enjoy his new dominion that the single horn on his head suddenly fell off and in its place grew four new horns. (Dan.8: 1-8)

We can rightfully assume that this portion of the vision displayed a prophetical analogy of what would be a future conflict between the Macedonian forces of King Alexander and the armies of the great Persian Empire under King Darius III.

We know from history that there were several previous battles between these two Kings before this final battle in BC 331 wherein Darius was defeated and his vast Persian Empire was taken over by Alexander, who went on to conquer regions of India and the Middle-East, before returning to Babylon, where he died in BC 323.

He had no heirs for his empire, so it was subsequently apportioned among four of his top generals, of whom at least two made themselves 'kings' by right, with one of them founding the Syrian dynasty from which the President would ascend.

In this revelation, his forbearers have been depicted as coming out of one of the 'four horns' on the goat, and for want of a better delineation of which of those four 'horns' he was descended from, Daniel makes the designation that it was one who oversaw the most northerly province of the Empire, which included a portion of the ancient Babylonian Empire called Assyria.

From this we gather that the President is a descendant of the Syrian ruler General Antigonus, who later made himself a king by proclamation, and in the process generated a new 'royal dynasty' into which the European President would eventually be born. This would not only confirm the President's 'royal' background, as it were, but also his heritage on one side, from Arab stock, which becomes a vital factor in the future fulfillment of the prophecies of his life.

So this early portion of the vision actually serves a double role. It not only defines the heritage of the present day President, or Anti-Christ, as he would come to be recognized, but it also provides a marker for the positioning of the judgment period in the future. This marker is in reference to a later scene in the vision where two individuals are discussing Alexander's death in relationship to the forth-coming judgment period. (Dan. 8:13)

But now we come to the highlight of this revelation when Daniel learns that the primary reason for the extended number of his visions and revelations was to reveal the Lord's intricate plan for sending Satan down to earth in the tribulation. However, for the plan to succeed, it was vital for the transfer to be kept in utmost secrecy, for what happens in those critical moments on the final day of the indignation lies at the heart of the Lord's plans for the redemption and deliverance of both the Jewish remnant and the Tribulation saints. For at any point in time, should either the President or Satan balk at their respective roles in their missions, the plans of God could be thwarted.

So it's understandable, that the Lord would want to keep the advent of the incarnation at least obscured, if not hidden altogether while still revealing the concept of the plan to Daniel. And He does this through the use of allegorical language, which falls right in line with keeping the anonymity of its participants. For as you have probably realized by now, the true identity of the President has been kept hidden behind the term 'little horn,' and the word 'Satan' or 'Devil' never actually appears in the writings.

For whatever reason, the revelation now couches the actual transfer of Satan, or the incarnation event, in extremely figurative language, by depicting it as an 'evolving process' which takes place within the man, much like the 'evolvement of the little horn' when it grew into a man's face in the last revelation, only in this instance the 'evolving process' takes place within the heart and soul of the President, while his outward appearance remained the same.

The narrator explains this transformation process by first directing our attention to the amazing 'career' development of this 'little horn,' who has moved up the social and political ladder from a 'commoner' in society to the esteemed political status of the Presidency of the European Union. The narrator describes this 'moving up' process as "*waxing great.*" Meaning that his stature in the world community had risen to a higher level, similar to the recognition Daniel received when Belshazzar made this former slave the third ruler in the Kingdom.

But his Presidency was far from trouble free. It came with grave responsibilities that were not discussed in Daniel's journal, such as the bearing his Presidency will have on the troubles that have surfaced within the universal Church.

The Apostle Paul, in his epistle to the Thessalonian church, writes very poignantly about the man and his election to the Presidency, pointing out his deep concern over the influence this man will have on the fragile faith of the believers following his inauguration. Paul intimates that the President will be at least partially responsible for the apostasy that has arisen within the Church body at this time. (II Thess. 2:3-8)

Without skipping a beat, the narrator propels us three and a half years in the future, where we find the President's political status now being expressed in glowing, almost regal terms. He has suddenly *waxed exceedingly great,'* which meant that he has reached the top rung on the ladder. No longer a mere President, he is suddenly endowed with a greater authority and prestige than he had ever imagined Needless to say, this sudden change in stature could only have come about through one thing, and that was the incarnation of the Devil.

The President has figuratively reached for the stars and laid hold of the scepter of his career, or as Daniel expressed it,

"He was able to reach into heaven and draw out from there some of the host of angels and cast them to the earth where he stamped on them." (Dan. 8:10)

Witnessed but unseen and certainly unheralded, the movement of Satan into the frame of the dead President on earth had been accomplished, and what immediately followed was this creature's audacity to rebuke the Lord and throw out a challenge to Him as the 'Prince of the host.' (Dan.8: 11)

You can imagine that this was a gesture that was made in great anger and a challenge that could only come from a proud and boastful angel who suddenly finds himself in this disdainful earthly condition. Satan was bitterly angry at being put in this position, and this wrath spewed out at every occasion.

It was this 'new President' who immediately instituted a total ban on the Jews' daily worship practices, and committed a profane act against the Jews and the Lord by "casting down" or desecrating the Holy place in Israel. (Dan.8: 11) All of which, and much more, took place in the closing hours of the judgment period. Incidentally, this 'thing' as it were, would be the infamous "abomination of desecration" that Jesus referred to in His description of the event. (Matt. 24:15)

Though both Daniel and John envisaged the emergence of this 'super human,' in the tribulation period, neither of them realized the purpose for this union.

Now we realize that Satan will perform two vital functions for the Lord in the tribulation period. But to successfully perform these functions, it was essential that he be incarnated into a human frame, and preferably that of the President. From which unique union a new personage will evolve who will be given a title of "the Beast," whose immediate task after his 'emergence' will be instigating the mass exodus of the Jews from the Holy Land. Later, during the great tribulation, he will be given dominion over the world, and for the first two years of the great tribulation period he will perform a miraculous work for the Lord in the Deliverance of the tribulation saints. This latter work was the reason for him being inducted here in the indignation period.

But getting back to the incarnation, the successful conclusion of which will be the 'desolation' work, as the exodus of the Jews is called. This work is discreetly veiled in Dan. 8:12, which reads:

"And a host was given him against the daily sacrifice by reason of transgression, and **it** *cast down the truth to the ground; and* **it** *practiced and prospered."*

When you realize that this is Satan's mission against the Jews, the message of this verse becomes abundantly clear, for it says, that because of their rebellion, the Jews will be turned over to him for punishment, and he will successfully discharge his duty, as the phrase *'practiced and prospered'* implies. This desolation of Israel turns out to be the closing act of the indignation by the incarnated President, and the closing scene of this portion of the vision.

CALCULATING THE DAYS

With that closing episode on the President, Daniel's revelation and vision now reverts back to positioning the judgment period, and our attention is given over to a scene in the vision where two unidentified individuals are discussing the previous scenes of the ram and the goat. Their limited conversation went something like this:

One asked,

"How long shall be the vision concerning the daily sacrifice, and the transgression of desolation, to give both the sanctuary and

56

the host to be trodden under foot?"

And the other man answered;

"Unto two thousand and three hundred days; then shall the sanctuary be cleansed." (Dan. 8:13,14)

The conversation in this episode will be explained in a moment, but let's go back to the three specific actions of the President following his incarnation. These were the cessation of the daily sacrifice in Israel, the blasphemy of the Creator, and the desecration of the Holy place.

Following these actions however, Daniel mentions another event that was alluded to in the conversation between the two men. That event was; *"the treading under foot of the sanctuary and the host."* This was an action taken against the Jews that turns out to be more terrible than any previous persecution and desecration. Apparently, when the Beast initiated the desolation program he had no intention of just letting the Jews ramble off into the sunset without further trying to destroy them in their exodus. These words speak of that intended 'slaughter of the innocents,' which would take place in the refugees' flight from the armies of the 'Beast.' And he almost got away with it, but fortunately the Lord intervened and his intended slaughter was blocked at the onset. The pursuing armies were destroyed instead. (Rev. 12:15,16)

This partially successful atrocity against the Jews is what the witness in the vision calls *"the transgression of (the) desolation,"* or the terrorization of the Jews in their exodus from their homeland. This sentence should have been written in capital letters to emphasize what happens in the end of the indignation. It's no wonder that Daniel was so distraught for days after hearing of this intended slaughter.

THE ANGEL'S INTERPRETATION OF THE VISION

At this point there seems to be to an intermission following the scene of the two men, during which time Daniel apparently remained in his trance-like state of deep contemplation over the recent revelation of the Beast and his atrocities against the Jews. While still in that state of mind, he envisions the Lord at some distance, standing on the surface of the water in the middle of the river, and with Him stood the Angel Gabriel.

Apparently Daniel's bewilderment over the revelation showed on his face, even from that distance, because he overheard the Lord saying to Gabriel,

" Go and interpret the vision for Daniel."

At that time, the Angel came over to Daniel, who had already prostrated himself before the Lord. But with the Angel's soft touch and gentle assurance, he was lifted up to listen to the Angel's next words.

"Daniel, I have come to help you understand what's going to happen in the last end of the indignation, for at the time appointed the end shall come." (Dan. 8:17,19)

And with that simple introduction, his interpretation of the vision began.

But first, notice that the Angel is using a new word for the Jews' judgment period. That word is 'indignation.' That particular word will surface again by Daniel, (in 11:30 and 11:36) and in common usage of the day it typified a period of 'wrath or great fury,' but as it is used here and in the book of Ezekiel, the word carries a narrower definition, which inferred a period of 'God's anger over sin,' and more specifically, a time of the "wrath of God in judgment." (Ezek. 21: 31,22:31)   However in this instance, with the definite article "the" before the word, it denoted a specific period in which God's wrath would be expended, which is to be the judgment period of the Jews.

But at the time, Daniel's mind slipped over the Angel's terminology because he wasn't aware of any judgment period other than the Jewish one, nor was he cognizant of anyone else being involved in any type of judgment. However the issue of 'other peoples' involvement will arise in the next revelation when Daniel is made aware of the actual part this 'indignation' had in the overall scheme of the judgments.

And if you hadn't caught it, the words *'last end'* of that indignation threw a new light on the picture, for it wasn't to be the 'last days' of the tribulation period as some have supposed, but the last days of the Jewish judgment period.

Nothing in the revelations thus far have revealed what the punishments will be like during the three and a half year period, and with this announcement it's apparent that we still won't be told because the Angel has been restrained from passing on any information about the individual punishments except for the last two, which are the war and the entrance of Satan.

It should be noted however, that the scenes of the incarnation event that Daniel had just witnessed, and which will be reinforced by the Angel' interpretation, will occur in the 'last end' of the indignation, or more specifically, the last three days of the first three and a half years. The Lord is stressing this point because His plans for the remainder of the seven-year tribulation period hinge on the successful completion of the events of those last three days.

Ironically, the last four of the five revelations deal with four events that happen to, and by, the Anti-Christ. These are; His signing of the peace covenant, his assassination by the Jews, his incarnation by Satan, and his death at Armageddon. The signing of the covenant initiates the tribulation period, his death at Armageddon ends it and the other two events happen in the middle. And this revelation deals with those two events.

The Angel Gabriel continued to expound on his interpretation of the vision, beginning as Daniel did, with the scene of the ram and the goat. And with little explanation, as though he were summarizing what Daniel already knew, he quickly described how the ram with the two horns represented the two kings of Media and Persia, and the goat with the single horn represented the king of Greece. He then reiterated the story of the Grecian king's death several years after a battle between them, and the ultimate partitioning of his vast empire between his four generals who were less noble than he.

From secular history, we understand that once the division of Alexander's Empire was made, the four generals immediately made themselves regents over their respective provinces. The province of Macedonia went to Cassandra, the province of Thrace to Lysimachus, Egypt to Ptolemy Soter, and the one we are interested in, Asia Minor, was given to one named Antigonus. And while the Angel omitted detailing the events following the split-up of the Empire, he made

59

this comment, that *"in the latter time of their kingdom, when the transgressors are come to the full, a king of fierce countenance, and understanding dark sentences, shall stand up."* (Dan.8: 23)

Here we are being told that in the latter days, or in the tribulation period, when the Arab invasion of Israel has been accomplished, the President will 'stand up,' as he says, or come to the forefront, which he does following the incarnation incident.

And it's not incidental that the President had his roots in one of the four kingdoms, but from which of the four is not indicated here. However, from the following earlier verse, the conclusion can be made that he came from the line of Antigonus of the 'northern' province of Assyria.

"And <u>out of one of them came forth a little horn, which waxed exceeding great,</u> toward the south, and toward the east, and toward the pleasant land." (Dan. 8: 9)

And because this 'little horn,' is ascertained as <u>coming out</u> from one of the four larger horns, it signifies the parentage of this man as coming from the royal bloodline of the 'kings of the north,' which was obviously not a Semetic line. Moreover, from other scriptures in the Bible we understand that his mother would have been of Jewish ancestry dating back to the tribe of Dan, which was one of the tribes of Israel that had been deported to Assyria as slaves some 400 years earlier. Suffice to say that this dual heritage of Arab and Jew will cause him a lot of grief when he is forced to pledge his allegiance to one side or the other after he becomes the European Union President.

As for Daniel's questions concerning the dramatic change in the character that came over the President, the angel would only say that a certain power was given him, which allowed him *"to destroy wonderfully, prosper and practice, and destroy the mighty and the Holy people."* (Dan.8: 24)

Which was no more than he already knew, but it did add confirmation that the 'Beast' was successful in destroying the Jewish people, although not to the extent that he would have probably preferred.

There was an addendum to the Angel's interpretation however, which seemed to sum up the career of the Anti-Christ;

"And through his policy also he shall cause craft to prosper in his hand; and he shall magnify himself in his heart, and by peace shall destroy many: he shall also stand up against the Prince of princes; but he shall be broken without hand." (Dan. 8: 25)

This statement may be somewhat confusing because it is actually an extraneous reference to the Beast's activities beyond the desolation in Israel. It speaks of his dominion over the world in a period after the indignation, which had no bearing on the Jewish situation. In fact, it's strange that the Lord allowed it to be included in the dissertation unless He believed it was so abstruse that not even the Devil would comprehend it. For what it says is, that the Beast has grandiose aspirations about his future as the world leader, which included the predilection of becoming equal with God. But his bubble is burst when he chooses to do battle with the Lord at Armageddon, where he meets his demise instead.

All of this information will be picked up later by John for his writing of the book of Revelation, however there is one other important feature about this vision which is the time element of the incarnation event, or when all this takes place, and how it becomes relevant to you and I in the twenty-first century.

As the Angel had said, these things would happen in the 'last end,' or in the last few days of the indignation, which was the moot point in the discussion between those two by-standers in the vision. They were trying to determine how long it would be from the time of Alexander's death to this 'last end,' and they came to the conclusion that it would be twenty-three hundred "days." There is some discrepancy between Biblical interpretations as to whether the word 'days' was the legitimate word to be inserted here. A better interpretation would be 'years,' which would correlate closely with the twenty-three hundred years from Alexander to the present.

CHAPTER 3

The Drawstring

The year was BC 538, an important year for the Jewish community in Babylon for they had finally been granted their freedom by Cyrus, the new Persian king. And in the same city, Daniel had just been called into the great room of the palace before Darius, who had just been made prince of the newly conquered Babylonian Empire. He had been summoned there to hear the reading of that proclamation, and as he listened to the droning voice of the court attendant, his mind wandered back over the past sixty-eight years to the time of his youth, when he was brought into this very room and forced to bow before the great King Nebuchadnezzar, fearful of whether he was to live or die.

And he remembered how, many years later he was again brought into this court to stand and tell the mighty king of his dream of the great image, and how at the time the Lord gave him the wisdom to answer the king rightly, and by doing so he was lifted up in honor and position to rule alongside the great king.

And it was in this room that Prince Bel-shazzar, the grand-son and heir of King Nebuchadnezzar, had summoned him on that fateful night, just over a year ago, when he was asked to interpret the meaning of the words that had mysteriously appeared on the wall behind him. And again his interpretation of the writing so pleased Bel-shazzar that he removed his royal scarlet robe and put it about Daniel's shoulders. He also removed his golden chain of authority from about his neck and placed it around Daniel's while declaring him to be third in power in the kingdom.

Daniel was never quite sure whether it was the royal apparel and the King's signet that saved him from being killed that very night when the invading Persian army swept through the palace and into the drunken court where all of the revelers were destroyed. By the next morning, however, the city had been taken and the king in whose presence he now stood was installed as the reigning monarch over Babylonia, and again Daniel was chosen to be second in command.

The news of the captives' release that he was hearing had not come unexpectedly. Some years back the exiles had received a letter from their own prophet Jeremiah, wherein they were informed that the captivity would last for seventy years, and as it turned out, by the time the refugees were fully prepared to return to Jerusalem it was right on seventy years.

But while this news gave new hope and expectancy to those who would be making the journey, one of those who wouldn't be returning was Daniel. He was well into his eighties and felt too old and frail to trek those hundreds of miles over the desert, besides, the Lord had other plans for him in Babylon. But in his heart he carried a deep concern for those who would be making the trip and for the situation that they would be finding themselves in when they arrived in the old abandoned city of Jerusalem.

In the succeeding generations of the Jewish exiles, nearly all of them had either abandoned their true faith in Jehovah God, or had been seduced into worshipping the heathen gods in Babylon. There were synagogues for the dedicated few, but the many years with neither relics nor sacred scriptures to sustain them had taken their toll, and now that the time for their return was near, Daniel feared that they would be ill prepared to meet the challenges of rebuilding the Temple and the city. All of these things weighed heavily on Daniel's heart, and coupled with those concerns was the remote possibility that the final judgments might just be waiting for the returnees.

You can well imagine that with these thoughts on his mind and remembering the scriptures which deemed a curse upon those who would abandon their true God, Daniel was oft compelled to fall to his knees before the Lord and plead for mercy for himself and his unworthy brethren in their state of sin and rebellion. And this time was no different. He fell to his knees and prayed long and earnestly, not only for his people but also for the land of his fathers, and particularly the city of Jerusalem, which lay in desolation and ruin after so many years of neglect. His words were, *"O Lord hear; O Lord forgive; O Lord hearken and do; defer not, for thine own sake,*

O my God; for thy city and thy people are called by thy name."
(Dan. 9:19)

When you read his fervent prayer, you get a real sense of Daniel's apprehension over the dire misfortunes that could await the refugees on their return, as though they were heading into the maelstrom of the judgments. And it's more than likely, that on hearing these words the Lord sensed this trepidation in Daniel, and wondered if somehow he had misunderstood the timing of the judgments, so even while Daniel was still praying about the situation, the Lord sent the Angel Gabriel to him with instructions to help him understand the content of the former visions and make him know when the judgments would come.

From Daniels's point of view, it was understandable why he had been having second thoughts about when the judgments would arrive, because there had been a lengthy dry spell as far as visitations from the Lord were concerned. The last revelation had been some fourteen years earlier, and at that time he was led to believe that it would be the last one because everything about the judgments was confirmed and there would be no need for further revelations. As a matter of fact, the last thing the Angel said to him was, *"Shut up the vision, for it won't happen for many days,"* and many, many days had gone by since those words were spoken.

But whether or not the Lord actually planned on giving Daniel further visions was answered when the Lord chose to send two further revelations that would include further deep secrets about the future that went well beyond just affixing the time period of the tribulation. He would eventually pour out all of the secrets of the last days of the indignation, along with a preview of the great tribulation that is extremely relevant to our generation.

In past revelations, as you recall, when a vision was given to Daniel, he would record what his impressions of the vision were, and then he would accompany them with the Angel's interpretation. And although there were some minor differences between the two versions, it was usually in the Angel's abbreviated version that some of the features of the vision were left out. Still, the dual dissemination of the revelation was highly profitable because of the extra information that it contained.

But for some reason, the Lord chose to revise His method of transmitting the revelations, and instead of receiving a vision for his verification, Daniel would be afforded only a visitation by the Angel, who in this case is purportedly sent to give him 'skill and understanding,' or in other words, clear up the situation about the past visions so that he might better understand the distant future status of the judgments. So, under these new conditions of transmittal it was imperative that Daniel pay close attention to both the message and the messenger.

There may have been various reasons for the Lord doing this, such as the impracticality of transmitting what will be a large biographical package about the President or it could be because the Lord wanted to categorize this new up-coming information separate from the judgments. However, this method of information transferal also has its drawbacks, because, in the past the Angel has tended to abbreviate his interpretations, which turns out to be the case in these next revelations.

Here again, whether it was God's original intention to divulge all of the information that we find in this revelation, or whether He was more or less coerced into it by Daniel's apparent confusion over the timing of the judgments, the Lord does oblige him by opening up more of the mysteries surrounding the judgment period, which, by the way, are solely applicable to the Jews and the nation of Israel. He will however bring in the issue of the Gentile involvement.

As an aside, it's difficult to ascertain who came up with the concept that the book of Daniel was a prophetic message for the Gentiles, but it's of fairly recent origin, and unfortunately many contemporary theologians and students of eschatology have perpetuated this theme, which is based solely on Daniel's practice of dating his revelations to the reigns of Gentile kings. With this conviction in the back of their mind, the prophecies of Daniel, and by implication the judgments and prophecies of Revelation also, have been systematically assigned to the Gentile masses.

And because the 'seven year judgment period' falls within this scope of so-called Gentile prophecies, it too is parlayed into a single universal tribulation period. But this idea couldn't be farther from the truth. As you have come to realize, all of the visions and revelations in Daniel revolve around and appertain to one people and one nation, those being the Jews and the nation of Israel.

The reason I bring this up now is because the one and only inference of a Gentile involvement in the punishments is mentioned here in this fourth revelation, and there is reason to believe that even this reference was an oversight at the time. In fact, the Lord has been adamant in His desire to keep any recognition of a Gentile involvement in the tribulation a secret until the book of Revelation was released.

But we are going to find the Lord taking a new tack in this revelation and He will be opening His secret vault on a whole array of subjects concerning the judgments, including a background check of the Union President, his launching of the judgment period and his involvement in the closing days of that period, with just a sneak preview at what's coming as far as the Gentile world is concerned.

Not that this added information about the Gentiles will effect the status of the Jewish punishments in any way, for their period will be just as severe and will endure for its intended 31/2 years as prophesied, with its close being the dreaded desolation of Israel. However, much to Daniel's surprise and consternation, he finally finds out that the Lord has added another judgment period which extends beyond the "indignation" for another three and one half years.

THE FOURTH REVELATION

Daniel's fourth visitation came fourteen years after the previous one, and as he writes, it was in the first year of Darius the Median, who was now the Crown Prince and ruler over the realm of Babylonia.

And just as the third revelation might well have been the concluding one because of the climactic nature of the information it contained, so this fourth revelation, although very brief compared to the others, would fit beautifully into second place because it supplies the answers as to why there is a projected judgment period in the first place, and how the program of judgments would be set up in the manner that it is.

This is a three part revelation, with the first part laying out six reasons why God is seeking indemnity for mans' treatment of Him through these end-time punishments. The second part deals with several important stages in the history of the Jews, including the reconstruction of the city of Jerusalem and the Temple, the advent and death of the Messiah, and the second Diaspora of the Jews with the heartbreaking destruction of their beautiful city and its Temple. These last events occurred in the first century A.D., and provided verification of the prophecies that Daniel had recorded some 600 years earlier. They also provide a stepping stone to the next events, which will be the judgments.

The third part of the revelation is contained in the closing verse of the ninth chapter, and it encompasses all of the key elements of the judgment period along with a brief resume of its chief advocate, the Union President. In this one verse, the angel highlights the judgment period's beginning, its middle portion, wherein the division of the period is made, and finally the conclusion of the seven-year period, which, taken in its entirety forms the backdrop for the other revelations.

This revelation is extremely abbreviated, (Dan. 9: 24-27) and it's unfortunate that the Angel decided to make it so, but then again, it is more or less a summation of the three previous revelations, with the prime objective of spotlighting the three 'time elements' of the judgment period. The first of these time elements is the 'seventy-week' overall time period, the second is the final 'one-week' restitution period, and the third or key element being the division of those seven years into two equal portions.

The angel delves right into the revelation by informing Daniel that **"SEVENTY WEEKS would be determined upon his people and upon his holy city."** (Dan.9: 24)

This doesn't sound like the Angel is speaking about a coming global judgment period, but a narrowly defined acknowledgment about the Jews and the city of Jerusalem. They are awesome words, like the dire pronouncement that a judge might give to a condemned killer, but the intention behind the announcement was to relieve Daniel's apprehension about the judgments just sitting and waiting for the refugees to return to Jerusalem. It also assures Daniel of the judgments' pre-determined location in the distant future.

Some readers might wonder how the term "seventy-weeks" is converted to 490 years. The explanation starts with the terminology of the period in which the book of Daniel was written. The Hebrew word for the English term 'week' was *Shabu'im,* which literally meaning 'sevens,' and was invariably used by Jewish scholars when they were contemplating a particular time period in terms of years. If any other time period was being considered, such as a 'week of days,' for instance, the writer would add the word 'days' (yamim) after the word *shabu'im.* In this case the consideration is for years and the *seventy weeks* or *seventy-sevens* (70x7) of years is 490 years.

The city of Jerusalem was included in this time envelope because it too must share the burden of responsibility for the punishments sent down by the Lord.

However, if we off-handedly dismiss this opening sentence as merely being time related, or that it simply declares a certain period of time between two events, we miss the full import of the pronouncement. The ensuing verses, which speak of certain events taking place within this time frame, as well as our own realization that over two millenniums have passed since these verses were written, suggests that this seventy-weeks of years was not thrown out as a simple time period of so many years, but that it was to be a period wherein severe tribulation and trouble would be determined upon the Jews and the city of Jerusalem, of which the final week of those years would be a time of 'great tragedy' or, as Daniel states it, '*a time of trouble, such as never was since there was a nation..*' (Dan. 11:1)

Historical records as well as the scriptures verify the tragic ordeals that the Jews went through under Gentile domination from the time they returned to their homeland after the Babylonian captivity, until the second Diaspora in 135 A.D. With that Diaspora, however, their tribulation was interrupted, and will remain so until the final week when the tribulation begins anew. This partially explains why the list of prophetic events in this revelation ended with the desolation of Jerusalem in 135 AD.

The Angel points out to Daniel that this 490 year period would begin with the issuance of a decree by the King of Persia and Babylonia, (Neh.2) (Arta-xerxes Longimanus, in BC 445) which stated in part that the refugees would be allowed to return to their homeland and rebuild the city. This predicted future date from Daniel's standpoint, should not be confused with the original decree of freedom for the Jews which was issued by King Cyrus in BC 538, some 93 years earlier and to which Daniel was a witness. At the earlier time, some of the refugees did return, however the numbers were somewhat insufficient for the task of rebuilding the city and the Temple. And though it sounds incongruent when you consider the time that has already elapsed, the end of this 490 year time period is supposed to coincide with the future setting up of the Kingdom on earth when the Lord will be anointed the most Holy.

This aspect we will take up later, but meanwhile, Daniel was given a list of six 'things' that would have to be accomplished during this 'seventy-week' time period, first and foremost of which will be the removal of Satan's presence from heaven and the earth, with all vestiges of sin that accompanies him. This will remedy the situation between man and God with respect to the affront made on His Holiness and Majesty, as well as subduing and expiating sin as a whole in the world. This riddance of Satan will be accomplished on the last day of the period, at the conclusion of the battle of Armageddon.

These six accomplishments are as follows:
1)" *To finish the transgression,*
  2) *To make an end of sins,*
    3) *To make reconciliation for iniquity,*
      4) *To bring in everlasting righteousness,*
        5) *To seal up the vision and prophecy,*
          6) *and to anoint the most Holy.* (Dan 9:24)

Getting rid of Satan will take care of the first two on the list, but the third has to do with God's retaliation on mankind for their rebellion and disobedience.

As you recall in an earlier revelation we encountered the phrase *"the indignation,"* which was determined to be "God's time of recompense upon the Jews," or the judgment period. This was to be a time when He would receive recompense from the Jews for their sin and rebellion against Him. However, that word has herein been replaced with another descriptive phrase, *"make reconciliation for iniquity,"* which seems to carry the same connotation as 'indignation,' but decries of a different judgment period. Actually it encompasses the whole seven years, whereas the indignation only reflected the judgment period of three and a half years for the Jews. Incidentally, this statement about a 'reconciliation' was Daniel's first inkling of the existence of another time of judgment, which will give him a problem later.

And it should be noted, that while Daniel's passionate prayer in the earlier part of the chapter expressed his deep concern over the sinfulness of his own people, and for which he sought God's forgiveness and mercy, the Lord appropriately took this opportunity to confront Daniel's assumption that only the Jews were going to be involved in the tribulation. He let him know that the judgment period was intended to be a time of retribution and vengeance from *all* peoples, which is why we find this extended list of the works that must be accomplished.

Some have attributed these six works to the Lord's atoning death and resurrection, and from a first glance that might appear to be the case, but the particular atonement spoken of here had to include the transgressions of the Beast for his desecration of the Holy place, which can only be achieved through the punishments. This also is the lone remedy for repairing the wide chasm that now exists in the fellowship between man and God, and makes possible the establishment of the everlasting kingdom on the earth.

However, the fifth accomplishment on the list, which is *'the sealing up of the vision and the prophecy'* is one that doesn't fit in the mold of recompense, though it also will be accomplished in this same time period.

This work requires the Lord **to seal all end time visions and prophecy from man's understanding** "until the latter days," when the seal will be broken. This apparent sealing of the prophecies could only have been accomplished after the writing of the book of Revelation, and from all indications that 'sealing of man's understanding' could still be in place today because of the seemingly limited number of people who contemplate end-time prophecy. And though we cannot comprehend all the parameters of the sealing process nor is it likely we will know when the sealing has been removed, if this is truly the end-times, it likely should be soon.

After assuring Daniel that all would go well with the returning refugees, the Angel began to expound on the second portion of the revelation which sets forth three significant happenings over the 490 year time period, beginning with the re-construction program of Jerusalem.

From other writings, notably the books of Nehemiah and Ezra, we are furnished with a complete scenario of the re-building efforts, both of the city, its walls, and the Temple, and as mentioned, those were troublous times, with constant interference from the neighboring peoples who didn't want to see the re-construction program completed. But as it turned out, the Temple was not only rebuilt, it was enlarged and beautified over the original Solomon design.

This rebuilding effort was accomplished in the forty-nine years outlined, but then there was a time lapse of some four hundred and thirty-four years before the second mentioned event took place, which was the advent of Christ.

Without going into details about the birth, life and ministry of our Lord, which he knew would be thoroughly portrayed in the Gospels, the Angel cites the Messiah's death as a signpost of the times along with the terrible upheavals in the nation that followed. However, the wording of the revelation doesn't imply that these catastrophic events were instigated by the Lord's crucifixion, in fact they happened nearly a hundred years later, when revolts in Palestine against Roman oppression brought the legions of Rome against the nation in retaliation and terrible devastation followed. The populace of Jerusalem took the brunt of the destruction when thousands died of starvation during a year's siege of the city, and when the city was finally overthrown, those who were still alive were deported as slaves and the city was pillaged and destroyed. So once again the land was made desolate of its people and city of Jerusalem was abandoned.

The following is the Angel's encapsulation of those 483 years:

71

"Know therefore and understand, that from the going forth of the commandment to restore and to build Jerusalem unto the Messiah the Prince shall be seven weeks, and threescore and two weeks: the street shall be built again, and the wall, even in troublous times. (26) And after threescore and two weeks shall Messiah be cut off, but not for himself: and the people of the prince that shall come shall destroy the city and the sanctuary; and the end thereof shall be with a flood, and unto the end of the war desolations are determined." (Dan.9: 25-26)

It seems strange that Daniel didn't interpose on the Angel to tell him more about the Messiah, especially when His death was mentioned, because the Messiah's coming had always been a much anticipated event in the lives of the Jewish people. But the Angel was hastening on with his interpretation, and he now deliberates on those last seven years of the 490-year period, which have been popularized as 'the tribulation period.'

THE SEVEN LAST YEARS

In an unusually quick succession of phrases, the Angel by-passes a broad spectrum of time and events, of which our present Church age is a part, to zero in on the events of those last seven of the 490 years, but, here again, the brevity of his outline on the subject shows up like a flat stone skipping over the surface of a still pond, where only the salient points of those years are being touched upon. Here is the way he tells it:

"And he shall confirm the covenant with many for one week: and in the midst of the week he shall cause the sacrifice and the oblation to cease, and for the overspreading of abominations he shall make it desolate, even until the consummation, and that determined shall be poured upon the desolate." (Dan.9: 27)

Bear in mind that the Angel is still endeavoring to help Daniel understand the previous visions, and this 'he' that is being spoken of here evidently refers to the same individual or 'little horn' that had been mentioned in the previous visions, which would undoubtedly be the Union President.

Here again, the full disclosure on this person will appear in the next revelation, but the purpose for mentioning him here is to reveal his 'extra-curricular' activity in initiating the judgment period. He is the one who brings it into being, as the scripture states, through his generation of a peace agreement between "many peoples," referring of course to the Arabs and the Jews.

The duration of this agreement was obviously intended to be seven years, with the implication that the same period of time applies to the span of the tribulation, however, our attention is not directed to the seven years per se, but to the unique way in which the Lord divided those seven years into two parts.

He arranges for the President to depart for Israel 'mid-way' through the seven year term, which illustrates a division of that time period. It may seem like a strange way to make a division, but Daniel understood the connotation from his knowledge of the previous revelation when he was told that the Jews would be undergoing a three and a half year punishment period, but what confuses him now was the purpose for this extra period. "What was it for?" he wonders, and "Who was it for?"

Now the signing of any peace accord between nations is of historical significance and this one maybe even more so, because it will be the first such major agreement in a long while between Israel and its Islamic Arab neighbors, and quite frankly something that had been said would never happen. And while the world views this covenant as a means of bringing peace to the region as well as quelling terrorist activities, in the grand scheme of God's plans for Israel, its primary purpose will be to guarantee the borders of Israel from outside interference or aggression while the judgments on the Jews are in progress.

In reference to the President's sudden trip to Israel midway through those seven years, you might get the impression from Daniel's wording, that immediately on his arrival in Israel he arbitrarily banned all normal Jewish religious worship and, in an act of defiance toward God and the Jews, he desecrated the Holy *place*, which by the way, is not a newly constructed Temple as some have imagined, but the existing Western Wailing Wall, which was the only 'Holy place' left intact after the great earthquake two years earlier. It's strange that God singled out these particular activities for mentioning here if they were not important, but on this we will have to wait until the next revelation

In this one concluding verse of the revelation, (verse 27) and in his own inimitable way, the narrator has compressed all of the vital elements of those whole seven years into one sentence. He begins by confirming the peace treaty's existence for seven years, which at the same time initiates the tribulation period. He then notes the division of the tribulation taking place with the entry of the President into Israel, followed by the President's incarnation, as illustrated by the abominable acts of persecution that were made against the Jews just prior to striking his final blow of the desolation.

For a third time those several judgments on the Jews and the nation during the three and a half year period have been passed over, and we are instantly brought from the inauguration to the final day of the indignation, where we find the incarnated President standing on the plaza in front of the Wailing wall trying desperately to hold back the wrath that was ready to explode.

Blasting the airwaves with his venomous rhetoric against God he issues his demand for the cessation of all worship of the Creator, then without waiting for the uproar from this to subside, he blares forth the command for the forcible expulsion of all of the Jews from their homeland.

Daniel was dumbfounded by the edict for the expulsion of his people, but the fact that troops would be sent after the refugees to destroy them on their way was more than he could take. On top of that he learns that their expulsion will last until the consummation of the tribulation period, which would be another three and a half years.

But then came the final straw, which were in the final words of the Angel who spoke them slowly and deliberately:

"That (which has been) determined shall be poured upon the desolate."   (Dan. 9:27)

Daniel must have listened carefully to those words and rolled them over in his mind while he entered them in his journal. He looked up at the Angel to see if there was an explanation coming, but the Angel kept silent.

With the Angel's continued silence on the subject, Daniel might have assumed that they spoke of yet another round of

74

punishments, and from our viewpoint, if this predictive sentence had been written in the concluding chapter of Daniel's book, it could easily have been construed as encompassing all of the judgments that had been poured out upon Israel during their time of trouble. But because they immediately followed the decree of the desolation, they were really intended to be conciliatory words of encouragement that would be directed to all of the Jews in an act of appeasement by the Lord. This was His way of announcing a series of Divine salutary acts that would begin the moment the refugees entered into the desert on what they assumed would be their death march. For the phrase *"That which is determined"* speaks not of punishments but of blessings that will be poured upon the fleeing refugees, the first of which is revealed in this relieving statement that was later given by the same angel when speaking of the refugees:

"Thy people shall be delivered, everyone that shall be found written in the book." (Dan. 12:1)

If this is any indication of what's ahead for the Jews, it certainly won't be further punishment that the refugees will be facing, but their *deliverance,* and it won't be persecution from the Satanic army that drives them forward, but protection from all harm in their flight under the Grace and Mercy of God. For the Lord has determined that from the moment their exodus into the wilderness begins, so does their Deliverance into a secluded place. There they will remain safe and secure for the next three and a half years of the tribulation (Rev. 12:14)

CHAPTER 4

The Divided Tribulation Period

Through the past three revelations the Lord has effectively targeted the last day of the indignation to draw our attention to the emergence of Satan into the world. It seems that the supplanting of Satan was uppermost in the Lord's mind almost to the exclusion of other major facets of the tribulation period. But in the fourth revelation He takes time out to deftly lay out the master plan for the tribulation period. The significant feature of which appears in a one-verse brief synopsis of the whole seven year period. (Daniel 9:27) Here the Lord's typically masterful touch is seen in His calling upon the President to light the fuse of the judgments, and then call on him again to come to Israel and put out the flames of the terrible sixth judgment war. But this is no surprise. With the Lord every action serves a double purpose, and the President's trip to Israel was no exception.

The President's decision to make the trip came at a judicious time which unobtrusively divided the judgment period into two equal portions at just the right moment, thus baring the divisional secret at this juncture so that He might conclude the list of endangering events for the Jews in the following revelation without need of interruption.

As I mentioned earlier, the crux of the Lord's revelations to Daniel lies in the events that transpire in those last fateful days of the indignation. And virtually all of the information in the second through the fourth revelations, as well as a goodly portion of the fifth revelation, serves as a setting for those climactic events which happen in the final 72 hours of the indignation, beginning with the death of the President, his incarnation three days later, and the concluding desolation. And this divisional feature was vital for the projection of that particular point in the judgment period when all of these things would come together, and ostensibly quell any notions by the Jews that the Lord was going to set up His Kingdom at the conclusion of the indignation.

That scenario, which predicted the return of the Messiah immediately following the Jewish punishment period, had been set forth by several of the Old Testament prophets, including Daniel, who, at the time of their writings had no knowledge of a Gentile punishment period.

If another reason were needed for making such a division in the judgment period between the Jews and the Gentiles, it would probably be because of the positional differences of the two groups.

God has always considered the Jews as a different people, set apart from the rest of the world. They are His chosen people regardless of their rebellious attitude toward Him, and have always been under a mandate to live according to the ancient Sinai covenant between them and the Lord. That covenant was never done away with, and their future punishment is based on their refusal as a nation to live up to that agreement.

Consequently, their punishments will be much harsher than those put upon the Gentiles who have had no like covenant. Because of these differences, a separate time and a place of isolation had to be provided for the Jewish indignation, which the peace covenant was supposed to provide. Granted, the existing borders of their nation seem open for inspection and travel, but when the time comes they will be sealed and virtually all communication with the outside will be cut-off while the nation is being judged and punished for their sins of disobedience and rebellion.

Immediately following their punishment period, the judgments on the rest of the world's inhabitants will begin. This was the format John would follow in his listings of the judgments in the book of Revelation.

Daniel exhibited some anxiety and frustration at not being made privy to this information about the Gentiles' judgment period. He couldn't imagine that others beside the Jews would be subjected to similar judgments as his people, and yet there was a time set aside for them. And though he tried every means of persuasion to have the Lord reveal the information, his pleas went unanswered. In fact he was told to quit asking and close up his journal. (Dan 12)

But God had His reasons for withholding the information from Daniel, and one of them was for secrecy. Had Daniel been given the information he requested and included it in his journal, there is every reason to believe that Satan would have acquired that information directly from his journal. And had he done so, it would have afforded him ample opportunity to plan a different strategy for disrupting the future redemptive process at Calvary. For this very reason, the plans for the development of the Church were kept secret from all of the Old Testament prophets until the advent of Christ, some 400 years later. And if the Church was to remain a mystery so must the second part of the judgment period.

However, the veil of secrecy surrounding the Gentile judgment period did open a little when our Lord Himself, during a conversation with His disciples, acknowledged the existence of the second half of the seven years. And although He referred to it in couched terms, He came very close to revealing the whole thing. And it happened like this:

THE GREAT TRIBULATION

A few days before going on the cross, Jesus and His disciples had left the Temple area in Jerusalem and gone up into the surrounding hills for a respite, and at some point along their way they happened to stop and rest on a grassy knoll which afforded a view of the Temple in the distance.

In their casual conversations the subject of the beauty of the Temple came up, which opened the door for Jesus to make the remark about the Temple being be torn down one day. (Matt.24:2) His words may have seemed innocuous to the disciples at the time, but I have an idea that this was a leading statement, meant to elicit the disciples' further inquiry into it, and it was successful because the disciples immediately picked up on His remark and asked Him when that destruction was going to happen. But before He could prepare an answer, they continued their inquiry by asking Him to tell them of the wondrous signs of His second coming and of the end of the age. These were really three questions in all, but they were legitimate questions because He had told them previously that He would be returning to earth. (Matt. 24:2-3)

The Old Testament prophets had testified of the marvelous

celestial manifestations that would take place in the heavens when the Lord returned in Glory, and the disciples may have been curious to learn more of this event. It's obvious that they had no interest in hearing about the judgment period which came before His return, and yet this was exactly what the Lord was going to bring up.

So He deliberately bypassed their first question about the Temple and went on to answer the other two questions which dealt with events at the end of the age. However, knowing beforehand that they had little knowledge or interest in the judgments, and not desiring to confuse them about the events of that period, He spoke only in general terms about the killing and hatred, and the offenses of betrayal, the deception, and the sin and rejection that will take place in the world prior to the judgment period. He described these conditions as being the *"beginning of sorrows."* (Matt. 24:8)

He also by-passed commenting on the punishments during that period, except for one gray area in which Daniel had already disclosed, which had to do with the desolation of the Jews from their land, and for some reason the Lord chose to expand on the information that Daniel had supplied. He led into it by expounding on the persecution of the Jews by the Beast during those last fateful days of the Jewish punishments. Then He came to the pivotal point in His story which described the Beast's deliberate acts of defiance against God and his desecration of the Holy place. Jesus spoke of this event in a very poignant way:

"When ye therefore shall see the abomination of desolation standing in the holy place, let them who are still in Judea flee into the mountains." (Matt. 24: 15) (Dan.11: 31)

This was not simply a message to a few disinterested Disciples, it was obviously intended to be a prophetic warning to the Jews in present day Israel, cautioning them of a perilous situation that they will encounter in the judgment period. And at that time their choice must be to flee into the mountains rather than face the enemy.

But these same words carry an underlying message of submission to the dangers of the desolation in preference to a far greater and imminent danger, which Jesus refers to as the great tribulation;

*"**For then** (following the desolation) **shall be great**

tribulation, such as was not since the beginning of the world to this time, no, nor ever shall be." (Matt.24: 21)

Moreover, this tribulation would be a time of punishment on a people other than the Jews, and although Jesus wouldn't reveal who those people were, there are answers to that question elsewhere in the Bible. Buried in the book of Isaiah, for instance, there are two key verses of scripture that were written purposely to identify those people:

"Come, my people, (speaking to the Jews) **enter thou into thy chambers,** (secret place) **and shut thy doors about thee: hide thyself as it were for a little moment, until the indignation be over passed.** (21) For, **behold, the LORD cometh out of his place to** *punish the inhabitants of the earth for their iniquity:* **the earth also shall disclose her blood, and shall no more cover her slain."** (Isaiah 26:20-21)

Recognizing beforehand that the seven-year period has been divided into two separate three-and a-half-year periods, you will readily see that these two verses apply to those closing days of the first period, when the Lord beckons to the refugees with these words

"Come and enter into your sanctuary where you may rest secure until the tribulation is over."

If you will notice, the verse following that speaks of peoples who are not Jews but 'inhabitants of the earth,' in clear contrast to "His people," of the first verse. These inhabitants are the ones who are about to come under punishment. The understanding here is that all who are **not** Jews are simply "inhabitants of the earth." But note that this generalized term of "inhabitants of the earth" speaks not only of the Gentile peoples in contrast to the Jews, it also connotes that the punishments of the period will be "world-wide," in contrast to the localized area of Israel.

These verses possibly revealed more information than what God really intended, but then again they were sufficiently hidden away from prying minds that the Lord permitted Isaiah to write them, but at the same time we are reminded of the restrictions that the Lord was under when He was conversing with His disciples.

We saw earlier that because overt exposure of the punishments on the Gentiles would have compromised God's secret, Jesus used the term "great tribulation," when He was speaking of the second judgment period. This would be a time of widespread or universal tribulation, which in itself alludes to the "other peoples" as being the Gentile nations of the world.

Note also, that when He was speaking to His Disciples about the persecution and desolation that would come upon the Jews in that era, He purposely refrained from designating that period as a tribulation, or even as the time of "Jacob's Trouble," however, when mentioning the period following the desolation, as is the case in point, He purposely selected the word "tribulation" rather than referring to it as a time of 'plagues or judgments.' This term gave no hint of a dedicated time of judgment. And when he coupled that word with the Aramaic word for "great," the tribulation was characterized as simply being "exceedingly wide in scope," or worldwide, without actually defining it as a time of judgment.

But there was one other interesting disclosure that Jesus made concerning the identity of these "inhabitants of the earth," and it's found in Revelation chapter 10. This verse relates to a vision of John's, wherein he was engaged in a conversation with the Lord. What is particularly interesting about this visitation, was that it came at a time when six of the seven Trumpet judgments had already fallen upon the Jews and the seventh plague was about to come down. This infers that the seven remaining Vial judgments for "the inhabitants of the world" were still sealed within the book.

And, as you could well imagine, all the while that the judgments have been coming down on his people, the Apostle has been as heartsick over the situation as Daniel was before him. He is unsure as to when and how it was all going to end and he needed reassurance badly.

And incidentally, it's no wonder that the book was sealed with seven seals, for in it was not only the mystery of the great tribulation, but of the people, the judgments, and most importantly the destruction of Satan's seat in Rome, the battle of Armageddon, and the final defeat of Satan. We can only imagine what Satan would have done had he been able to learn of these secrets in Daniel's book.

But now the time has come when Jesus must reveal all of those secrets, and He begins by informing John that he must start a new sheet in his journal, on which would be written a whole new series of judgments, but of particular note to John was the Lord's mentioning of who these recipients of the judgments would be. And he finally learns from the Lord that they were to be the *"...many peoples, and nations, and tongues and kings"* of the world.

Just as we figured, it turns out to be all of mankind except the Jews, and when Jesus had made that final identification for John, He handed him the book and said, " There it's done, the Mystery of God is finished." (Rev. 10:7)

The Apostle John was also mindful of the divided period when he accommodated the separation of the fourteen judgments into two groups of seven, one of which he designated as the Trumpet judgments, which would be applied on the Jews, and the other he labeled the Vial judgments, which would be applied on the rest of the world's inhabitants. And it wasn't by accident that he placed the two groups in their correct order, with the first group being dispensed on the Jews in their time of indignation, and the second group being dispensed on the world's population during the great tribulation.

Unfortunately, many well-meaning Christian writers have misunderstood the purpose of the separation, and some have even considered it as inconsequential, even though it's importance should have been obvious from the different group names used.

Others have recognized the separation but for some reason have been unable to probe its purpose, and so have chosen to ignore the subject altogether and follow the well beaten path of a single universal seven-year tribulation theme, with one continuous series of punishments discomfited on the whole world's population and distributed over the whole seven-year period. But contrary to this popular belief of a universal seven-year deployment scheme, the Lord has purposefully divided those seven years into two equal but adjoining periods of time, wherein the fourteen judgments would also be apportioned equally in number, but independently bestowed upon the Jews and nation of Israel in the first period, and upon the Gentile nations in the second.

And while there still exists a popular consensus among contemporary writers for a division of sorts, or a 'middle ground' in the seven years, this break has never been considered by them to be anything more than a 'lull before the storm of God's great wrath,' wherein some adherents actually tout that a "mid-tribulation" departure of the Church will occur.

CHAPTER 5

The Heir Apparent

"And out of one of them came forth a little horn, which waxed exceeding great, toward the south, and toward the east, and toward the pleasant land." (Dan.8: 9)

Such was the angel's only commentary on the ancestry of the Anti-Christ. But it speaks volumes about a man who we shall find is descended from a royal line of Syrian kings dating back to BC 323, and whose political status skyrocketed from a commoner of mediocrity to a Presidency and 'exceeding greatness,' as Daniel states, in describing the man who ultimately becomes the leader of the free world.

In the previous revelations we were afforded only brief glimpses of this person, but because this was to be the Lord's final dissertation on the judgment period, He had the Angel Gabriel pull out all the stops and furnish us with a complete picture of those last electrifying weeks of the Jews' tribulation period, including an extensive dossier on this individual with all of his faults and redeeming qualities displayed, his noble and his ignoble sides portrayed, and his failures and his achievements revealed. All of which was dispensed with the expectation that the reader would grasp the reason why this particular man was chosen by the Lord to be the great betrayer of His people, just as Judas in his time became the betrayer of His Christ.

The dissemination of the Lord's plans for the judgment period were thought to be complete in the four previous revelations, but for some reason the Lord decided to add this extra one to fill in the voids of the plans. For instance, the only time that God will use mankind to implement one of His punishments during the tribulation is in the sixth judgment war, when the Arab legions become His 'instruments of punishment' on the Jews. The Lord uses this revelation to explain His reasons for doing so, one of which was to punish the Arabs for what He claims is their eternal hatred of the Jews. From what the Lord says, this eternal hatred or enmity of the Arabs for their half-brothers has existed in the their culture from time immemorial. And because of this continued hatred, the Arab nations will have to be punished in return with an overwhelming number of casualties.

Also, in the previous revelations the career development of the President was never fully explored, whereas in this revelation we find him playing a major role in the activities of those last days. Which is why the Angel follows the man's every move from the moment he steps foot on Israeli soil until the time of his death forty days later. And in the Angel's coverage of those troublous days, you can almost sense the tension growing in Israel as the President attempts to usurp more and more authority over the Jews..

Throughout his stay in Jerusalem he was undoubtedly warned more than once that his continued presence was tenuous at best and fraught with terrible danger. But he apparently brushed off the warnings right up until the day he was brutally murdered, which happened just three days before the close of the indignation.

With the disclosure of the President's death, the Angel abruptly ends this fifth revelation, because the events that followed in those last three days had already been covered in the previous revelations.

Not to be left in the shadow of this gripping story however, the Lord makes one last effort to project the judgment period in its future time slot. This has been His consistent aim throughout the revelations, but rather than leapfrogging over the centuries as He had done previously; He now takes more diminutive steps through time.

Daniel begins this last and longest of his revelations in his typical manner of referencing its occurrence to the contemporary reigning Gentile king, which in this case was King Darius I, monarch over all Persia and Babylonia. (BC522-485) He then inscribes in his journal the beginning words of the Angel Gabriel, who was busily predicating the four successive monarchs that would follow King Darius. The last one of which was Darius III, whose armies would battle frequently against the armies of Greece before his final defeat by King Alexander.

Alexander also was briefly mentioned as having died without

heirs, and because there were no rulers in either Greece or Macedonia who would step forward and accept the challenge of ruling such a vast Empire, the decision was made to divide the vast Empire into four provinces with the designations of the provinces being 'northern, western, southern and eastern.'

With the division of the Empire thusly determined, the narrator continues his revelation with a lengthy account of the constant battling that went on between the successive 'kings of the northern province' and the 'kings of the southern province,' lasted for 160 years following the partitioning. But it's also from this lengthy dissertation that we learn of a hitherto unrecognized dynasty of Kings who reigned in the Middle East, in a 'pre-Roman era,' circa BC 323 to BC 160.

Secular historians have typically cast these 'provincial rulers' as being merely governors of the Greek Empire, which implies that the Greek Empire continued to maintain its dominion over Asia and India through those years, but according to the Lord this was not so.

As you know, most of Alexander's army, including his top Generals were foreigner mercenaries derived from the lands that had been conquered by Alexander, and one of those mercenaries was a certain Arab General by the name of Antigonus who became 'governor' of the northern province. His territory would, through time, greatly expand its borders, and his heirs would gain the power and supremacy equal to that of the former Assyrian Empire. In secular history this 'Grecian' northern province would become known as the kingdom of Syria, however, in this revelation it is referred to by the narrator as simply the 'kingdom of the north.'

The purpose for the Angel's digression through this relatively unknown era was at least two-fold. First, it would reveal the surprising royal background of the President, whose ancestors came from this line of Arab kings. This Arabian heritage is a factor that will certainly have an effect on the President's actions in his dealings with the Jews. And secondly, the Lord wants to provide us with information on a certain distinctive feature that exists in virtually all Arab peoples, but will be more profound in the warriors who will be going into battle against the Jews in the tribulation.

Oddly enough, this unique feature that seems to have been

86

reared in their culture for generations, is the Arab's inherent hatred for their Jewish half-brethren. The Lord speaks of this hatred as being 'eternal' because it has prevailed through time and continues to be displayed in every communication and confrontation between the Arabs and the Jews. Yet there is no real basis for this hatred and certainly no reason for its continuing undiminished for over three millenniums. And it is because this intrinsic hatred that the Lord has chosen the Arab armies to be His instrument of choice to punish the Jews in the coming sixth judgment war.

In this revelation, the narrator will illustrate this peculiar temperament that exists uniquely among the Arab peoples. And he will do this by exposing us to an array of battles that were fought between the rulers of Syria and Egypt from the time these nations came into being in BC323 until their assimilation into the Roman Empire in BC165.

Actually, through this exposure, the Lord will not only be prophesying the battlefield situations that will be found in the sixth judgment conflict, He will be displaying the ancient military strategies that will be duplicated by their contemporary Arab counterparts in the coming war. Also, through these incessant battle scenes, the relentless antagonism and hatred of the Arabs for their antagonists will also be displayed like cream rising to the top of a milk pitcher

To underscore the similarities of the conditions and peoples between the battles of the past and the one in the future, the narrator progressively analyzes the days of each of these Arabian kings, beginning with Antigonus I, the first self-proclaimed monarch of the northern province and continuing through Antiochus IV, who was the last monarch of the Syrian Empire before it was conquered by the Romans.

Coincidentally, the royal background and heritage of the future President will also be unveiled, providing us with verification of his 'evil kingship,' as Daniel pictured him and the 'seventh king,' as John purports him to be in his book.

Although his inheritance to the throne of the defunct Syrian kingdom is not being stressed in this narrative, it will certainly taint his decision making in his dealings with Israel. In this aspect, he will

87

undoubtedly emulate the talents of his former mentor and predecessor Antiochus IV, who, during his short rule over the vassal province of Judea, persecuted the Jews mercilessly, even to the desecration of their new Temple and sacrificial Altar.

What will also be shown in this coverage of the many battles, is the distinctive brutal nature of the fighting that should be expected in the sixth judgment war, when hatred for the enemy emanates from the soul of an opponent whose sole purpose is to eradicate his enemy, rather than punish him for gain or spoils.

While the Lord could predicate the war and it's outcome, the element of hatred was something over which He will have no direct control. But then again, He chose the Arab forces on the basis of this eternal hatred and knows that it will come into play, so He will exploit it to full advantage in order to meet the requirement of the sixth judgment which called for the destruction of one third of the Jewish population through war. (Ezek. 5:12)

It may be difficult for us to rationalize the Lord's use of Arab legions as His instruments of punishment, but remember that He has used Babylonian and Roman legions in the past for the same purpose. Uniquely in this case though, the punishment requires the destruction of His people. However, in their pursuit of destroying the Jews, the Arab legions will also suffer at least equal punishment in retribution for their perpetual hatred of the Jews.

In addition to this background information on the battles of the past, we are furnished with somewhat of a biographical sketch of the President, disclosing his many hidden talents as well as his aspirations that not only brought him into leadership of the European Union, but which will continue to propel him into world leadership.

In the last third of the revelation the scene of activity is no longer situated in the past, but is fast forwarded to the closing weeks of the indignation period. Here is revealed the invasion plans of the European Expeditionary forces on the shores of the Gaza and the battle strategy of the troops after their landing. From this point the Angel's revelation progresses rather rapidly until we come to the President's assassination. At this point the revelation ended.

Also in this last section, which is really the heart of the revelation, the narrator presupposes that a war was still going on in

Israel, which was the reason for the Union forces being sent in, to end the conflict.

Bear in mind that five of the seven Trumpet judgments had already run their course in Israel, and this sixth judgment war, which is just coming to a close, has brought much suffering and death. The stimulus of the war was the unfounded rumors of the Jews' intent to re-build their Temple on the former site of the Muslim Mosque, the edifice that had been destroyed in the earthquake of the fourth judgment. These rumors persisted and fanned the smoldering embers of an existing hatred against the Jews. These in turn ignited the fierce blaze of conflict, which by now had destroyed almost a third of the Jewish population through violent death or starvation. Soon after the Union forces intervened however, the fighting was brought to an end and all remaining Arab troops were expelled from Israel.

Now, with the war and the sixth judgment ended and the days of the indignation waning, there was a common reflection, or perhaps it was just wishful thinking that wafted throughout the land, that the punishments were at last over, especially with the intervention of foreign troops on their soil. But the Lord hadn't forgotten, and it was in this unsettled situation that the final drama of the indignation played out.

THE FIFTH REVELATION

Daniel affixes the date of this last revelation as being in the first year of the reign of Darius the Mede who is now King over the whole Persian Empire. Some 17 years earlier, when tagging the date of his fourth revelation, he referenced it to this same ruler, who at the time only reigned over the Chaldean, or Babylonian kingdom. He had been installed in that position by King Cyrus following the overthrow of Babylonia by the Persian forces. Therein the two reigned simultaneously for over ten years (Dan. 6:28) until Cyrus died in BC 529 and his son Cambyses took over the Empire. Seven years later the son was killed in battle, and the Persian mantle fell on Darius. So the year of this writing would be circa BC 522; Daniel is close to a hundred years old and still in Babylon some 85 years after his exile in BC 607.

With the positioning of the judgment period still on the front burner, the angel Gabriel opens his revelation by projecting Daniel through roughly 350 years of the times and the tides of a series of monarchies, from Darius I in Persia to Antiochus IV of Syria, who ascended to the throne of this relatively new kingdom in BC 175. He ruled for nearly ten years before the Romans hordes swept over the land and reduced his kingdom to that of a vassal province of the exploding Roman Empire.

This Angel's journey through the kings begins with a brief announcement of four Persia monarchs who were undoubtedly selected for remembrance because of their favorable treatment of the Jews who still remained in their land. These four kings would probably have been Xerxes I, (BC 485 to 465) whose Jewish Queen Esther interceded on behalf of her kinsmen in order to save them from being destroyed by an edict of the same king. Following Xerxes would be his son Artaxerxes I, and then Artaxerxes II, with the fourth likely ruler being Darius III, who only reigned for seven years but those years were filled with battling against the armies of the Grecian King Alexander. Alexander finally defeated him in battle and took over the great Empire of Persia. As was noted in a previous revelation, Alexander had succumbed to a serious illness in BC 323, and with no legitimate heirs to assume his throne, his vast domain was parceled out among his four top generals.

Now one of these generals, by the name of Antigonus, received as his portion the combined northern territories of Assyria, Syria, and Babylonia, and soon after setting the boundaries of his domain he had himself crowned Antigonus I of what would be his newly formed 'kingdom of the north,' with the adopted name of 'Syria.'

However, in the break-up of Alexander's Empire, another powerful kingdom also came into being. That was Egypt, with its vassal territories of Palestine, Edom and Moab, and a ruler by the name of Ptolemy Soter.

As you have already been made aware, a large portion of this revelation has been given over to the wars of rivalry that were fought between these first two kings and their descendants. Invariably the

Syrians were the instigators of these skirmishes which were usually fought over claiming rights to the buffer zone of Palestine, whose borders were being constantly shifted to placate the victor and dominate the Hebrews. Each generation of the Syrian kings seemed to follow in the footsteps of his father, continuing *ad infinitum* for 150 years. (Dan. 11: 5-19)

With respect to the coverage of these many battles, there has been a considerable amount of controversy among Bible scholars over the detailing of these conflicts, as to whether they were written prophetically by Daniel or after the fact by some mysterious historian in the first century BC. The reasoning behind this later writing seems to hinge on the profuseness of events and the minute detailing of rather mundane happenings, which in some aspects, the pundits say, doesn't seem to correlate with Daniel's journalistic abilities. But then again, that may be the very reason they were included, in order to prove the prophetic abilities of God.

There is one aspect of the revelation that tends to prove the fallacy of a later writing, and that is in the 'prophecy of a prediction' that is hidden in the phraseology. In other words, the descriptions of the battles between the Syrian and Egyptian kings were prophesied by the Lord and recorded by Daniel as coming to pass some 200-250 years in the future, while simultaneously prophesying the same antagonists battling some twenty centuries later in a duplication of the former battles. Only the Lord could prophesy the battles in both the former period and in the judgment period, and predict the outcome. The Lord prophesied the events in both occasions, and it was Daniel who recorded them.

But these verses reveal a great deal more that just about the battles and the people involved, they also speak of a people whose nature and character can be seen in their typical affinity for warring and revenge. It seems that the temperaments of both the earlier Syrian warriors and the Arab peoples of today are more or less identical, notwithstanding their general hatred for the Jews that continues to this day. So it's not strange that the Lord would have Daniel replicate this temperament as well as their enmity of the Jews so that we might recognize that it was these qualifications that became the deciding factor in His choice of the Jews' antagonists.

THE WARS BETWEEN THE KINGDOMS

The conflicts between Egypt and Syria started soon after the consolidation of the new kingdoms in BC 300, and though relatively small military forces were involved in the battles there were still considerable casualties. Until finally a day came when the 'king of the south' realized the futility of the constant warring and decided to send his daughter as an ambassador to the 'king of the north,' to try and settle their differences in a diplomatic way. And as was the custom in those days, she took with her a large entourage of servants and bearers, as well as an appeasement offering of precious silver and gold for the king

However, when she came before the Syrian king with the petition of peace, he refused to accept her as the mediator of the king, and instead, held her as a valuable prize for ransom. As a result, she and all her servants and bearers were cast into a prison. Ultimately, word of her imprisonment got back to the king of the south, and in retaliation he sent his eldest son with a vast army in an expedition against the stronghold of the north.

Daniel doesn't describe the battle that ensued, but sufficed to say that the prince prevailed over the northern armies and rescued his sister along with the rest of her entourage, and retrieved all of the treasures that had been sent with them, and after lingering in Damascus for several days, they all returned safely to their home in Egypt.

Many years later and in retaliation for the humiliation of their father, his sons raised a large army and again marched southward. When they came against the sparsely manned garrisons of the Egyptians in the land of the Israelites, for at that time they were the honorees, they easily over-ran them and continued on toward Egypt. But their element of surprise had been lost, because runners had been sent ahead to warn the king of Egypt, who was both surprised and angered by the audacity of the Syrian princes. He quickly dispatched his armies north to meet the invaders. (Dan. 11:10,11)

On this occasion the armies of the north greatly outnumbered the defending Egyptians, however their vast numbers still proved to be no match for the skill of the defenders, and when they met in southern Judea there was a bloody combat for survival. When the tide of battle began to turn on the invaders, they were forced to retreat with heavy losses. But the initial victory could not assuage the anger of the Egyptian King, and he ordered his troops to pursue the fleeing remnants of the northern army until they were completely destroyed. (Dan. 11:12)

Several more years went by and yet another king came to the throne of Syria who had not learned the lessons of his father, and he also determined to take revenge upon the king of the south. He spent all the money in the treasury to raise and equip a vast army which far outnumbered the army that his father had used. But to supply such a large army on the march required a great quantity of food and supplies, which was almost broke the treasury. He knew that if he were to be defeated everything would be lost and he also knew that what he was doing was a dangerous gamble, but his pride wouldn't let up on him, and by then it was too late anyway.

These preparations in Syria became well known in Egypt, and they too began to assemble their armies. In the meantime, things were not all that peaceful in Judea. The land and peoples had taken a terrible toll in the last war, and insurrections against their Egyptian overlords was bubbling in the land. But there were also many pacifists among the Jews who preferred the treatment they received from the Egyptians over that of the Syrians, so they wanted the Egyptians to retain control of their land.

As the story continues, we find the massive northern armies slowly advancing south, coming down the eastern side of the Jordan River before crossing over into Samaria and Judea and then on down the coast. And once again the hapless and defenseless Judeans were forced to abandon their homes and animals and lands and flee from the torches of the Syrians. And once again the few Egyptian fortified garrisons in their path were overrun and destroyed under the massive onslaught of the Syrian army that slowly plodded south.

Eventually the invaders reached the borders of Egypt, but the defenders were there waiting for them. In this confrontation however, the Syrian forces were so large and well equipped that they never gave up the offensive. Now the tables were turned and the defenders were forced to flee back to their cities, while the invaders continued to march down into chief cities of Egypt. The King of Egypt tried desperately to negotiate a peaceful settlement with the invaders and offered his wealth and even his daughters to them, but to no avail.

Now the raiders from the north ruled over Egypt, at least temporarily, but there must have been some sort of amicable agreement reached between them because it wasn't long before the Syrians departed Egypt. Their departure could also have been the result of a message that the king received from Damascus, informing him that during his long absence he had been deposed by his brother. Needless to say, he hastened to return home, but not forgetting to leave guardian troops in various cities along the way, so that his Syrian presence and control would remain over their newly conquered lands. But alas, somewhere on the route home the deposed king turned up missing, and it's presumed that he was killed by traitorous men under his command. (Dan. 11:13-19)

Here the episode should have ended, but it turned out that the usurper on his throne, Antiochus III, went on to be a great ruler who extended the Syrian dominion over all of the former Persian Empire. But he too was killed in an ill-fated campaign against Greece in BC 190, and when the Egyptian king heard the news of his opponent's death, he took advantage of the embroilment among Antiochus's heirs, and sent his legions into Judea to regain control of the land.

Meanwhile in Damascus, the eldest of the two sons of Antiochus gained control of the empire, but he was no match for the determination of his younger brother to dethrone him. His dominion experienced a severe setback in relations with the people when he was forced to raise the already burdensome taxes in order to pay for the continuing war effort against the Greeks. The younger son seized upon the peoples' growing dissatisfaction of his brother, and put pressure upon him to abdicate, however, before the king could convince himself to step down, he was assassinated. From there the reign of the country were handed over to his evil brother Antiochus IV, who, once he was safely enthroned, proceeded to destroy all opposition to his rule. (Dan. 11: 20-22)

The scriptures go on to reveal the devilish exploits of this young upstart, who ventured to take back control of Judea, but he did so under the guise of a peaceful ploy, wherein he and his army infiltrated the Holy Land, which was an insidious thing to do for a king, and something that his venerable father before him would never have done. Once inside its borders however, he covertly seized control of the land in a bloody coup from the Egyptians. And as he was wont to do, when once he was in control of the situation, he destroyed all opposition to his authority. (Dan. 11: 24)

From this new base of operations in Judea he waited for the remainder of the army to regroup and then he marched southward. But even before he could cross the border he found himself confronted by waiting superior armies of the south. His battle went poorly and many of his troops deserted in the face of the enemy. He could continue fighting no longer, which meant that he had to either seek a peaceful solution or retreat in disgrace. So the two kings met and agreed to a standoff, so that neither would suffer anymore losses. But the handshakes of agreement between the two were insincere, for both kings remained determined to "do mischief" another day. But for now, all Antiochus could do was to return to his own land and wait for another opportunity to strike a blow against Egypt. (Dan.11: 25-27)

That opportunity came a year later, when he and his armies marched south again. However, the Egyptian king was forewarned of the Syrian troop build-up, and had prepared a surprise for them. A flotilla of ships containing loyal troops was sent north to a port on the Isle of Cyprus for just such a contingency, and when spies sent word of the Syrian armies' movement to the south, the flotilla immediately sailed to the mainland and discharged the friendly troops behind the enemy legions. And by the time the Syrians realized that they were caught in a pincers movement between two Egyptian armies, there was nothing to do but abandon their invasion plans and flee to sanctuary inside Judean territory. (Dan.11: 28-30)

Being thwarted in his invasion plans and now surrounded by hostile Egyptian troops didn't bode well with Antiochus, and he vented his frustrations and anger on the hapless Jews. He had sought shelter in the walled city of Jerusalem where his only way out of the city was through the enemy divisions.

Confined as he was for many days, Antiochus took out his abger on the Jews in many ways. He offended them greatly by polluting the 'Sanctuary of their strength' in an abominable profane act of entering through the veil into the Holy Place. In doing this he committed a most grievous act against the Talmudic Law, that of polluting their Temple with his presence on a Holy day. And moreover, he offered a swine on the Altar, and thus prohibited the daily sacrificial offering of the Jews. Both of these were heinous acts against God and His people, and it sparked an immediate uprising among the faithful Jews, an uprising that continued to grow into a full-scale revolt under the leadership of Judas Maccabaeus.

The Jews, though few and ill-equipped in comparison to the Syrian troops within their walls, were emboldened enough to assemble an insurgent force and strike against the Syrian army, and summarily caused them to withdraw from Jerusalem and the land in disgrace. Antiochus returned to Damascus with only a handful of his army in tow, and was later slain in ignominy by his own people. Meanwhile in Jerusalem, Judas Maccabaeus began cleansing the land and rededicating the Temple. (Dan.11: 29-34)

With that last disabling rout, Syria's domination of Judea came to an end, and some thirty years later its own demise as a nation came to an end when the Roman armies swept over the region and dealt a crushing blow to the Syrian army. This also brought the reign of the royal line of Antigonus to an end.

In considering the question as to why the Lord chose to prophecy these many battles and have Daniel document them, the most credible reason would be His intention of preparing the stage for the future Arab and Israeli war. In contrast to the Angel's normal brevity of disclosures, we have this lengthy detailed dissertation of the wars between the north and the south. Evidently the Lord's primary purpose for the detailed story was to establish a correlation between the combating kingdoms then and the predicted war between the Arabs and the Jews in the sixth judgment. Only this time the war won't be for a territorial gain, but to exterminate the Jewish nation.

The story also provides us with a unique character analysis of the peoples of that time, such as the reticence and timidity of the Egyptians versus the aggressiveness and belligerence of their Arab foes.

Aside from the details of these past conflicts, this revelation is filled with the Lord's intricate workings, from His disclosures of the President, his royal heritage, his ascendancy to power in the European Union and even unto his death at the hands of assassins. All of which are skillfully woven into the picture to display the real purpose for the President's involvement in the seventh judgment, and ultimately the great tribulation.

THE PLANS FOR THE DESOLATION

The basic plan for the last days of the indignation was to inculcate Satan into the workings of the judgment period, in particular the seventh judgment, where he will become the Lord's instrument in bringing about the desolation of Israel. In order to accomplish that total evacuation though, it was imperative for Satan to reside in a fleshly body while he was on the earth, which deepened the plot considerably. And time was a factor in the transaction. His transition from the pit into the human body must be made on the last day of the period, which called for an adroit disposition of both events and peoples to make this happen. The first step was to bring the President to Israel at the precise time to end the fighting between the Arab forces and the Israelis. And in this invasion action it was imperative that he be judged as an intercessor into an already existing war rather than being an interloper who breaks his own treaty to initiate a war. In this way the prophecies about this action would be accurate.

Then the fighting in the sixth judgment must be brought to a swift conclusion so that the next phase of the plan could begin. This was the crucial phase of the whole operation and required the complete cooperation of the President. The plan required him to become overly involved in the affairs of the Jews to the point where his intrusion would become so deeply resented by the Jews that they would assassinate him three days before the close of the Jewish judgment period. Now there was the problem of coordinating his death with the heavenly battle that was going on between the angels of Satan and those of the Lord, and hopefully, when everything is coordinated perfectly, the expeditious expulsion of Satan will occur right on schedule and the final segment of the incarnation plans will fall into place on the third day after the President's death.

The closing section of this revelation (Dan. 11:36 through 45) was intended to cover those problematical events in the days prior to the incarnation. But in order to do that the Angel had to begin with the entrance of the Union Expeditionary force as it came ashore on the beaches of Gaza. He then traces the movements of the armies following the landing and their eventual movement inland to Jerusalem.

From there, the narrator picks up on the actions of the President as he becomes involved daily in the affairs of the nation. From that point the Angel moves swiftly to the day of his assassination which closes out the revelation.

THE SHIFT IN TIME

What hasn't been brought to light in this intriguing story, is the way the narrator relates all of this background information on the battles of the past to the future war. In other words, how does he take all of the ingredients of those past battles, including the locale, and transpose the whole scenario into the future sixth judgment battle?

He manage to do this by succinctly overlapping the 2150-year separation of the battles with his use the same designations for the future battle as he used in the past. For instance, the term 'king of the north,' still applies to the northern country of Syria, even though it will become allied with other Arab nations, and Egypt continues to be the 'king of the south.' (Dan.11:6-19) He makes it seem as though the gap in time doesn't exist and his coverage of the hatred between the nations continues its momentum from the past into the future tribulation battle.

Incidentally, if there were ever any question as to whether the sixth judgment war would be fought between the Arabs and the Israelis, this portion of the revelation settles that question..

It now becomes evident that the Angel had another motive for tracing through the kings of Syria, other than the continued use of the terms 'north' and 'south,' and that was to reinforce the President's position as being the rightful heir of Antiochus IV. Which brings up the possibility that one of the reasons the President went to Israel was to secure that inheritance. The Angel adds support to this possibility with his use of the phrase *"and in his estate shall stand up a vile person...,"* which speaks of the President's inheritance being passed down from Antiochus IV to him, which would conform to the traditional disposition of an inheritance from father to son.

In this instance however, the President will not be able to claim his inheritance until after he has been incarnated. (Dan.11: 21-28)

And while we're on the subject of 'kings,' we note from the Angel's descriptions of those various Syrian kings, as well as from historical records, that they can be identified with considerable accuracy.

They were Antigonus I, Antigonus II, Seleucus II, Antigonus III, Antiochus III and finally, Antiochus IV. (Epiphanes) And while their identities are not that important to our study, a unique correlation can be seen between these rulers and a group of kings mentioned by John as being the predecessors of the Anti-Christ. This group is mentioned in Rev. 17:10,11 where it says:

"And there are seven kings: five are fallen, and one is, and the other is not yet come; and when he cometh, he must continue a short space. And the beast that was, and is not, even he is the eighth, and is of the seven, and goes into perdition"

The person being spoken of here as *'the other one who has not yet come on the scene, and when he does come he will remain on the scene for only a short while,'* is the President, who is rightfully the seventh king in the royal line of Antigonus. He will come into Israel in the closing days of the indignation. And as the scripture states; *he will be there for only a short space of time* before he is assassinated.

Thereupon, Satan enters into the slain body and gives it new life, but in this new life he is neither human nor celestial but a rare combination of both, which is why John refers to him as the 'Beast.' And it is this 'Beast' who becomes the eighth king by royal decree.

When the Angel concluded his dissertation on the Syrian kings and their endless battles, he began an exposition of the President's involvement in the affairs of the Jewish people during those last forty days of the indignation. And as his story unfolds, we can see a distinct similarity between the cruel behavior of the President during those days and that of his ancient predecessor Antiochus, who, as you recall, also entered into Judea rather surreptitiously on a supposedly peaceful mission, and once he was in, he overthrew the Egyptian caretakers and took control of the land. And when he was forced to abort his failed expedition against Egypt a year later, he retreated within the walled city of Jerusalem where he expressed his frustration and anger toward God and the Jews by profaning the Holy Place in the Temple. He did this by his presence in a place where Gentiles were forbidden to trespass. He also desecrated the Altar of sacrifice.

Obviously, the reason for including these selected incidents about Antiochus was to give us a preview of the President's future 'invasion' so to speak, of Israel, which also is purported to be a 'peaceful mission.' And he too will desecrate the Holy Place, when he stands there as the 'abomination of desolation' and blasphemes the Lord and His anointed before sending them off into exile. (Matt.24:15)

The narrator pictures the President invading the Holy Land just as Antiochus had done before him, however, twenty-two centuries have gone by and everything but the topography of the land has changed. The vast Syrian Empire is long gone and the country that now exists by that name is but a signet of its former greatness, while Egypt, that great Empire of the past, has lost its status among the nations with her last failed attempt to conquer Israel in 1967.

What could be recognized as the 'northern Empire' in Europe today is an alliance of nations called the European Union, which still retains a shard of the glory-filled days of the magnificent Roman Empire. And though the title of 'king of the north' is yet to be conferred upon him, the coming leader of that Union will be just as ruthless and ambitious as his forefathers.

PASSING OF THE MANTLE

When we read the first 35 verses of this revelation, it's as though we were on an excursion into the past where we have been able to view new and exciting things, yet they were seemingly irrelevant to the events of the tribulation. Then all of a sudden we come upon verse 36, and immediately we are drawn back to the storyline and made witness to the renaissance of the old monarchy of Antiochus. But it's this new 'evil king,' or the President who comes to the forefront. There is no hint of the years that have quietly slipped by. It is as though the writer were re-introducing us to this same evil king of the past who is now draped over with a mantle of dark secrets, while at the same time disseminating all of the qualities of his leadership in the European Union. And from the portfolio we have been given of this man, he will be just as evil and pernicious as his forefather and just as eager to commit the same terrible acts against the Lord and His anointed. And surprisingly to many, tucked into the pocket of his cloak is a *carte blanche* that the Lord has given him to carry out his program.

THE TRIBULATION INVASION

Quickly though, the angel ends his re-introduction of the man and we find ourselves drawn into the conflict between present day antagonists who react somewhat differently from those in the ancient past. (Dan. 11:37-39)

There is a strange irony in the way this revelation unfolds. Your first impressions lead you to believe that the invading armies from the north are again seeking possession of Israel in what looks like a re-run of the battles in the past, not only because of the continued use of the descriptive phrases 'king of the north' and 'king of the south,' but because the region of conflict is still the same. Then you come to realize that this is a new era being referred to, and while the expressions 'king of the south' and 'king of the north' are still being used, they are depicting Egypt and an Arab coalition rather than just a Syrian force. Moreover, these former enemies are now allied against a new intruder of their domain. And to top it off, this new intruder is being projected as the rightful heir and descendent of Antiochus IV, although he is not the king of the north as you would expect, but a foreigner and an invader who surreptitiously sneaks into the land under the guise of peace, in much the same way as his father had done many years ago. (Dan.11: 21, 40-42)

In these several passages, the Lord is not only prophesying the coming invasion, He is actually laying out the detailed plans for the European invasion of Israel in the last month of the Arab-Israeli war. Those European forces who will be under the command of the President who will enter Jerusalem after the 'mop-up' operation has been completed.

To get a complete picture of the situation in Israel in those days, it is necessary for us to go back to the fourth revelation where we read of a peace accord that had been struck between Israel and the Arab nations. That covenant was supposed to ensure peaceful relations in the Near East for at least seven years, but barely two and a half into that peace, the Arab coalition along with Egypt, breached the accord and invaded Israel with the sole purpose of driving the Jews into the sea. Now, its eleven months later and the Union forces are disembarking troops on the Gaza shore on a crusade to end the fighting in Israel.

And here is a leader, ready to engage in combat, so to speak, with an even greater conflict within him. With whom should he side in battle? His ancestry is from both Arab and Jew, and he is now confronted with making a decision between his loyalties. From his childhood he has known no loyalty to either the God of his fathers or the heathen gods, but has only honored the god of power, which ultimately meant Satan. With that uncertainty still lingering in his mind, he vacillates in every action he undertakes, whether it's on the beachhead at Gaza or later on when he tries to ameliorate his position with the Jews by promoting himself as their Messiah. (Dan. 11:37,38)

When the European troops do come ashore on the beaches of Gaza and northern Egypt they are met with minimal resistance, allowing the troops to move swiftly up and down the coast. The hurriedly assembled Egyptian troops quickly folded under the onslaught of the superior European armies. Meanwhile, the main task force was moving northward, hugging the coast line of the Mediterranean and avoiding the temptation of going inland toward the Dead Sea areas of Edom and Moab. But in this course they inevitably run into heavy resistance from Arab forces that had been pulled from fighting the Jews to combat this new enemy. (Dan. 11: 40,41) Incidentally, the reason for by-passing those particular areas around the Dead Sea was to alleviate the threat of destruction to those areas, particularly the city of Petra, where it is presumed the Jewish refugees from the desolation will be headed in just a few short weeks.

The war is soon brought to a close and relatively peaceful conditions restored, but in the succeeding weeks the tensions continued to ride high over the terrible loss of life and the tremendous effort that had to be expended by the weary survivors in their endeavor to bury the dead and cleanse the land of the rubble.

Adding to the turmoil and frustrations of the people was the authoritative presence of the Union President who took over the reins of government after the war was over. This obverse act on the part of the President can readily be seen as a fulfillment of the ancient prophecy of his forefathers. But the man was very arrogant and disdainful of his Jewish brethren to begin with, and his efforts in ending the war has only made him more narcissistic. Daniel describes his attitude at this time as being particularly contemptuous of both God and the people he came to save, which was reflective of his domineering and cavalier treatment of them. And it is this overbearing attitude that the Jews couldn't handle. (Dan.11: 36)

However, once he was ensconced in Jerusalem and had set up his permanent headquarters there, his attitude softened somewhat, and he even made an effort to ingratiate himself to the Jews by politicizing that he was their kinsman. But when he began to make ridiculous claims, telling them that they needn't wait any longer for their Messiah to appear for he was the long awaited one, the people only became more infuriated, and within a month after his triumphal entry into Jerusalem he was assassinated. And with that cliffhanger the angel closed this electrifying episode of the man who would be king. (Dan. 11:40-45)

However, there was one area of the story that hadn't been elaborated on because it had been described in an earlier revelation. It has to do with verse 44 of chapter 11, which speaks of the President's reaction to some disturbing news that came to him while he was in Jerusalem. Apparently this news brought on a complete change of character within him, causing him to explode with wrath against the Jews. His reaction to the news was to *"go forth with great fury to destroy"* and *"utterly to make away many."* Terms that could hardly describe the actions of the President during his short tenure in Israel but would explain his demeanor after being incarnated by Satan.

But what was the communique that troubled the President? The scripture mentions the news coming from two directions, the north and east, which suggests the possibility of two different messages. One might have been a warning from someone who knew that there was going to be an attempt on his life, and the other was possibly from the Lord, telling him to accept what was coming. Either one or both of these messages would have been extremely troubling to say the least. The first he could have prepared for, but for the second there was no alternative but to submit.

In retrospect, we can assume that he knew that it was his lot to die and somehow he knew that his death was imminent. In fact it had come down to the precise day. The end of the indignation was only three days away, and the conflict between the angels in heaven was already in progress. Satan was about to be cast out of heaven and driven to the earth. All of these things would happen in rapid succession, including the final desolation of Israel, and immediately following the desolation would come the great tribulation on the Gentiles. (Dan. 12:1)

In the attack on his life, the President suffered a severed right arm and facial stab wounds by his attackers, but whether these were the cause of his death, the fact remains that he died and the plans for the incarnation would be right on schedule. (Zech. 11:16,17)

104

CHAPTER 6

The Fourth Trumpet Judgment

Happenings like the incarnation of Satan, or the waters being turned into blood, or the disappearing fish, or even the descent of the Lord to battle the Beast at Armageddon are incredible and mystifying feats, but topping them all will be the most baffling and intriguing accomplishment of the whole tribulation period, that of shortening the length of the days.

If you are not familiar with this life saving development, it's a merciful operation of the Lord to reduce the number of casualties that would otherwise occur during the tribulation. But it's the way He does it that makes the feat so amazing. Figuratively, He extends His strong arm into the workings of our solar system and gently nudges our planet to make it spin faster on its axis, and He does it without disturbing other parameters such as the planet's yearly cycle around the sun or the moon's orbital path. And He does this twice during the seven-year tribulation period. Once near the beginning of the period when He speeds it up, and again near the close of the period when He slows the earth's rotation down to its original speed.

The 'speed-up' happens some time after the first three rounds of the Trumpet judgments have pounded the land of Israel. There were two separate eruptions of a volcano in the southern desert regions of Israel, with the first eruption blanketing much of the area with several inches of ash and debris, which made the land uninhabitable. The second eruption created fireballs of lava and sent out firestorms that further destroyed large areas of the Holy Land. A short time later a meteor cascaded out of the sky and exploded like an atom bomb in the northern section of the country where it destroyed or otherwise contaminated much of the fresh water sources in the region These punishments were bad enough, but it was the fourth judgment that really did the damage.

The first noticeable sign that something was amiss was the worldwide earthshaking that lasted for several minutes and caused tremendous damage and destruction the world over. From the collapsing of entire cities to the crumbling of mountain ranges, from the draining of vast lakes to course alterations of mighty rivers. It was an earthshaking so great that it caused great tidal waves to rise up and devour islands and shake continents. Both polar ice caps were moved and great masses of ice broke free to drift aimlessly out to sea. Yet none of these happenings are even remotely envisioned in the simple announcement that came from the writer's pen when he ushered in the fourth Trumpet judgment with these words;

"The fourth angel sounded, and a third part of the sun was smitten, and a third part of the moon, and a third part of the stars; so as a third part of them were darkened, and the day shone not for a third part of it, and the night likewise." (Rev. 8:12)

As you can see, nothing written in the above verse suggests that such catastrophic events would occur, yet the sounding of this Trumpet in heaven will cause the greatest number of casualties and incomprehensible destruction that the world has ever experienced.

The words read as though the Lord smote the heavenly bodies, such as the sun and the moon, and in so doing destroyed a third part of their surface, so that no light could be emitted from that area. However, it was not the heavenly bodies that were effected, it was the earth that was 'smitten' by the Lord, causing it to rotate faster on its axis and thereby reducing the number of hours in a day.

Jesus made a reference to this 'shortening of the days' when He was answering some questions put to him by the disciples concerning other end-time events. However in His response to them, there was no mention of how this 'shortening' would be accomplished. He commented only on the excessive loss of life that would result from the ensuing judgments if this shortening were not done. His words went like this;

"Unless those days are shortened there will be no flesh saved: but for the elect's sake, those days shall be shortened." (Matt.24: 22)

These words may have sounded innocuous to the disciples at the time, but they were predicated on what the Lord already knew was going to happen.

Strangely, until the last century there had been little attempt to expound on the implication of the Lord's words, and many of our recent scholars have also failed to recognize the significance of this event or even that it is a credible judgment. But if the Lord's statement about the shortening of the days was important enough to be included in the tribulation experience, it is certainly important enough to understand its relevance to the situation.

We know that the fourth judgment was not of John's making, for it came straight out of the seven-sealed book of the judgments that was composed by God and later revealed to John, who incidentally was in the group of disciples that was listening to Jesus when HIs comment about the shortening of the days was made. There is also no reason to believe that the Lord was simply hypothesizing about such an adjustment being made when He already knew that the change was in the works. He was confirming the fact, while at the same time reaffirming a commitment to prevent the complete annihilation of the Jews during the projected time of the indignation.

However, if we continue that train of thought in a larger context, the inference can be made that shortening the punishment period would also reduce the number of Gentile casualties. This concept gains support from the conjugation of the sentences, which could, and should be understood to mean that once started, the days would remain shortened through the remainder of the seven years. Here is the Lord's complete statement about the event:

"For then shall be great tribulation, such as was not since the beginning of the world to this time, no, nor ever shall be. (22) And <u>except those days should be shortened</u>, there should no flesh be saved: but for the elect's sake those days shall be shortened." (Matt. 24: 21,22)

Thus, in concert with the program of saving lives in both the Jews' judgment period and the great tribulation period, the Lord begins the 'shortened days' just before the last three lethal judgments are administered on Israel, and allows them to continue until the seventh judgment of the great tribulation when the length of the days are returned to 'normal' by the slowing down of the rotational speed of the earth. At this time another great earth-shaking takes place just five days before the close of the tribulation period.

Ironically, the shortening of the days will also result in the saving of a myriad of unbelievers, for the term the Lord used *"there should no flesh be saved"* was not an indicative conclusion "that all flesh would be lost." His decision to shorten the days may have come about because of His concern for the welfare of those people who would become believers during the tribulation, and as for those who remained 'spiritually lost,' they were extremely fortunate to be caught under the same umbrella.

To many Bible scholars however, the reason for shortening the time of punishment time was of less importance than the problem of how it was going to be accomplished. And to get around that problem, it has been suggested by some that the Lord will make His triumphal entry as Lord of Lords some time before the judgment period was scheduled to end, and thus cut short the punishments. The language being put forth for this early action follows the line of;

"The Anti-Christ's violent measures will be cut short by the sudden appearing of Christ, who will destroy the wicked one."

Certainly, an early appearance by the Lord would result in some of the latter punishments being either be cut short or eliminated altogether. However this concept attaches little significance to Jesus' words on how the shortening action fits into His overall plans. And although the idea of simply 'lopping-off' a number of days from the tribulation period seems to solve the problem, this concept is nowhere hinted at in the time frames that are given in the books of Daniel and Revelation where the number of tribulation days has been pre-determined by God and sealed up in His book. That number is to be 2520. And with the number of days established it leaves little room for our Lord to either decrease the total number of days or short circuit the program by arbitrarily breaking in on the process. It was mandatory that all of the devious plots of the Beast to take place and be completed as planned, and all of the judgments of the Lord be fulfilled as prophesied.

So, with everything else locked in place, including a specific number of days for the punishment period, the only door left open for the Lord to shorten the length of punishment time was to shorten the length of each day. If this were to be done, the days could still be reckoned as 'days,' which would fit the requirement of the judgment even though their duration time would be drastically reduced. The judgments could continue to be administered in the prescribed manner, but the time element of their administration would be dramatically reduced, resulting in the saving of millions of lives.

Through this minor adjustment, the total number of days will remain the same, at 2520, the seven-year period will continue as is, but the "punishment time" will be far less, which is exactly what the Lord had in mind.

As you well know, 'a day' is the designated term signaling one complete revolution of the earth on its axis. Thus, if the earth could be made to rotate faster on its axis, the period of time for each revolution would be lessened, and the 'day' as we know it would become more diminutive. To accomplish such a 'speed-up' of the earth's rotation however would require a supernatural input to our planetary system to give the planet a nudge. It sounds simple enough, but no matter how quickly or slowly the adjustment of the speed is made, the change itself will induce other dramatic changes in the mechanics of a planet that is already delicately balanced between its centrifugal and gravitational forces. Any sudden change in speed, however slight, will loose tremendous energies that will in turn bring about catastrophic physical changes on the surface of the planet, and it's these changes that will be witnessed in the fourth judgment. Even so, because God considered these cataclysmic events as secondary consequences to His primary goal of shortening the length of the days, He had John relegate the information on this sudden energy release to a brief announcement under the sixth Seal opening, where it reads:

"_And I beheld when he had opened the sixth seal_, and, lo, there was a great earthquake; and the sun became black as sackcloth of hair, and the moon became as blood;   (13) And the stars of heaven fell unto the earth, even as a fig tree casts her untimely figs, when she is shaken of a mighty wind.   (14) And the heaven departed as a scroll when it is rolled together; and every mountain and island were moved out of their places.   (Rev. 6:12-14)

When we consider the effects of the increased speed on our planet's surface, the devastation reaches far beyond the initial shocks and strains and into seasonal and climatic changes. And unless the

109

Lord makes suitable adjustments there might also be a somewhat rarefied atmosphere and lessened gravitational effect. But as for the earth itself, the catastrophic effects from the earthquakes will be far too numerous to give account.

Like the scriptures describe, islands will disappear into the sea, great mountain ranges on every continent will break down and raise such a cloud of dust particles in the atmosphere that for days on end the sun will be completely hidden. For a time, the natural winds will be whipped into a maelstrom of hurricanes and tornadoes and fierce hailstorms. Volcanoes will erupt in many places over the earth and add to the residue into the atmosphere. Great wave formations, called tsunamis, will sweep in from every sea, destroying numerous coastal cities and killing thousands of people while forcing untold millions to flee to higher ground.

And in the aftermath of this devastation, nothing short of a massive reconstruction effort over many years will erase the scars from the land. Many coastal cities will never be rebuilt to their former beauty and function, while others will be simply abandoned.

The earth will continue to spin at this higher rate until the closing week of the seven year period, when God will again intervene and slow it down to its original 24 hour day, which will bring on a similar cycle of destruction.

This second earthshaking is described in these words:

"And there were voices, and thunders, and lightning's; and there was a great earthquake, such as was not since men were upon the earth, so mighty an earthquake, and so great. (19) And the great city was divided into three parts, and the cities of the nations fell; <u>*and great Babylon came in remembrance before God, to give unto her the cup of the wine of the fierceness of his wrath.*</u> *(20) And every island fled away, and the mountains were not found."* (Rev.16: 18-20)

Footnote:

This wasn't the first time that God has intervened in the cycle of the earth. In the book of Joshua 10: 12-14, there is an account of His slowing the rotation of the earth in answer to a soldier's prayer, so that the Israelites might win the battle that they were waging at the time. The sun was said to have stood still in the heavens, but it was the earth that stood still, or slowed in its rotation.

Other Old Testament prophets mentioned the latter earthquake as one of the events that would precede the Second Coming of the Lord, as in the book of Psalms, where we read this detailed account of the earthquake as though it were already in progress:

"Then the earth shook and trembled; the foundations also of the hills moved and were shaken, because he was wroth. (8) There went up a smoke out of his nostrils, and fire out of his mouth devoured; coals were kindled by it. (9) He bowed the heavens also, and came down; and darkness was under his feet. (10) And he rode upon a cherub, and did fly; yea, he did fly upon the wings of the wind. (11) He made darkness his secret place; his pavilion round about him was dark waters and thick clouds of the skies."   (Psalm 18:7-11)

In the fierceness of His wrath, the Lord descended through the black storm clouds surrounding the earth, and His anger was vented in all places in strong winds and heavy rain with hailstones and embers from volcanoes. The brightness of the lightning and the deep thunder was His voice to the earth. Earthquakes opened fissures in the earth and the seas ran into them. The volcanoes broke apart and the lava spewed forth as a blast from the rebuke of the Lord.

(12) "At the brightness that was before him his thick clouds passed hailstones and coals of fire. (13) The Lord also thundered in the heavens, and the Highest gave his voice; hailstones and coals of fire. (14) Yea, he sent out his arrows, and scattered them; and he shot out lightning, and discomfited them.

(15) Then the channels of waters were seen, and the foundations of the world were discovered at thy rebuke, O LORD, at the blast of the breath of thy nostrils."   (Psalm 18: 12-15)

111

CHAPTER 7

The Pretender

In yielding to a preemptive judgment of the man who would be king, I might have overlooked a certain aspect of his background which guided him in the direction he was meant to go. For this man's life and destiny was not determined capriciously by him in the twentieth century. Those decisions were made for him by his ancestral father, some 3500 years ago when the Hebrew people were still under Egyptian bondage. However God has known all along who this Anti-Christ was going to be, and He has steered his life accordingly.

His forefathers were from the Hebrew tribe of Dan, who was the fifth son of the twelve sons of Jacob, and the great grandson of Abraham. As the story goes, his father was nearing the end of his years and the time had come for the traditional pronouncement of a father's blessing upon his offspring.

Now these blessings were usually of a prophetic nature, and were intended to be both uplifting and goal setting for the recipient. However, in Dan's case, the blessing would turn out be more of a dismal premonition of his progeny's future than a worthy promise. This was the pronouncement that was given him:

"Dan shall judge his people, as one of the tribes of Israel. (17) He shall be a serpent by the way, an adder in the path that bites the horse's heel, so that his rider shall fall backward." (Gen.49: 16-17)

At the time, Dan may have considered these words to be somewhat of a mixed blessing, as they began innocently enough with a prediction, that one day one of his descendants would find himself in a position of prestige and authority over his people. In that aspect, his father could not have given a more appropriate prophecy, for indeed a man from the progeny of Dan will fulfill that ancient prophecy, by rising from virtual political obscurity to the leadership of the ten-nation alliance in Europe, and when he arrives at that

112

exalted position he will have authority over his people, which comes about when he will be called upon to adjudicate a peaceful settlement between his own people the Jews, and their hostile Arab neighbors. And it is through his administration of that particular treaty that he gains a modicum of authority over his people during their time of indignation.

The second portion of the blessing speaks of a serpent which lies coiled and waiting in the path of an unsuspecting rider. At the proper moment, the serpent strikes the heel of the horse and the rider is thrown from his saddle. This analogy aptly describes the President's waiting on the sidelines for nearly 3 1/2 years before he makes his 'strike' against his kinsmen. This waiting is envisioned in the invasion of Israel by the armies of the European Union in their effort to quell the long prevailing war.

When the Hebrews returned to the promised land from Egypt, the Dannite tribe received a small inheritance in the south-west area of their new homeland, but because of internal rivalry a portion of the tribe was forced to migrate to the northern boundary of the country and squat on a small section of land called Laish that was already occupied by the Sidonians. This land was promptly renamed Dan by the new settlers

The Sidonians resisted these warring newcomers throughout the years, and proved to be a constant threat to their existence, which made it necessary for the tribe to resort to frequent battles just to retain their precious land. This brings to mind a similar situation that exists in the Near East today, where Israel has to maintain a constant vigil against neighboring terrorists.

On the death of King Solomon, the nation of Israel was split into two factions under different kings, with the ten northern tribes of Israel, including Dan, coming under the reign of King Jeroboam, and the two southern tribes under King Rehoboam.

Jeroboam was a wicked man who rebelled against Jehovah, and in his rebellion he refused to allow his people to journey to Jerusalem to worship in the new Temple. Instead, he set up his own temples, with one located in the north country of Dan, and another in Bethel, near the southern border of Samaria, neither of which were sanctioned by the Lord.

113

Two hundred years later and still ostracized from Jehovah, who was no longer able to stomach their continued rebellion and idol worship, the ten northern tribes were sent into exile in Assyria as a punishment for their rebellion. It was an exile from which they were never expected to return. Through time, those displaced tribes became assimilated into the Arab culture, though they never lost their identity as Jews.

Over many generations the members of the various tribes, including Dan, migrated to Western Europe, from which the most recent ancestors of the European leader emerged. Thus making it possible for the ancient blessing of Jacob to be finally realized in this one modern individual, who, with God's help and direction will rise from obscurity in diplomatic circles to the esteemed position of the Presidency of a realigned European Union, the last hurdle that must be overcome before the tribulation can begin.

Digressing for a moment on the matter of the European Union set-up, it appears that the stumbling block in the path of the tribulation period's beginning lies in the charter of the present European Union which has permitted the membership of the Union to grow well beyond the original small group to the present fifteen and growing yearly. One day there will be a tightening of the requirements for Union membership, which will allow only those nations that are amenable to surrendering their sovereign rights to obtain membership With that limitation, it's very possible that the number of federating countries would dwindle to ten, with a more unitized governing Council located in Brussels.

As for the Presidency, the Lord has already selected the man. One of the pre-requisites for filling that position, other than having an extremely limited fellowship with other political associates, will be his total anonymity before the election. Thus his nomination will come as somewhat of a shock to the new governing Council, and the fact that he has won unanimous approval as President will be even more astonishing. With the re-aligned federation formally adopted and functioning, and with the new President installed, the Lord quickly removes all restraints holding back the activation of the end-time events.

The early months of his Presidency progress relatively

uneventful, with most of his activities and responsibilities having to do with internal machinations of the Union and gaining mastery in manipulating people and concession making. But it is also a time when his true character begins to emerge and his alter ego is frequently displayed with its megalomaniac symptoms of grandeur. A certain amount of this egotism is typical in all leaders, but for some reason, in this man there seems to be a sinister aspect to it. In one of the few characterization of this man made available to us, Daniel removes the mask and offers this picture.

(He) neither regarded the God of his fathers, nor the desire of women, nor regarded any god: for he shall magnify himself above all.   But in his estate shall he honor the God of forces: and a god whom his fathers knew not shall he honor with gold, and silver, and with precious stones, and pleasant things.   (Dan. 11:37,38)

It appears that this man has a personal drive that seems to have no fulfillment, as illustrated by the descriptive phrase " for he shall magnify himself above all." Daniel, who was privileged to be able to recognize the 'Hyde' personality in him, pictures him here as a man who esteems himself above all other men and even boasts of being greater than the God who put him there, and apparently would take every opportunity to ridicule Him.

The Apostle Paul, in the New Testament, articulates the man's dual personality in similar words to Daniel, when he describes him as a man *"who opposes and exalts himself above all that is called God, or that is worshipped; so that he* (imagining himself to be) *as God, sits in the temple of God, trying to prove to himself that he is God."* (II Thess. 2:4)

While the world sees none of these innate evil traits in the man, both Daniel and the Apostle Paul were aware of his treacherous aspirations, only they saw them from different points of view.

Paul was more concerned about the dangers the Church would face after his arrival on the world scene, while Daniel, who knew nothing about the coming Church age, was understandably concerned about the welfare of his people under this man's despotic authority. In his journal he writes of this new President's authority as being evil and threatening, but it was his attitude towards God that offended him the most.

Whereas Paul views his presence as a diabolical threat against the Church that is still on the earth during the early months of his Presidency. He believes that the Church members will be susceptible to all of this man's deceitful words and persuasiveness to revoke the Lord in their lives. Which ironically, is the probable reason for his appearance on the world scene well ahead of the scheduled judgment period, so that he could, if not initiate the apostasy in the Church, at least assist in the Harvesting process that will be going on at the time. But the President's plans in this area are not disclosed

The Apostle Paul's letter to the Thessalonian Church indicates that this winnowing process, or apostasy within the fellowship, will begin soon after the President's inauguration and continue until the signing of the peace covenant several months later. During this time, Paul envisions the President using all of his deceptive powers to drive a stake into the heart of the Church in his attempt to succor the weaker Christians as well as the non-believers away from the fellowship.

The Lord spoke of this end-time separation in several of His parables which are recorded in the book of Matthew. In alluding to this particular time and situation, He states that the angel's will be the ones who will actually be doing the separating.

Paul views the man's deceptive efforts as an open attack on the Church that he has so carefully and lovingly nurtured, and he warns the believers in that generation, that they must be vigilant and recognize the man for who he is and what he is, which is the epitome of sin against God and the "mystery of iniquity" who chips away at the foundation of the Church.

In the same letter he uses words similar to those of the Prophet Daniel in his description of the evil king. (II Thess.2: 4, Dan.8: 8-12) In one instance used the same term as Jesus when he called him the "son of perdition," or the son of "eternal ruination," as opposed to eternal life with God.

Certainly, with Satan being the father of eternal death, both physical and spiritual, this pretender, like Judas before him, should rightfully be recognized as the "son of Satan" or the "son of perdition." And even though Paul was not privy to the man's incarnation by Satan, it didn't stop him from referring to the President as a man "whose coming is after the working of Satan."

As an added bulwark against the wiles of this Judas, Paul beseeches the Lord to intervene on behalf of the believers and prevent this individual from destroying the Church. And God acquiesces to his request, but only to the extent of sending a delusion over the non-believers which would encourage them to make a hasty acceptance of the lies of the Anti-Christ.

Of course, the secular world will be totally unaware of the strife this man is causing in the Church during this time, which could very well be smoke-screened by the enemy as being an ecumenical movement. But when all is said and done, it would have been better if this man had never been born, for when his work in the judgments is finished, and the seven year period comes to an end, the Anti-Christ will suffer the condemnation of the Lord without ever appearing before the Judgment Seat, and he will be sentenced to the lake of fire:

"Wherefore it shall come to pass, that when the Lord hath performed his whole work upon mount Zion and on Jerusalem, I will punish the fruit of the stout heart of this king of Assyria, and the glory of his high looks." (Isa. 10:12)

"And I will break the Assyrian (Anti-Christ) **in my land, and upon my mountains tread him underfoot: then shall his yoke depart from off them,** (Israel) **and his burden depart from off their shoulders."** (Isa.14: 25)

117

CHAPTER 8

The Harvest

The return of Christ for His Church is almost a forgotten hope today. Unsung by many modern preachers because of its questionable expectancy, the Blessed Hope of the Believer has lost its efficacy in drawing souls to Christ.

With the passing parade of deteriorating social structures, incessant wars and civil disobedience, plagues and the depreciated values of human life, and still no sign of His return, expectations of the fulfillment of what will be the pinnacle of the redemption process have all but faded away, and disillusionment has been allowed to take over. Until today, in the lives of most Christians, little remains of the Blessed Hope but the heavenly persuasion.

But the Rapture has never been hobbled with the vicissitudes of men, nor shackled to the whims of gainsayers. Since the time of creation, the Rapture of the Believers has been the crown jewel in the plans of God for mankind, and its brilliance will continue to exalt the Lord forever.

The issuance of those words of the Lord, when He said, *'I am going to prepare a place for you, that where I am you may be also,'* revealed to mankind the essence of His coming to earth and giving up His life, and when He made that announcement the separation process of the believers from the world had already begun. He was speaking of course, of a dwelling place in heaven for the resurrected believers, which was radical departure from former concept of a physical resurrection to an earthly Kingdom.

The Apostle Peter received a revelation about this heavenly calling, and in his excitement over this new realization, he penned these beautiful words describing how the earthly body would be exchanged for a spiritual body;

"*Salvation,* he said, *was of the soul to an incorruptible inheritance, and that same salvation* (or that new spiritual body) *is to*

118

be brought to us at the revelation of Jesus Christ." (I Pet. 1:3-13)

And united with that concept of the transformation, the Holy Spirit also informed him that this 'revelation of Jesus Christ' would be a uniquely different visitation from the familiar second coming of the Son of man, when He is expected to make His entrance "in the clouds of heaven with power and great glory."

This must have been an astounding revelation to Peter, even though he still didn't know all the particulars about it. But he now understood that when the Lord does come for the believers, to present them with their new spiritual bodies, the secular world will not see Him, whereas on that great and terrible day of the Lord, when He returns to set up His Kingdom and seek justice for those who have been downtrodden, He will be dressed in His full regalia as the King of Kings, and mounted on a white horse at the head of a vast army. This is the picture of the Lord that every one on earth will see when He comes to stand on Mt. Zion at the battle of Armageddon. (Joel 2: 30,31) (Rev.19: 11-16)

Incidentally, there are believers today who still hold to the ancient concept of the Lord's 'dual purpose' return, albeit they have modified their ideas somewhat to allow for the two distinct appearances to appear as one. In this they defer to the Lord's own description of His spectacular return, when He said that it would be at a time when *"The nations will mourn in the expectation of terrible judgment,"* (Matt. 24: 30,31) And by simply including a momentary 'side trip' in His descent to the earth, He will accomplish the Rapture.

In this aspect, it has been suggested that the angels will have been sent beforehand to trumpet His elect from their graves to stand by for their departure. Then, it's hypothesized, without a hesitation and while yet approaching the earth, the Lord will draw the saved unto Him, whereupon He leaves them in reunion and fellowship in the lower heavens while He continues on his journey to the earth. Once there, He will punish the wicked, set up His Kingdom and judge the nations, before making His way back to the Throne of God with His 'raptured saints' in tow.

This 'dual objective' approach is nothing new, for the same message was circulated by the Disciples in their early ministry, and to which for a time the Apostle Paul also acceded. (II Thess.1: 6-10)

Through time though, the Holy Spirit began to reveal more of the plans of God for the Rapture event, which allowed the Apostle Peter to be able to write convincingly of the believer's salvation, as a time when all those *"Who are kept by the power of God through faith unto salvation, will be revealed in the last time."* (I Peter 1:5)

This assertion evidenced his personal belief that the 'salvation rapture' would be a time of revealing all of its own, but, as we shall find out, it is not an isolated event, as expected by most Christians, but the final experience of a separation process called 'the Harvest.'

It will be the 'grand finale,' so to speak, of God's redemptive Grace of the earthly portion of His eternal plan for mankind. It is the reason for sending His Son into the world and sacrificing Him on the cross that His resurrection from the tomb might serve as the perfect example of the Harvest of the 'first fruits of a Holy people.' And with every accomplishment and effort that the Lord has put into it, that Harvest and the final Rapture of the Saints will be one of the most glorious and wonderfully committed endeavors of God.
(Matt.13: 39-43)

We can only imagine what takes place in those fleeting moments before the final parting, when out of the dust of the earth there suddenly arises the transformed bodies of the dead in Christ, who join in ecstasy with the living saints who have been likewise transformed, and together they are taken up in the Shekinah Glory of the Lord that surrounds the earth. (I Thess. 4:16,17)

That momentous event will hardly be visible to the world, but that's not to say that the celestial fireworks and celebration of the inaugural will be unseen, for at that very moment the whole universe will be lit up like the explosion of a super nova. The heavens and the earth will begin to shake from the great sound coming from heaven's trumpets and all the while the Archangel's voice will be resounding over the earth: "THE KING IS COMING!"

And with those proclamations still ringing throughout the universe, the Glorious cortege of our Lord, made up of His myriad of angelic host and the souls of the already redeemed, will pierce through the clouds and sweep to the earth like a bolt of lightning that erupts over the earth into an exceeding brilliance that momentarily encircles the globe. And in that flashing moment the earthly believers will be caught up into heaven. Then just as suddenly as it began, the Rapture is over; the sound of the trumpets fades and the magnificence of the moment disappears, leaving behind an eerie pall of gloom over the earth.

"What a day that will be, when our Savior we shall see!"

To accomplish that momentary deliverance of the believers from among the millions of peoples who will remain on earth, requires a skill far greater than that of a master surgeon, for not one mistake will be made, nor one believer left behind even though families will be divided, husbands and wives will be separated, brothers and sisters wrenched apart by their individual decisions, churches splintered, friends and loved ones separated, and on and on over all the earth. But while this is a moment of great joy in Heaven, it is also a time of deep sorrow in the heart of God, for He has never been desirous of anyone missing this salvation.

The only fortuitous element for the people left behind, will be the suddenness of the Churches' departure, in comparison to the Jesus' slow departure from the Mount of Olives. His rising then was almost gentle before His aghast Disciples who continued to follow His ascent until He disappeared into the clouds. If the ascension of the believers were that slow, you could well imagine the shock and consternation of those on the ground as they were to wave good-bye to their loved ones until they disappeared from sight.

In this same aspect, the Lord's unseen descent to whisk the believers into heaven in a split second of time was a blessing in disguise for the unbelieving world. For *"He changes our vile body, that it may be fashioned like unto His glorious body, and in a moment, in the twinkling of an eye, at the last trump, the dead first and then we which are alive, shall be caught up together, to meet the Lord in the air."* (Phil.3: 21, ICor.15: 52, I Thess.4: 16,17)

While this news about no one missing the Rapture was comforting to the early Church it hadn't alleviated their concern of the Rapture's immanency. They were told then, even as we are told today, that the believer should be ready at all times, for the Rapture could happen at any moment. Today we are reminded that there are no more prophecies that need to be fulfilled before the Lord returns, therefore He could quietly and surreptitiously appear at any moment. However, due to the indifference and independence of men, the prophecies that we already have, such as the reorganization of the European Union, for instance, are still waiting to be fulfilled.

It was this prediction of the Lord's sudden return that worried many of the early believers, lest they go to sleep at night and miss His appearing, or that He would come while they were off to work, while still others were concerned that their loved ones who had already died would miss His coming.

At the time there seemed to be no adequate answers to these concerns, until the Holy Spirit revealed to Paul that the Lord would not return for His Church until it had passed through a testing period wherein the faith of the believer would be recognized. This testing period will apparently coincide with the first months of the President's term in office, and its forthcoming will be marked by recognizable signs which Paul conveniently outlines in his letter to the Thessalonian Church.

"Now we beseech you, brethren, by the coming of our Lord Jesus Christ, and by our gathering together unto him, (2) That ye be not soon shaken in mind, or be troubled, neither by spirit, nor by word, nor by letter as from us, as that the day of Christ is at hand. (3) Let no man deceive you by any means: <u>for that day shall not come, except there come a falling away first, and that man of sin be revealed, the son of perdition;</u> (II Thess. 2: 1-3)

Here we are told of two of the four events or signs that will precede the Lord's return for His Church. All four should be easily discernable by Christians who have been made aware of their existence, however Paul leaned heavily on the two signs given above, which he deemed would be more obvious than the others. But he was also more apprehensive about them, because, in their execution he could see the whole embodiment of the antagonism and deceitfulness of Satan being paraded against the believers by this 'man of sin,' and the disastrous results that could arise from those tactics. Paul knew that this man's enticing words of doubt and rebellion could destroy the Church just as easily as loosing a ravenous wolf among a flock of unsuspecting sheep.

He had previously seen fellowships torn asunder by false teaching, and he fully suspected that the wiles and deceit of the Devil in this man could bring about such an apostasy within the flock that the breech could not be mended. For this reason he warned his converts of the potential harm that could come to the Church, and cautioned them, as well as us, to hold tightly to the precious beliefs that he had taught them.

But when Paul wrote those lines he didn't realize that the plans of God called for the man of sin to be revealed at this time to implement the testing of the believer's faith as well as the pseudo-believers, by the vary methods Paul was warning about, namely the seduction of the ambivalent church goers from the fellowship and the Lord. The fruits of this seduction mature from the seeds of doubt and deceit that will be planted by the man of sin, causing dissension among the flock.

The other two signs, though less conspicuous, are nevertheless workings of the Lord. One has to do with the removal of the restraints that are presently preventing this individual's entrance onto the world scene. Meaning that his offering of the Presidency of the European Union is presently 'on hold' until the Lord determines that the proper moment has arrived.

The other event is a delusion, which the Lord will put into the minds of the unbelieving sector of the fellowship, in order to persuade them to heed the solicitations of the President and separate themselves from the fellowship of believers. The purpose of this delusion is to influence or otherwise encourage those who have not accepted the 'Word of Truth unto Salvation' up to that point in time, to make their choice known. This delusion is neither a witness of the Holy Spirit nor a testimony of the Devil.

However, for the Church, the only recognizable by-product of this delusion, other than the obvious departure of an unusual number of people from the fellowship, will be the typical excuses that will be given for leaving the fellowship. Unfortunately, if the Church has never been forewarned of this coming situation, the believers in the church will not recognize the true situation until it's too late, and thus be ill prepared to witness to their brethren.

The angels, who will be coordinating the separation effort will recognize the non-believers by the delusion within, and they will determine who is be cast back into the world of unregenerate men, or as the parable of Jesus states, 'which of the fish are to be thrown back into the sea.' (Matt. 13: 48,49)

This second pair of signs is given in these scriptures:

"And now ye know what withholdeth that he might be revealed in his time (7) for the mystery of iniquity doth already work: only he who now letteth will let, until he is taken out of the way. (8) And then shall that Wicked (one) be revealed."
(11) And because they received not the love of the truth, that they might be saved, God shall send them strong delusion, that they should believe a lie: (II Thess.2: 7,8 and11)

Below are the Harvest events or 'signs' in the sequence that they will occur, concluding with the Rapture itself:

* **The restrainer is removed, allowing the Wicked one to be revealed.** (Ver.7)
* **The man of sin is made known for who he is** (Vers.3, 8)
* **The Lord sends a strong delusion to convict the unbelievers.**   (Ver.11)
* **There is a falling away, or apostasy, within the fellowship of believers.** (Ver.3)
* **The Rapture**. (Ver.2)

1.   THE RESTRAINER REMOVED

The verse that states " Only he who now letteth will let, until he be taken away," imparts the belief that the restraining force is a personage (he) rather than the power that this individual exhibits, because it is he that is directing the activities of mankind. And in this particular event, the man of sin, who will be known as the President, will be prevented from making his appearance on the world scene until the opportune moment.

Paul writes this under the assumption, that while it is the Father's program, the Holy Spirit (or possibly one of the Archangels) is the 'co-restrainer,' and when the Father determines that all is in readiness for the last days to begin, all restrictions will be lifted and the man of sin will emerge on the world scene as the President of the ten-nation federation now known as the European Union.

One factor among many impeding the process of revelation, is the requisite number of nations that must be in the European Union when the President or Anti-Christ comes into power. It has been designated as ten in the scriptures, however the present affiliation exceeds that amount by several more. And certainly one sign that we may watch for in the coming days will be the Lord's expertise in diminishing the present number of member nations to the required ten, and apparently the only hindrance to this change is the reluctance of the affiliated nations to relinquish their individual sovereignty to Brussels. When this eventually happens though, I would expect that the new ruling Council of the Union would immediately select their permanent President.

Men have speculated on 'what 'or 'who' this restrainer may be, and have come up with a variety of ideas, such as the Roman government, the Emperors of Rome, and even the church, with the pre-conceived notion that God has taken a "hands off" attitude in the control of events. There is also the possibility of the angel Gabriel being the restrainer, because God's pattern of using angels for such activities is more consistent with events in the past, while in the Christian era all revelation emerges through the Holy Spirit, thus He would be the informant to Paul, who could rightly assume that the Holy Spirit would be the restrainer.

2.   THE REVELATION OF THE MAN OF SIN

With the restraints on his emergence lifted, the man of sin comes boldly to the forefront in world politics as leader of the European Union. While ostensibly not the world leader yet, it is from this platform that the Lord uses him to harass the Christian element in society.

As you recall, the revelations to Daniel highlighted the existence of an evil king who would one day wield great power after being indwelt by Satan. But prior to this incarnation the actions of this king were limited to expressing defiance against God and attempting to usurp the position of the Messiah, but this only won

125

him his predestined assassination.

Paul was given a similar revelation of this same individual, but rather than refer to him as the evil king, he gave him the titles of the "man of sin," and the "son of perdition," which reflected the same underlying nature as the evil king of Daniel. But where Daniel envisioned this man as persecuting the Jews, Paul envisions him as persecuting the believers, and he penned this message of what he conceived as our future peril under this man of sin.

Paul may not have been totally aware that the actions of this man were purposely orchestrated to generate a rift between the believers and the non-believers, but he was cognizant of his deceitfulness and persuasive powers which could cause the weaker Christians to stumble and fall, so he cautions all Christians, in every age, to *"Stand fast and hold to the traditions which you have been taught, whether by word or our epistle."* (II Thess. 2: 15)

Similar warnings about this man and his capabilities were given by the Apostle John to 'the believers of the second chance' in the tribulation period.   (Rev.14: 12)

We mustn't loose sight of the fact, that for whatever else he is, the Anti-Christ is a brilliant strategist, and a believable orator who could deceive the very elect if he were allowed to continue, and he will use every trick in the book to not only put himself across as the real Messiah to the Jews, but also to set himself up as the New World Utopian leader to the universal Church, and as Paul warns us, his words will become a siren song that can pull on the heart strings of both the weaker Christians and the pseudo-Christians to entice them to separate from the fellowship of true believers.

The visible signs surrounding this man's appearance will be there for everyone to see, but unfortunately, not all to understand, which is as the Lord intended it should be, but the believers must be made aware of this man's potential to harm the Church as Paul so strongly admonished.

3.   A STRONG DELUSION

There is no definitive way to describe the working of a delusion. The dictionary defines this word as 'a trick of the mind,' 'a hallucination,' 'a false impression' or even a misconception, but what ever it is, in this instance it is applied by God on the unbelievers in the congregations at some unknown point in time to work in concert with the lies of the Anti-Christ and thus cause divisions within the Church body.

Paul uses some strong language in describing the wickedness of the Anti-Christ, with the lies and deceitfulness that he used to achieve the presidency of the European Union. What form those lies come in we are not told, but Paul feels that they will have a dramatic affect on the Church, and that concerned him deeply. He expressed this same fear about the division that would occur in the church in Ephesus when they were forced to fend for themselves after his leaving. At that time he said,

"After my departing, grievous wolves shall enter in among you, not sparing the flock. Also among your own shall men arise, speaking perverse things, to draw away disciples after them. Therefore watch, and remember, that by the space of three years I ceased not to warn every one night and day with tears." (Acts 20:29-31)

While Paul doesn't go into any lengthy explanation of how the words of the Anti-Christ will cause such a problem in the Church body, he reasons that the canker must be cut out to save the fellowship, and he knew that the only way that could be done was to have God intervene in this battle of decision-making in the Church. And God does intervene by sending a 'strong delusion' upon the unbelievers.

Whether the term 'delusion,' which has somewhat of a deceitful connotation to it, correctly defines the 'mind impression' that God intends to use on the unbelievers, the purpose for it is to have them accept a lie from the Anti-Christ over the truth of the Gospel, and provoke them further into disassociating themselves from the Church fellowship.

The pressure or compulsion from God will not be a degenerative reaction to forcibly doom the unbeliever against their will or abandon what faith they might have, but to abandon their inner struggle of trying to make up their own mind of accepting Christ.

127

The time for mankind to make its choice of accepting the Lord as their Savior will have reached its limit. We have all known that there would come a time when the 'building of the Church' would be completed, and this is it, that defining moment that is initiated by the removal of the restraining force which allows the 'harvesting process' to begin, and incidentally the Anti-Christ to be revealed.

From that moment on, the separation of the 'wheat from the chaff' begins, and the team effort of the Holy Spirit and the angels takes over the precise and delicate operation of separating the true believers from the pseudo-believers. It will be a very crucial time in the life of the church, as there will be a restless unsettled feeling running through the congregations, some more than others, depending upon the number of non-believers in the fellowship.

The arguments of the non-believer might follow a line of disdain for the "extremists" and "super-fundamentalists" that are preparing to leave this earth, or there may be simple reasons given to leave the church and find a more liberal-thinking group. But for whatever the reasons given for the exodus, there will be no mistaking the 'falling away' within the church body because it will not occur before the Anti-Christ appears on the scene.

The delusion, so to speak, lasts only until the Rapture is accomplished, at which time all those left behind will be free to rescind their former choice of following the Anti-Christ, and repent to the Lord for their sins and rebellion, and hopefully prepare for the 'second chance' during the tribulation.

We never seem to doubt the capability of Satan to impress thoughts in a person's mind, but we shake our heads at the thought of God doing the same thing. But it will happen. The Holy Spirit's capability of impelling men in a direction of their lives is not nearly as difficult as restraining Satan in his dealing with men.

4.   THE FALLING AWAY FROM THE FELLOWSHIP

The mystery surrounding this verse has baffled the church from its inception. How could six words slip into the epistle and cause so much confusion. It can't be disregarded, or God wouldn't have put it in the scriptures. But this is a letter to the Believers, and as such, it deals with a falling away, or a desertion within the ranks of the church fellowship.

In every age the church has tried to reason if this apostasy was taking place in their time. They knew it had to be a recognizable separation within the fellowship, but that didn't appear to be happening. Then in our age began the "Jesus movement" and "free love" Hippie sects that seemed to be a sure indication of the collapse of the recognized churches. But it wasn't, and that too is past, and now the rapid growth of the Muslim movement, and the eastern religions, is being studied by the church.

No, this apostasy that Paul is speaking about, is on a grander scale, and it will be a distinctive separation within every fellowship of believers. In some cases it will have the appearance of a split in the church that occurs over some disagreement within the body, except this time the excuses will be different.

Since the Church first came into existence there have been people attending Christian fellowships who have considered that their regular attendance in a church, whether it was in a fundamental gathering or not, classified them as a Christian. And thousands of recognized church assemblies accept such attendees into their fold without ever questioning the individual as to whether they had accepted the Lord or not. And as may be expected, these same churches seldom if ever give an invitation to believe in Christ for salvation, so that person remains as lost as the one whose heart has been seared by the word of God but allowed his pride to come between him and the Savior.

For whatever the reason, their remiss in believing in Jesus, marks them for separation from the believers, and this is something that the individual has no control over. Visitations and prayers by the pastor or other believers will have little effect on his decision to leave the fellowship at this time because the unfortunate one will have already received a delusion from the Lord compelling him to either choose the Lord or leave the fellowship.

The separation process is best illustrated in the following Biblical parables depicting the worldwide harvest in those last days:

The Church fellowship is likened to a field that the Lord had planted to wheat, but in the early stages of the crop growth the Devil

129

surreptitiously sowed tares, which in the early stages of growth look surprisingly like the wheat plants. But rather than trying to remove the tares during the growing process, the harvester allowed the plants to grow together until time for the harvest. Now in what we would consider a normal harvesting process the fruit and the chaff would be reaped together, but the Lord harvests in a slightly different way. In the words of the parable, the tares are first separated from the fruit before the harvest begins.

"He that sows the good seed is the Son of man; (38) The field is the world; the good seed are the children of the kingdom; but the tares are the children of the wicked one; (39) The enemy that sowed them is the devil; the harvest is the end of the world (age); and the reapers are the angels. (40) As therefore the tares are gathered and burned in the fire; so shall it be in the end of this world. (Age) (41) The Son of man shall send forth his angels, and they shall gather out of his kingdom all things that offend, and them which do iniquity; (42) And shall cast them into a furnace of fire: there shall be wailing and gnashing of teeth. (43) Then shall the righteous shine forth as the sun in the kingdom of their Father. (Matt.13: 37-43)

In a second parable depicting the same separation process, the sea represents the world in which all varieties of people live. The harvest at the end of the age is depicted by a fisherman who stands on the shore and throws his net into the sea from whence he draws it back to shore with fish of every kind. After the net full of fish has been drawn to shore the fisherman separates them by throwing the undesirable ones back into the sea and keeping the edible fish.

The Lord interpreted the parable in this way:

"So shall it be at the end of the world (age): the angels shall come forth, and sever the wicked from among the just, (50) And shall cast them into the furnace of fire: there shall be wailing and gnashing of teeth." (Matt. 13:49-50)

It should be noted that this separation takes place only among the living. The separation of the dead takes place at the moment of their physical death, when the soul of the believer is taken to be with the Lord, whereas the soul of the non-believer is sent to hell.

In our churches today we have both believers and pseudo-believers worshipping together, but in due course the angels will begin their task of removing all of the pseudo-Christians from the fellowship.

In summarizing, it has always been assumed that the Rapture of the Church was an isolated event that could happen without warning and at any time, when in fact, the Rapture event is the climax of the 'Harvest of Believers' that had begun several months previously.

Paul has told us that the Day of Christ would NOT come before the man of sin came on the scene and the separation process of the unbelievers was completed. He spoke of that separation process as the 'apostasy' or "falling away," which in turn will not begin before the delusion is sent upon the unbelieving world to urge the unbelievers within the Church fellowship to part company.

Meanwhile, the Anti-Christ has also added his persuasive abilities to entice the unwary Christians. However, each of these steps in the process is precisely and deliberately controlled by God and directed through the efforts of His angels.

There will be a moderate time span, perhaps as much as a few months, during which the separation process continues. And it will be a time when the Christians see their faithfulness to Christ being tested, but not as some have intimated, through the experience of the tribulation. On the day that the Anti-Christ signs a covenant with Israel that separation process ends. That day is known as the 'Day of Christ,' and within moments of the signing, the Rapture of the Church takes place, and the judgments begin.

CHAPTER 9

The Seals on the Scroll

The tribulation period has been frequently likened to a three-legged stool, with the Seal openings and the Trumpets and Vial judgments forming a triad of punishments that are equally supportive of the campaign. So it's not surprising that the Seal openings, which come first in the order of events, would be assumed to set the standard for the remaining punishments in the period. And because the so-called 'horsemen' are the first four on the list of the Seal openings, they have come to symbolize, not only the period itself, but the apocalyptic end of all civilization.

It seems that Christians and non-Christians alike have viewed them as 'doomsday' warriors of wanton death and destruction who gallop madly across the tundra on their fearsome stallions while wringing desolation everywhere they go. So its no wonder that an unsuspecting reader, who has scarcely begun perusing the book of Revelation, is suddenly confronted with these terrible omens of death who are just waiting to pounce upon the unwary. Like gargoyles protecting the gates of a castle, they threaten all those who would dare to enter the book. Surely, it is believed, these horsemen must epitomize the horrors of the tribulation. But the scriptures reveal otherwise.

These mystifying horsemen with their cascading exploits neither propound such horrifying mortalities upon civilization, nor do they elicit the theme of the judgments. Their sole purpose is to exemplify modern man's predilection toward violence and death, and attempt to give him a warning of preparedness for the impending Trumpet and Vial judgments. These horsemen actually characterize the Lord's spirits, whose function is to provide the backdrop of the tribulation period with the common situations of upheavals, strife, pestilence and famine that are prevalent in our society today.

The fourth rider, which depicts 'death,' has been routinely

portrayed in the secular world by a shrouded skeleton carrying a scythe in his right hand and hovering over the planet earth like an omen of death to those below. This is a typical symbolization of man's propensity for death which is exactly what John is attempting to portray by the use of the horsemen, which in many ways illustrates the powder-keg situation that exists in eastern Europe and the Mediterranean area today. In direct antithesis to the theme that 'death takes a holiday,' violence and death still runs rampant over a many areas of the earth today, and John simply paints a composite picture of this situation with the words;

"And I looked, and behold a pale horse: and his name that sat on him was Death, and Hell followed with him. And power was given unto them over the fourth part of the earth, to kill with sword, and with hunger, and with death, and with the beasts of the earth." (Rev. 6: 8)

Another reason for disclaiming these 'Horsemen' as being judgments, lies in their posture of 'generalizing death.'

As you recall from the visions of Daniel, it was God's prerogative to apportion the punishments between the Jews and the Gentiles, which means that He selected them and proportioned them with respect to both time and location. This demonstrated a certain specificity of the punishments, which is totally unlike the activities of the four horsemen. There is no indication of any selectivity whatsoever in their course of action, but to the contrary, they demonstrate a supposed random distribution of punishment over all of humanity.

Furthermore, while the singular purpose of the tribulation judgments is to punish the wicked and the unbeliever, as dictated by the "Trumpet" and "Vial" judgments, there is no such directive shown in the actions of the four horsemen. The only directive that might possibly be construed as showing partiality or purpose on the recipients is indicated in the phrase " *the fourth part of the earth,*" taken from the verse above, which, if taken literally implies that a selected portion of the world and not the whole will suffer death, but then the question could be raised, "Which portion?"

If this common death sentence was part and parcel of the tribulation, then the rapture of the Christians, the redemption of the

144,000 selected Jews, as well as the deliverance of the faithful remnant of both Gentiles and Jews would be without merit, for these believers would all be under the same umbrella as the wicked and unbelievers, and such is not to be the case

Admittedly, the words "to kill with sword, and with hunger and with death, (pestilence)" in the above verse do in fact typify the means of punishment that will be used by the Lord during the tribulation period, however the inference of a seemingly aimless administration of these punishment by these horsemen actually negates their actions as being judgments.

Somewhere down the line, these 'Four Horsemen of the Apocalypse,' as they are called, have gotten the bad reputation of being the perpetrators of all the dastardly deeds upon mankind, when in fact, they are God's spirit messengers, sent from Heaven to PREPARE the earth for the tribulation ahead. They have been depicted as first century warriors for John's benefit, that he might be able to visualize the spirits and pass the information on to us, much the same as similar revelations that were given to other prophets, wherein these selfsame spirits were effected in the guise of horses and chariots. (Zech. 6:3-7)

Moreover, when Jesus commented on this same concert of wars, starvation and pestilence and civil strife that would precede the tribulation period, He made no mention of any involvement by the spirits. He labeled these turbulent times and events as 'the beginning of sorrows,' and noticeably refrained from considering them as tribulation judgments. Here is the description He used:

"Take heed that no man deceives you. (5) For many shall come in my name, saying, I am Christ; and shall deceive many. (6) And ye shall hear of wars and rumors of wars: see that ye be not troubled: for all these things must come to pass, but the end is not yet. (7) For nation shall rise against nation and kingdom against kingdom: and there shall be famines, and pestilences, and earthquakes, in divers places. (8) All these are <u>the beginning of sorrows</u>." (Matt. 24: 4-8)

I can just imagine the puzzled looks that came over the Disciple's faces when they heard Jesus tell of these things in the future. For certainly these announced signs were far removed from their original question about the signs of His Second Coming, however they have a great import on our world today.

Being general in nature, they could apply to just about any time period in the past two thousand years if it weren't for that last phrase. When He said that all those events were the precursor to the "sorrows," He was using a term that only the Jews would recognize as being the time of Jacob's Trouble, or the judgment period. Thus, His words served as a preamble to the judgment period, without ever having to divulge the actual judgments.

In the book of Revelation, we find John following the same idea with his writing of the seven "Seal" visions. And as Jesus' remarks were both a prediction and a warning of things to come, so also was it John's reason for including these Seal events. However, because there seems to be no definitive break in his journal between the listing of the seven 'Seal' visions and the summoning of the 'Trumpet' judgments, the demarcation between the preface and the beginning of the judgment period goes almost unnoticed, leading many Bible expositors to believe that the Seal opening events were a part of the tribulation punishments.

Then again, a reader might mistakenly consider these Seal openings as being the opening phase of the punishment period because of the auspicious circumstances surrounding their introduction in heaven, which happened to follow on the heels of a memorable moment when the seven-sealed scroll was being used as the scepter of royalty, which was offered by the Father to Jesus in recognition of His becoming the King of Kings and Lord of Lords.

Through two full chapters of John's book we are made witnesses to the magnificent Coronation of the Lord and the recognition of His royalty, but with His coronation came the awesome responsibility of administering the judgments.

Following His acceptance of the scroll, and while still standing before the Throne, He turned to the congregation and raised His arm with the scroll over His head. And for what seemed a long while he remained standing there while the ovations of praises and Glory rolled through the heavens. Then He lowered His arm and stepped back to the Throne where He sat down at the right hand of the Father,

On this, the praises diminished and all of heaven became stilled when it appeared that the seals were about to be broken.

The first seal parted, and almost immediately one of the four creatures that circled the Throne called to John from outside of the Throne room,

"Come and see!" So John hurried to where the creature was, and as he did so he looked down and gasped in amazement, for never had he been in such a position before. It was as though he were standing on that same hill overlooking Jerusalem many years ago. But he was much higher now, and he could see all over his beautiful homeland, and far out to distant lands.

And while he was looking at the scenery below, he saw a warrior wearing a crown and carrying a bow in his hand, riding swiftly on a white horse all over the earth below, and at every swift step of the stallion he saw the people bow to the ground. Wherever the feet of the horse touched the ground people could be seen giving honor and obeisance to the warrior, but John could not recognize who this king was.

Meanwhile, Jesus had continued with the opening of the second seal, and the second creature from over the Throne called to John,

"Come and see." So he turned to look at yet another scene on the earth that the creature was pointing to. There he saw another mounted warrior galloping across the tundra, only this time the warrior was wielding a large sword that he brandished at the men in the path of his galloping red horse.

The creature volunteered the information to John that this warrior was directed to take peace away from the earth, and to make trouble and war. And sure enough, even as he watched, wherever the warrior traveled, the people rose up in fighting and killing of one another. Then fast on the heels of that vision, the Lord opened the third seal, and now the third creature called, "Come and see:"

But this time the vision was not of war and killing, but of a man riding a black horse over the earth, and carrying a set of balances in his hand. And as John followed his path he heard a voice, but not that of the creatures, saying,

"A measure of wheat for a penny, and three measures of barley for a penny; and see thou hurt not the oil and the wine."

John might have turned then to see who spoke those words,

but at that moment he was watching Jesus open the fourth seal, and following hard on came the voice of the fourth creature, who said,

"Come and see." Now the vision was that of rider on a bay horse, but the rider was faceless and it startled John, so the creature told him that the rider was Death, and seated behind Death was Hell, and John was further told that these two would follow in the path of the other horsemen, namely war, pestilence and famine, and the beasts of the earth, over the fourth part of the earth.

Needless to say, John was awestruck by the visions under the four seals. He had no idea what to expect when he first came up to heaven, and had probably just settled down to enjoy the new experience. He might have even thought that he was up here just to view the Coronation. But those terrible scenes of death on the world below brought him up short, and he began to realize why he was brought here.

Now the scenes of the four horsemen didn't represent anything spectacular to John, as he had experienced the terrible siege of the city of Jerusalem only a few years back, when thousands of his brethren were killed by the Roman soldiers, and the scarcity of food brought about severe famine and even acts of cannibalism among his brethren. The only horseman that might have puzzled him, was the first one with a crown. He might have even conjectured that this was Titus, the Roman General, who led the assault on the city, but he dutifully recorded the visions with what limited information he had been given. Unlike Daniel of old, he failed to ask any probing questions of either the creatures or the Lord.

Each of these 'horsemen' appear to be depicting singular events, but the intention, at least of the last three, was to display the whole panorama of disastrous conditions on the earth that will be in progress at more or less at the same time prior to the tribulation period. In this aspect, any minor discrepancies that you might have noticed between the prophetic utterances of Jesus and the scenes that John had just described, are of little consequence, as the purpose of both recordings was to issue a warning to the world of what will be rapidly deteriorating conditions of peace and harmony among nations as the end-time approaches.

And although the whole world has been experiencing dramatic

climate changes which fostered terrible storms and related floods and hurricanes, in a certain respect the European continent and the Near East have been noticeably struck with increased civil strife and fighting between nations.

It should be pointed out that these developments on earth project the basic form of punishments that God has used since the Exodus. They are war, pestilence and famine. Other types of plagues have been associated with the pestilence at various times, as in the plagues of the locusts and the frogs that were used in Egypt and thirst for water was usually associated with such famines. But man's greed and pride, as well as his necessity for food, water, and health become the common ingredients that are invariably used by God for punishing humanity, particularly as we shall find out, in the great tribulation period.

To clarify the purpose of the other two 'horsemen,' who incidentally symbolized the Anti-Christ and Death, we need only look at this closing verse in the narrative:

"And Power was given unto them (the spirits) **over the fourth part of the earth, to kill with sword, with hunger, and with death, and with beasts of the earth."**

The word "power" in the above verse means that "authority" has been given to them by God, to reign over *"the fourth part of the earth."* Not the whole earth, however, but a bounded portion of the earth, and all of the people within that area. That bounded area would include Europe, the Near East, and portions of North Africa, which throughout Biblical history was the extent of the known and commercially traveled world. Though it was generally known that the earth was a planet of much greater expanse than just these mentioned areas, the Holy Spirit inspired John to designate that this area was the 'fourth part of the earth.'

As for the "beasts of the earth," noted above, they are not the wild carnivorous beasts that you are familiar with, but the "beasts" of Satan, the Anti-Christ, and the False Prophet, that have been described in Revelation chapter 13.

As you recall, God prophesied in the book of Daniel, (2:7-8) that there would be four major 'world' empires that would have dominion over the nation of Israel, and these would be the

Babylonian, the Persian, the Grecian, and the Roman. History has proven the truth of this prophecy, and the Roman Empire was the one that obliterated the nation of Israel in the great dispersion of 135 AD.

But it's political power waned after the third century AD, and eventually became dormant, until it stirred again in 1957 when a small number of the original colonies of the ancient Roman Empire signed a common cause agreement between them called the Treaty of Rome. This agreement formed the basis of the original 'Common Market of Europe.' From that humble beginning, the number of nations within its realm expanded, and its name was changed to the 'European Community of Nations,' which evolved still further into what is now the 'European Union,' or what the old Roman Caesars would have been proud to have called "the fourth part of the earth"

FIFTH SEAL OPENING

There was no requirement for the Lord to deal with the opening of the seals if it wasn't for the purpose of relaying information about certain peoples and events that were relative to, but not necessarily part of the judgment period. This was as true of the 'four horsemen' as it will be in this Seal opening and the ones following.

These last three seal-opening visions reveal several different groups of people and the situations they would be dealing with during this particular time period, providing us with a better picture of the tribulation period.

The fifth seal opening vision is an example of this format, where our attention is drawn to a specific group of people and the situation they find themselves in, that of being under the Altar in Heaven while the tribulation is going on. John describes this group thusly:

"I saw under the altar the souls of them that were slain for the word of God, and for the testimony which they held; (10) And they cried with a loud voice, saying, How long, O Lord, holy and true, dost thou not judge and avenge our blood on them that dwell on the earth? (11) And white robes were given unto every one of them; and it was said unto them, that they should rest yet for a little season, until their fellow servants also and their brethren, that should be

killed as they were, should be fulfilled." (Rev. 6: 9-11)

This vision was particularly poignant to John, for he was viewing the ancestors of his people, and they seemed to be distraught with their situation. Not because of where they were, but because of their vengeful attitude against their former oppressors on earth. They have been waiting patiently under the Altar for many generations and now they are told that they must wait a little longer until their 'brethren' are slain in the judgment period. The punishments have not yet begun, and they are becoming anxious about the promised revenge upon those who had punished them cruelly on earth. These "souls" are the 'Old Testament saints,' or Jews who had faith in God and who had dwelt in "Paradise" within the earth until they became the "first fruits of the Lord's resurrection" who took them with Him to heaven.

THE SIXTH SEAL OPENING

Under this Seal opening there are three separate visions describing three different groups of peoples. The first portrays an earth shaking situation and the desperation of those lost people around the world who find themselves trapped in a situation from which there is no escape. Unfortunately, John's record of this episode under the sixth Seal opening instead of being under the fourth Trumpet Judgment where it belongs, has caused considerable confusion among Bible scholars, particularly because of the phrase *"for the great day of his wrath is come: and who shall be able to stand?"* which appears at the close of the vision.

This situation is typical of all of the Seal visions in their depiction of future developments, even as the vision of 'the souls under the Altar' was a projected event. But this hasn't prevented some scholars from making a wrongful assumption about when the earthshaking occurs. Because the statement appears at this juncture of the book the assumption is immediately drawn that the Tribulation was already in progress, but this is not so. Moreover, the phrase at the end was intended to be a rhetorical question, to show the despair of mankind in their efforts to escape the real judgment. This expressed despair was either over the provocation of God's wrath

140

against the world or their own weakness in attempting to endure the wrath of God.

Following this vision, we are introduced to two other gatherings of people. One of which is a fairly small select group, whose identity the Lord wishes to keep secret from the Anti-Christ for the time being. lest they be put at the top of his list for extermination. These people are respectfully referred to as the 144,000 Jews chosen from the twelve tribes of Israel.

John's vision however, is not centered on the group, but on four angels seen standing on the earth, representing the four compass directions of north, east, south and west. It is suggested that the four angels have been given an objective of creating hurricanes and tornadoes over the earth's entire surface at the same time. However, before the four angels can start their work, another angel, recognized by the four as coming directly from the Throne of God, stops them long enough to allow the selection and 'sealing' of this Jewish group, that they might be the "First Fruits" of the Millennial Kingdom on earth. So one day, after the Judgment period has ended, and the Lord Jesus returns to stand on Mt. Zion, this group of young men will meet Him there, ready to serve and assist in the structuring and administration of the Kingdom. (Rev. 14:1-5)

There has been wide speculation among Bible expositors that these young men will be witnesses for Christ unto salvation during the Tribulation period, but there is no scriptural basis for they're being believers in Christ, let alone being witnesses.

However the timing of the selection of this group is critical. Being Jews, they must to be kept safe from all harm during the first three and a half years of the judgment period, as well as the great tribulation on the Gentiles, which means that their selection must take place sometime prior to the start of the judgment period. This seems to be substantiated by the event of worldwide catastrophic hurricanes and tornadoes being held up until the selection process was completed. (Rev. 7:1-3)

This leaves a narrow window of opportunity for such a phenomenon to take place. It could happen prior to the signing of the peace treaty, in which case the Church, being still on the earth would not only witness the disasters, but also be subject to their punishments. However, a more likely scenario would place these disastrous conditions shortly after the signing of the peace treaty in Jerusalem that initiates the judgment period.

The last vision under this sixth Seal opening features another group of people. This group has been called "the tribulation saints," because *'they have come out of the great tribulation, and have washed their robes, and made them white in the blood of the Lamb.'* (Rev.7: 14) They have been given a second chance for salvation and they reached for it, making them eligible for deliverance from the great tribulation to follow.

These folks are the 'gleanings of the harvest,' who have sacrificed their lives to gain deliverance soon after the Beast began his pressuring tactics on the believers. The stream of converts continues over a period of two years until the Vial judgments begin.

CHAPTER 10

The Seventh Seal
(Jacob's Trouble Begins)

One of the most provocative notations in the book of Revelation is the one that gives mention of a half-hour period of silence that followed in the wake of the Lord's opening of the seventh seal. Many explanations have been offered for this silence, such as it being a time of prayer by the saints against the perils that lie ahead, or a somber silence that was enlisted just before the judgments came upon the earth. But I would suggest that there was a burst of excitement and activity in heaven when the seal was broken, activity which included a 'preemptive strike' against the earth of unimaginable proportions. For in that slight pause between the breaking of the seventh seal and the opening of the scroll of the judgments, the amazing and wonderful Rapture of the Saints will take place.

John doesn't mention that only moments before this took place, the Anti-Christ had been preparing to leave Jerusalem immediately following the signing of the peace documents which officially opened the judgment period.

Looking back, it seems strange that of all of the significant happenings on the earth, with the great kings and their battles between the empires over the many centuries, the Lord would pick one of the least ostentatious happenings to tie His judgment period to, such as a lowly covenant between the Arab and the Jewish nations. But that is exactly what the Lord had prophesied would happen, which brings up the point, that until such time as the Anti-Christ does make his entry on the world scene as the President of the European Union, and drafts that peace covenant, the days ahead will continue to fold mercifully on as usual, until that day comes when a totally surprised world will sense for a moment the awesome presence of the Lord, as they gaze awestruck into the heavens at the most brilliant aura of light that ever enveloped the earth.

That brilliant light will signify to the world that the seventh seal has been broken, the Rapture has just been completed, and any and all restraints on the commencement of the Tribulation judgments have been severed. With those gone, the un-regenerate civilization will be free to slip quietly into the judgment period with no one on earth being the wiser.

But until that day arrives, the sword of justice will continue to hang over the earth by a slender thread, in anticipation of the seventh seal being broken and the plagues beginning. And while there is a great deal of anxiety being expressed on earth over the expectancy of the coming tribulation, (or as some worry that it's the end of the world) around the Throne in heaven there is an equal concern, which is why the scripture speaks of a silence that hovered over the whole congregation as they waited for the Lord to remove the last seal on the scroll.

The anticipation of the long awaited judgments has undoubtedly produced a mixture of emotions in those around the Throne. For those still waiting under the Altar this moment struck a responsive chord, because they knew that their time of retribution had finally come, whereas those closer to the Throne were beginning to get an uneasy feeling about the grieved expression they saw coming on face of the Lord.

They knew that the tempest on earth was just one broken seal and one roll of the scroll away, and everyone in heaven recognizes the expectations of the moment. There will be time for jubilation and the sound of 'hallelujahs' when the punishments finally get underway, but for some reason, John's only recollection of this memorable moment was memorialized in a dozen words announcing a half-hour silence following the opening of the seal:

"And when He had opened the seventh seal, there was silence in heaven for about the space of half an hour." (Rev. 8:1)

Immediately following that silence though, John reminds us of a flurry of activity in another direction, as plans were being readied for the judgments. But it's what happened during the half-hour interim that turns out to be so marvelous and inspiring.

Perhaps John intended to transcribe what went on during that

144

period but was cautioned against it by the Lord. Which wouldn't have been the first time that the Lord had made such a request of him, for there was another instance, when John was attempting to record the voices of the thunder, and the Lord told him to 'seal up those things,' or in other words, don't write about them. (Rev.10: 4)

But there's a greater possibility that during that mysterious half-hour period Heaven was bathed in silence because it was emptied of all creatures. It would have been interesting to know what the visions of this seal opening would have revealed about the goings-on in heaven and on the earth had he been allowed to record them.

But we can only surmise that what transpired during that time, not only had to be done as quickly and with as little fanfare as possible, but it also had to be squeezed into that small gap between the removal of the seventh seal and the unrolling of the scroll.

We know that the President of the European Union had come to Jerusalem just a few hours earlier to officiate at the signing of the peace covenant between Israel and the Arab States. Everything was going smoothly and right on schedule, and by three o'clock in the afternoon the dignitaries were gathered around the long tables with the President sitting between the two representatives in the middle of the group. Everyone seemed to be pushing themselves to make the atmosphere a little less somber, and you could hear the occasional jocular laughter being muffled behind cupped hands. But within the hour the documents initiating the peace agreement were dutifully signed by all.

Rather than staying for the festivities which followed, the President decided to return immediately to Brussels. A decision that was no doubt prompted by the thunderstorms that were beginning to move in from the south and threatening rain. So he had little time to ruminate over the successes of the day, nor would he realize that his departure from Jerusalem practically ushered down the two witnesses from heaven.

The President's plane had no sooner cleared the runway than a blinding corona of light filled the evening sky over Jerusalem. It only lasted for a few moments before the blackness closed in again and the rain and high winds took over.

Meanwhile, two of John's forefathers, namely Moses and Elijah, who had been taken into Heaven centuries ago in their resurrected bodies, were returned to earth in the city of Jerusalem. There they will be witnesses to John's countrymen to warn them of the coming judgments and the changes they could make in their lives to escape the judgments.

In heaven the trumpets had been resounding and the entire host of angels were at their assigned task of gathering the saints from the four corners of heaven to ready their course to the Rapture of the believers.

Thus, John found himself being taken from his records keeping after completing only one sentence, and along with the millions of other souls in heaven began the swift journey with the Lord back into the environs of the earth. There they would be united with their newly resurrected bodies, and share with the risen living saints, the wonders of that culminating moment of the Harvest. (I Cor. 15:52,53) (I Thess. 2:19)

And so, for that brief period which John claims was a 'half hour of silence,' the heavens were emptied, save for the Father and the four beasts. John also was away from his post and participating in the Rapture.

Side by side with the Lord at the reunion of the Saints, and even on his homeward journey, he opted not to write about any of it, but instead was caught up in the joyous festivities and the preparations for the sounding of the Trumpet judgments.

This one sentence in Rev. 8:1, was the closest John would ever come to letting us know what took place in that brief period of time, but he wouldn't have missed it for the world.

With the reunion fulfilled, the whole congregation gathered around the Throne and waited patiently for the Lord to open the scroll of the judgments, and when He did, silence again hung over the assembly. All were anxious for this moment, and it wasn't long before John realized that the scroll contained a list of punishments to be put upon his brethren in Israel, and that there was going to be a time of trouble and distress over all the earth. As one prophet had earlier described, "It was going to be a day of wrath, a day of trouble and distress, and a day of waste and desolation," (Zeph 1:15)

But the prophet Jeremiah gave one of the better descriptions of the hardship and the despair of the tribulation, when he said;

"It will be a day so great that there would never be another day like it. It would be the time of Jacob's trouble." (Jer. 30:7)

Quickly now, the preparations for the first judgment begin. Seven angels have already been selected to blow the trumpets, and they have been called to the Throne Room. (Rev. 8:2)

John watches closely as each of the angels goes forward in turn and hears that portion of the writing on the scroll that they will be initiating. And though he strains to hear what's being said, little of the limited conversations between the Lord and the angels are loud enough for him to understand.

Soon the last of the seven angels was dismissed and the scroll was closed.

Glancing across the room towards the Altar, John observes another angel holding a golden censer. Incense had been given to him, which he poured into the censor and lit from the fire on the Altar. And as the smoke from the incense rose gently before God, the saints surrounding the Throne lifted up their hands and offered their petitions to the Lord for Mercy upon those who were about to receive the punishments.

Watching the scene before him, John is reminded of a similar prayer offering that was made by Moses in the ancient tabernacle in the wilderness. Every morning and evening, Aaron, the High Priest, would burn sweet incense over the Altar, and while the smoke of the incense drifted upward, Aaron would offer prayers for God's Mercy upon his people. (Ex. 30: 1-10)

Here the same ritual is being repeated, except the prayers now being raised are from the believers in heaven along with those of the Jewish converts on the earth.

Suddenly, from the corner of his eye, John caught a movement which caused him to turn quickly and see the same seven angels again standing before the Throne, only now, each was carrying a trumpet as they waited for the signal from the Throne.

Until recent times, the trumpet had always been a necessary tool for every army in the world. The sounding of a trumpet in various ways was the only means of communication between the commander and his troops on the battle field, and to John, the sounding of a trumpet would be the same as the sounding of an air-raid siren to us today. It signals attention.

John wrote quickly, trying to encompass all of the activities going on at the moment, so he was caught unaware of the heavy silence that had fallen over the Throne Room. He looked up to see that all eyes were turned on the Lord as the vast throng anxiously waited for the commands from the Throne.

Moments slipped by, and still John heard nothing, and he sensed, as everyone there apparently did, that there was reluctance on God's part to issue the necessary order to commence the judgment. Was He having second thoughts? Was He striving to give His people on earth one more chance to heed those ancient words that said;

"In the latter days, when you are in tribulation, and all these are about to come down on you, if you will turn to the Lord your God, and obey His voice, He will not forsake you, nor destroy you." (Deut.4: 30)

From John's view of the Throne, he wasn't sure if he saw the nod of the head of the One sitting on it, but he did notice that one of the angels quickly moved to light a censer from the fire on the Altar and throw it down onto the earth, where immediately the elements exploded in response with thundering, lightning and an earthquake. Now the judgments will begin.

148

CHAPTER 11

The Beginning

It was the moment the world had long been waiting for, an opportunity for an ever-elusive peace process in the Near East to come into fruition. For the last half a century, since the state of Israel came into being, the Arabs and the Jews have been facing each other over weapons of war, and the almost daily acts of terrorism and reprisal have often brought the neighboring nations to the brink of war. But today there is a chance to wave the olive branch once again in the form of a newly engineered peace treaty by the President.

It was three o'clock in the afternoon and the treaty was on the table before the signatories from all of the Arab nations and Israel. A large retinue of the news media was on hand to witness the historic ceremony, the proceedings of which had gone smoothly, as the smiles and handshaking seemed to attest. The European Union President, being the last to sign, did so with a flourish of the pen that flaunted his proud achievement to the waiting world. And following his prolonged signing he added this brief statement for the press;

"We are pleased to announce that this historic treaty has now been ratified, guaranteeing peaceful conditions for a period of seven years. But we hope that it will continue for many times that, on into the millennium, and that this will settle the long-time differences between Israel and its neighboring Arab states, and ensure a lasting peace in this long troubled area"

The events leading up to this ceremony had begun some six months earlier in Brussels, Belgium, shortly after the newly elected President had been sworn in. He was destined to tackle many diplomatic challenges in the office, the foremost of which was the formidable task of finding a solution to the Near East crisis. This was an undertaking that had consistently eluded achievement by other national leaders, including former U.S. Ambassadors and Presidents.

Although many times over the years it appeared as if an

agreement had been reached, mistrust among the delegates inevitably reared its ugly head and the agreements failed. Attempts to settle their differences without a mediating third party were tried, but those proceedings also were doomed, and relations between the countries worsened. Ultimately however, both parties agreed to resume negotiations with the aid of the European Union representatives, and accepted another series of exhaustive meetings, with the leaders shuttling back and forth between neutral grounds, but eventually the effort paid off and a mutual agreement was reached.

This covenant would not only be a significant achievement for the President, and hoist his political status to a new level in the world community, but it would also be a milestone in the advancement of the end time events. For according to the Prophet Daniel, the signing of that necessary covenant would happen right on schedule and the judgment period would officially begin. (Dan. 9:27)

With that peace document in place, the conditions on earth were finally in readiness for the judgments to begin, and all that remained was the opening of the seventh seal by the Lord, which he quickly did. And with the brief remaining hours of that opening day slowly ebbing away, the Lord quickly sent two of His messengers back down to earth in Jerusalem, there to begin what would be a three and a half year ministry of witnessing and prophesying to the Jews of the coming judgments. Following that, He rather surreptitiously removed the Church from the earth, and when those two undertakings were completed, the curtain was raised and all was in readiness in heaven for the first of the Trumpet judgments.

In the meantime, on the earth in Jerusalem, the activities that normally followed such auspicious occasions were about to begin. However, the President graciously declined to stay for the festivities, choosing instead to fly back to Brussels well ahead of an approaching storm that had already begun to strengthen by late afternoon. In fact, the weather was deteriorating rapidly into storm conditions over the whole region, with light rain already beginning to fall as the President's plane taxied down the runway. It wouldn't be long before it would escalate into the heaviest of downpours, which gradually turned into the consistency of soupy mud. That's when the

150

seriousness of the situation became apparent.

Just hours earlier, in the southern regions of the Negev, there had been a sharp jolting earthquake from an existing fault-line that extended westward through the mountains from the Dead Sea. The earth movement went virtually unnoticed in the remote area and caused little destruction, other than shaking a long dormant volcano so violently that it developed a breach high in its wall, and what happened next was like steam bursting from a sealed bubbling cauldron. When the wall cracked it loosed the built-up pressure of gasses inside, and the mountain further exploded with a roar exuding great volumes of effluent clouds into the heavens.

The eruptions continued sporadically over the next several hours without showing any signs of diminishing, and after each eruption the mushrooming waste would mold into the brewing winds of a violent storm that was steadily pressing northward.

The deluge continued through the night, with the muck growing deeper and heavier by the minute. Roofs of homes and buildings began caving in under the ever-deepening mass, which also caused the trees and bushes to bow and give up their limbs. Live stock that had been left penned in the open, huddled together for protection while slowly suffocating to death. Soon the whole southern two-thirds of the country would be buried in a sea of mud.

What is happening in Israel is reminiscent of the eruptions of Mt. Pinitubo in the Philippines, in 1991. The eruptions of that equally dormant volcano continued for several days, during which time nearly a foot of ash and muck was deposited over hundreds of square miles. Everything beneath that covering of ash was destroyed and hundreds of villages had to be abandoned. And when it was over, 90,000 people were left homeless and destitute.

This is now Israel's plight. But through saving grace, most of the fallout has been confined to more or less desolate areas, which kept the loss of human life to a minimum, notwithstanding, thousands of domestic animals have been lost, and the once bountiful agricultural lands and orchards are no more. Access roads to many small communities lay buried under the thickening mud, deterring any form of rescue effort until the storm ceased. In some areas the

151

landscape was so completely covered in a blanket of mud that it was impossible to distinguish between human habitations and their surroundings.

But the eruptions finally eased off and the storms diminished sufficiently to allow clean up to begin. But the lack of adequate earth-moving equipment necessitated a great deal of manual labor, and, as happened in many small Philippine communities, where there was irreparable damage to buildings as well as water supplies and power services, many villagers simply salvaged what they could and abandoned the rest.

Following that first round of eruptions there was a quiet period for several weeks before the volcano started rumbling again, sending up large plumes of acrid smoke, which sent an ominous warning of another round of eruptions. And true to form, three months after the initial eruptions the mountain blew again, only this time the results were even more disastrous. Ash and the debris filled the sky as before, but along with the ash came a great quantity of molten magma that was thrown far out over the land and the distant sea where it finally descended like fireballs. There was no warning and precious little time for evacuation. Deadly molten lava rained down everywhere, killing thousands of people who were caught out in the open or under flimsy overhead protection, and of those who somehow managed to survive the onslaught of lava, many hundreds more were killed by the firestorms of hot poisonous gas that rolled over the countryside.

In this second attack, virtually the entire southern half of Israel was either destroyed by lava or covered again in ash. Vast sections of reclaimed desert lands now lay buried with little chance of ever being restored. But for some strange reason, the city of Jerusalem was spared from major damage. Could it have been because the two witnesses were in that city?

World news reports covered the tragedies live over television, with accompanying explanations, which attributed the disasters to a rare but natural phenomenon. This and similar explanation seemingly ruled out the prospect of these events being the Lord's handiwork. Nevertheless, there is every reason to believe that this was the same volcano that the Lord used to destroy the cities of Sodom and

Gomorrah in the plains of southern Edom, nearly four thousand years ago. In that instance, the inhabitants were destroyed along with the cities because of their total depravity, however the Bible indicates that it was the cities that were the prime target of His wrath, and they were destroyed so completely that no trace of them was ever found. This is the Biblical account of that incident:

"Then the LORD rained upon Sodom and upon Gomorrah brimstone and fire from the LORD out of heaven; (25) and he overthrew those cities, and all the plain, and all the inhabitants of the cities, and that which grew upon the ground." (vegetation) (Gen. 19: 24,25)

It's more than just a coincidence that what happened to Sodom and Gomorrah in ancient times had now happened in Israel, and you would imagine that by now the Jews would have considered the possibility of these two eruptions being judgments. For according to John's account, the Trumpet judgments began with these two eruptions.

The <u>first</u> angel sounded, and there followed hail and fire mingled with blood, and they were cast upon the earth; and the third part of trees was burnt up, and all green grass was burned up. (8) And the <u>second</u> angel sounded, and it was as though a great mountain was burning with fire and casting its embers into the sea; and the third part of the sea became blood; (9) And the third part of the creatures which were in the sea, and had life, died; and the third part of the ships were destroyed." (Rev. 8:7-9)

The land of Israel is under attack, just as the Lord prophesied centuries ago, and it's not as though the nation hasn't been warned that this would happen because it's evident from the following scriptures that God had repeatedly told the Jews that such a thing would happen if they continued to rebel against Him. And not only would their land suffer the same fate as Sodom and Gomorrah, but in the wake of the tragedies, even the neighboring nations would recognize that this was a just punishment on the Jews for their rebellious attitude.

"So that the generation to come of your children that shall rise up after you, and the stranger that shall come from a far land, shall say, when they see the plagues of that land, and the sicknesses which

153

the LORD hat laid upon it; (23) And that the <u>whole land thereof is</u>
<u>brimstone, and salt, and burning,</u> that it is not sown, nor bears fruit,
nor any grass grows therein, <u>like the overthrow of Sodom, and</u>
<u>Gomorrah, Admah, and Zeboim, which the LORD overthrew in his</u>
<u>anger, and in his wrath;</u> (24) Even all the nations shall say,
Wherefore hath the Lord done thus unto the land? Why the heat of
this great anger? (25) Then men shall say, Because they have
forsaken the covenant of the Lord God of their fathers, which He
made with them when He brought them forth out of the land of Egypt;
(Deut. 29: 22-25)

But if these eruptions were intended to unseat any deep-rooted convictions in the Jews, they have failed, for they exhibited no signs of apprehension over their future and their resolve to go it alone remains unchanged. And though their living conditions have been more than a little disrupted, their philosophy of life and more importantly their relationship with God remains as cold as ever. Though admittedly for some, the tragic circumstances have stirred a slight increase in synagogue attendance, though they simply attribute this sudden interest in religion to they're near destitute condition.

Then there is the possibility that the presence of God's witnesses, who have been showing up in various parts of the city, have had something to do with the heightened anxiety of the people. For wherever these witnesses appear, they're surrounded by a small crowd of listeners who hear the same warning message of God's anger and their own need for repentance, though sorrowfully for many it falls on deaf ears.

The months passed slowly by, and in the cities life was returning to at least a semblance of normality if not self-absorption in Israel. Nothing major had happened since the volcanic eruptions that even hinted of a punishment, and in the cities, at least, much of the debris from the eruptions had been cleared away. Aid was still coming in regularly from Europe and America and the peace agreement was still holding intact.

However in the scientific community there has been some new excitement revealed in the heavens. A meteorite of some considerable magnitude has apparently deviated from its usual orbit around the sun

154

and appears to be crossing over into the orbit of the earth. So far the news releases have indicated that even if it were on a collision course with earth it poses no threat. They remind us that the earth is being constantly bombarded by small meteorites and ice chunks that pass through our earth's orbit on their journey around the sun, and invariably, when one does enter our atmosphere, it is quickly disintegrated by the heat and friction of entry, with the residue falling harmlessly to the earth.

But frequently, they tell us, a sizeable piece will penetrate the atmosphere without disintegrating and strike the earth with a devastating impact, such as the time a large meteorite descended over the state of Texas on a bright October day in 1997. Thousands of people watched the cosmic fireworks display over the southwestern sky, but though few saw the flash on impact, the shock on the earth was felt over hundreds of square miles. In December of that same year a large meteorite was tracked to its landing in the snow and ice of Greenland.

And in this case, the meteorite that the scientists said wouldn't... did. It slammed into the mountains of northern Israel with the sound of a bomb, impacting at a point just north of where the Sea of Galilee used to be. The explosion on impact produced an immense mushroom cloud that spread out over a vast area. The shock sent all of the recorders in the Middle East off their scale readings, but more importantly, it sent shock waves of fear throughout a region that was already earthquake prone.

Tremendous damage was done to commercial buildings and homes throughout the immediate area, and Israel's main life-sustaining source of water was immediately destroyed, along with the viaduct that brought the precious water to the south. And what water storage facilities that hasn't disappeared in the blast, were too polluted for use.

Surprisingly, there were relatively few casualties, because the valley area was so sparsely populated and the high mountains directed the blast skyward. But the area has lost a crucial water supply, and where water is a critical commodity in this desert region, every source that is taken away becomes life threatening. Now the demand will be on those few remaining springs to try and fill the gap.

This third Trumpet judgment on Israel has developed into a major problem, as well as another source of trouble from the Arab communities that use the same water sources. This is the third time they have been made to suffer for Israel's rebellion.

The fiery meteorite that John describes, with its long white glowing extension of burning debris, is strikingly similar to the familiar satellite wreckage that we often see streaking across the sky and trailing flames behind as it burns up in the atmosphere. He pictured the meteorite as 'a star burning like a lamp' when it crashed onto the earth. And how aptly he named this 'flaming star' 'Wormwood,' a name that defined the purpose for its coming to earth right over the nation's water supply. For 'Wormwood' was a deadly chemical product that was used profusely throughout the Middle East as an ingredient in the making of intoxicating beverages, and now it connotes the poisoning of the waters.

It may be just coincidental, but sometime in the past, the Lord threatened the Jewish people, saying that He would feed them 'wormwood' and give them water of gall to drink, but whether He intended that to be a prophetic statement of this specific event is hard to say, but when that meteorite disintegrated in a fiery explosion, it produced a deadly ash and residue that poisoned all of the water in the vicinity. (Jer.9: 15)

This is the way John described the meteorite judgment on Israel;

"And the third angel sounded, and there fell a great star from heaven, burning as it were a lamp, and it fell upon the third part of the rivers, and upon the fountains of waters; (11) and the name of the star is called Wormwood: and the third part of the waters became wormwood; and many men died of the waters, because they were made bitter." (Rev. 8:10,11)

Even though the punishments so far have been directed at Israel, the Arabs are becoming increasingly incensed over the many casualties and considerable damage that they have sustained from these three happenings in Israel. And while they have surmised that these so-called 'natural catastrophes,' are judgments of God, they are also prone to voice dire threats against Israel over their losses, particularly over the disastrous water shortage.

One of the 'after shocks' arising from these 'natural calamities,' so to speak, has been the influx of immigrant Jews returning to their homeland. It's been estimated that close to a half a million Jews from all parts of the world have already immigrated to Israel since the tragedies began, which is putting a severe strain on the already depleted housing facilities and resources. These have always been acute, so those with any construction background are welcomed in the re-construction program that has been going on. None the less, it shouldn't be dismissed that the promotion of this exodus may lie at the doorstep of the Lord, who foreordained that the Jews in foreign lands must return to Israel for their time of punishment, and what may appear on the surface as a volunteer re-location, may very well have been a command to come home. (Jer.16: 15)

"Behold, I will take the children of Israel from among the heathen, whither they be gone, and will gather them on every side, and bring them into their own land;" (Ezek. 37:21)

But regardless of whether they felt spurred to return or did so voluntarily, the movement back to Israel came at the right time, for in the next few months a great earthquake, stemming from the fourth judgment paralyzes the nations of the world and cuts off all international travel.

While Israel has been suffering under these past three catastrophes, the rest of the world has been having its own tumultuous problems. Of note is a spirit of anarchy and rebellion that is sweeping over the nations. This may have fueled much of the latest outbursts of anti-Semitism around the globe, which helped foster the emigration, but its actions go well beyond that.

Man's penchant for evil has always been held in check by the Spirit of God, but during these troublous times those restraints have been removed and the soul of man is free to be drawn to lawlessness by the spirit of Satan. (II Thess. 2:9-11) Add to that, the worsening economies and the growing problems over national trade agreements, and it's easy to see why the Near-East problems are put on a back burner. But through it all, the west continues to send aid into Israel.

THE FOURTH TRUMPET JUDGMENT

Nearly a year had passed from the time of the meteorite episode, when the fourth Trumpet judgment made itself known. In the beginning, the movement in the earth was barely noticeable, and lasted for only a few seconds. Then it started moving in slow, almost rhythmic pulsations, with an occasional violent heaving motion that must have come from the sliding and collapsing of sub-surface faults. But unlike localized earthquakes, which develops quickly over a singular fault line then settle down, this earthshaking is being evidenced over virtually every fault line around the globe.

Few areas of the earth are unaffected by the movement, although some regions experience more catastrophic damage than others do. Typically the great mountain ranges loosed myriads of snow pack or rock avalanches which stripped the vegetation from the slopes and inundated any settlements at their base.

Untold millions of structures of all kinds were demolished, including several large flood control dams that buckled from collapsing foundations, which in turn loosed their latent deluge on everything below. Everywhere electrical transmission towers were toppled dragging the power lines with them. Endless numbers of highways buckled and railway tracks became serpentine.

And on the heels of the earth movement came great hailstorms, so fierce that it seemed as though the heavens were collapsing in on the earth. Hurricanes and tornadoes added their deadly fallout to the mixture of destruction, not to mention the many volcanic eruptions. In the oceans, great wave formations made their race across the seas, engulfing islands in their relentless journey to the continental shores. Rolling incessantly as they did, with no let up in size or ferocity, the great waves hammered the shores mercilessly and swept the residue back into the deep. Even the polar caps succumbed to the fury of the waves and displayed their hurt by shedding great islands of ice that drifted majestically out to sea.

But then the convulsions of the earth subsided and a frightening calm settled over the earth. The winds quieted, the waves abated, and in the heavens the dark clouds softened, turned white and then dissipated altogether, to reveal a beautiful azure sky with a sun that hastened from horizon to horizon with dizzying speed.

All of this happened because the Lord had made a promise to mankind, to shorten their time of punishment during the tribulation. To do that, He made the earth spin faster on its axis, which in turn caused the days and nights to hasten also. But this speed-up created an inertial shock to the planet that could only be dissipated through the upheavals and shifting of the outer layers of the planet, which ultimately was displayed in the earthquakes, the volcanoes, the collapsing of some high mountains and the massive ocean movements. This in turn brought on the cyclonic winds and violent storms. With the inevitable results from all of this being the excessive destruction of man's habitations and the death of millions of people.

To cap it off, the topography of the earth will be forever altered. Former low-lying islands will either have disappeared altogether or have been swept clean of all life and vegetation. There will be new lakes that will appear on the horizon while others will simply vanish. The courses of numerous great rivers will be dramatically altered and continental shorelines irrevocably changed, but in the aftermath, the days will be shorter and life will continue on.

Israel has taken its share of damage from the earthshaking along with the rest of the world, and its plight has been worsened because of it, but more terrible times are ahead for the Jews with the next punishment phase about to begin. And even though we might have difficulty in making this discernment, the past four Trumpet judgments have been directed toward punishing the land, whereas the next three judgments will be directed against the people in Israel, to punish them for their rebellion, and on the top of the list is the dreaded demonic plague.

CHAPTER 12

The Plague of Demons

"And the word of the LORD came unto me, saying, Son of man, set thy face toward the mountains of Israel, and prophesy against them, and say, Ye mountains of Israel, hear the word of the Lord GOD; Thus saith the Lord GOD to the mountains, and to the hills, to the rivers, and to the valleys; Behold, I, even I, will bring a sword upon you, and I will destroy your high places. In all your dwelling places the cities shall be laid waste, and the high places shall be desolate;... and your works may be abolished. (Ezek. 6:1-6)

In the previous chapter we witnessed the wielding of His sword of punishment over the land of Israel, just as the scriptures above describe. Vast portions of the nation have been twice destroyed with volcanic eruptions that buried the vegetation on the mountains and valleys alike under a deadly mantle of sulfurous ash. Then, using a wayward meteor He drove the sword of poisoning deep into the life sustaining waters of the region. And in a final stroke of retaliation, He brandished the sword of judgment again, only this time it was in the form of an earthquake that swept over the high places of Israel and made them clean, that the land, which had succored His rebellious people, might perish.

In the above scripture, the phrases *'I will destroy your high places'* and *'the high places shall be laid waste'* was not just an expression of denouement of the vegetation on the hills in Israel, but forecast the removal of all of the heathen idols and worship places that in ancient times were found in groves on the higher places throughout the land. These idol worshipping places had become very profuse under certain rebel kings such as Ahab and Ahaziah, the son of Jehoram, and even today there lingers such edifices as the Muslim Mosque which honors not Jehovah and which assuredly will be destroyed in the great earthquake.

However, now that His punishments against the land are over, the sword of vengeance will be turned against His people. But the remaining judgments will be vastly different from the former mild pattern of punishments against the land. In order to achieve His just retaliation for the disobedience of His people, the Lord will follow a rigid pattern of punishments which consists of pestilence, famine, war, and lastly, total banishment of the Jews from their homeland.

This sequence of punishments had proven successful for the Lord in the past when He was simply trying to punish the people for disobedience, but never before has He dispersed them upon any nation with the sole purpose of reducing their population until only a remnant remained. But during the tribulation things are going to be different. The following prophetic scriptures point out the terrible destruction of His people that this pattern of punishments will bring:

" Behold I am against thee, and I will execute judgments in the midst of thee in the sight of the nations. And I will do in thee that which I have not done, and whereunto I will not do any more the like, because of thine abominations." .... (1)"A third part of thee shall die with pestilence, and with famine shall they be consumed in the midst of thee: and (2) a third part shall fall by the sword round about thee: and (3) I will scatter into all the winds, and I will draw out a sword after them. Thus shall my anger be accomplished, and I will cause my fury to rest upon them... (Ezek. 5: 8,9,12,13)

As you can see, the Lord is going to do something that He has never done before and will never do again. It's no wonder that He wouldn't tell Daniel the full story about the annihilation of his people, but only reiterated the final dispersion, or, 'scattering to the winds,' as He puts it here.

In our finite minds, the concept of anyone arbitrary seeking the destruction of two-thirds of a nations' population in a seemingly vendetta of retaliation seems totally abhorrent, and in this instance there is a tendency to obliterate the numbers by spiritualizing the scriptures, or making them merely illustrative of the 'very severe anger' of God. In this way, the tragic circumstances of the judgments can be buried under euphemisms to make them more tolerable, which unfortunately, is the way much of the information on these terror filled days is transmitted to us in modern writings.

Generally in these same writings, such a colossal destruction of mankind is erroneously applied to the whole unregenerate world. But if the significance of the past four judgments has not been recognized by the reader for exactly what they are, that they are literal punishments from God and not some spiritual transformation that takes place in the Church, then it's unlikely that the reality of the next three terrible judgments against the Jewish people will be comprehended either, for sadly enough, it is in these three that the greater proportion of the population of Israel will be destroyed.

That being said, the first of these 'Woes,' or the fifth Trumpet judgment, sneaks unceremoniously on the scene with no sign-bearing marchers in the street or spot commercials on television decrying the tragic circumstances that will befall. It will come upon the Jewish people just as surreptitiously as a thief in the night, take its terrible toll on the unsuspecting people, and leave five months later in the same way.

Moreover, the catastrophic results from the plague will only arouse mild consternation in the outside world, where it's presence will undoubtedly be recognized but they will be so engrossed in their own tragic circumstances and the loss of millions of lives from the recent worldwide earthquakes, that it's highly unlikely that the circumstances behind the Jewish tragedy will ever be understood.

As overwhelmed as the nations are by the tremendous problems of re-construction that are draining every nations' finances as well as their materials and labor resources, many large and small countries alike are forced to recognize the need of a global effort to ameliorate the problems. And while this world unification movement is capturing most of the media's attention, the little nation of Israel, with it's interface effectively sealed from inquiring minds and certainly cut-off from all outside interference, suddenly becomes submerged in a cataclysm all of its own with no hope of escape.

The only witness to what really happens in Israel at that time is locked in the Biblical records of John, which even he has been somewhat reticent to reveal.

It's awesome to consider that the first inkling of these last three punishments come by way of an angelic messenger who circles the nation overhead and startles the population with this astounding announcement:

"Three 'Woes' are about to come upon the inhabitants of the earth, from the voices of the three Trumpets yet to sound."
(Rev.8: 13)

Again and again, the message came down as the Angel repeated it in every corner of the Holy Land, so that no one could miss the warning. Just hearing the voice of an Angel speaking from heaven would probably be as frightening an experience for the people as listening to the message that he brought. But this will be the only time that the people will get such an unusual warning about an entirely unsuspecting experience in which demon spirits will be administering the punishment.

This prior warning should have been a wake-up call for those in Israel who were at least partially familiar with the writings of the Prophets, because the message of the Angel mirrored the words of their favorite prophet Ezekiel, who, in relaying the words of the Lord, issued a stern prophetic warning to Israel, that in the last days there would come three judgments upon the people because of their abominations against His sanctuary and their continued rebellion against Him. (Ezek. 5:11,12)

However the message of the Angel was not intended to divulge the nature of the punishments, but only to make the people aware of what was coming upon them next. In this respect, the Angel's depiction of the judgments as "Woes" should have signaled the awfulness of the judgments in comparison to what they had already experienced. There again, it was not just a coincidence that these last three Trumpet judgments were referred to as 'Woes,' because they would come in the identical pattern and sequence as the punishments previously recorded by Ezekiel when he said:

"And I will do in thee that which I have not done, and whereunto I will not do any more the like, because of all thine abominations. (speaking of His unique use of demon spirits in the fifth judgment) **(12)** [First woe] <u>**A third part of thee shall die with the pestilence, and with famine shall they be consumed in the midst of thee:**</u> [Second woe] a <u>**third part shall fall by the sword round about thee;**</u> [Third woe] <u>**I will scatter a third part into all the winds, and I will draw out a sword after them.**</u> (Ezek. 5: 9,12)

These scriptures outline the sequence and procedure of the three judgments that God will follow in the last three 'woes,' as the Angel refers to them, or the fifth, sixth, and seventh Trumpet judgments, and unless the people repent and turn to Him for forgiveness, the course of the plagues will continue as planned.

In the past the Lord had invariably sought His vengeance through these same punishment tactics of famine, pestilence, and on occasion, war or hostilities with other nations. And in isolated cases, and as a last resort, He would go one step farther and cause the desolation of His people from their land, such as the situation in which the Prophets Daniel and Ezekiel found themselves in. A complete desolation of Israel will occur in the seventh judgment.

Needless to say, these forms of punishment, with slight variations, have been used consistently by the Lord throughout the ages, though sometimes He varies His methods a little to achieve a particular goal, which is exactly what happens in this case, with the use of demons.

The Bible lists many examples of these forms of punishment being used, sometimes singularly, but more often than not, using all three, depending upon the circumstances.

For instance, there are several incidences recorded in the Bible where the disastrous effects of famine followed in the wake of a long siege or war. One such incidence occurred in the eighth century BC when the Assyrian King Hoshea besieged the Jewish country of Samaria for three years before capturing it. During that time there was a terrible famine that destroyed thousands of Jews, and those who did manage to survive the famine were taken into captivity in Assyria.

One hundred and twenty five years later the Babylonian King Nebuchadnezzar besieged Jerusalem for several months, causing wide spread famine before the Jews finally surrendered. Following that engagement, over forty-two thousand refugees, including the Prophet Daniel and his friends, were sent as captives to Babylon.

Still later in 70 AD, another such example of this trio of punishments occurred. This time the Jews had rebelled against their Roman oppressors, and the Romans retaliated by surrounding the city of Jerusalem and besieging it for over a year. There again, this action brought on such terrible starvation among those under siege that acts of cannibalism were commonplace.

The last great siege of Jerusalem by the Romans occurred in 135 AD. And again, by the time the Jews capitulated to the Roman forces, almost one third of their population had perished by starvation. The rest were either taken into slavery or banished from the city altogether. That was the second Diaspora of the Jews, and a situation which they have vowed never to let happen again.

But in this fifth Trumpet judgment we have a totally different set of circumstances. There are no oppressive legions that can be called upon to bring a prolonged siege upon Israel with the consummate purpose of bringing the nation to its knees through starvation, and certainly there are no neighboring nations that would be willing to take in the hordes of refugees that would come after a battle.

So the Lord has chosen an alternate method, which incidentally, He has promised never to do again, and that is to use the existing legions of demon spirits that are presently languishing in a subterranean vault. He will bring them to the surface to use as His instruments of punishment, so that they in essence, will become His invading army, and the Jews will be their captors. However, instead of destroying their enemy, the demon spirits will be used to aggravate the necessary famine process.

Whether the spirits could be considered as 'pestilence' in this case, or whether they will simply induce various forms of pestilence, such as that which comes with starvation, the combined effect of the plagues will cause the decimation of one third of the population of Israel, just as the prophecy demands.

Waiting for the judgment to show itself became the most agonizing part. Days passed with no sign of it, and the people began to let down their guard waiting for something to happen. To them, the fear of going to bed at night and the worry of starting a new day, with every expectation of that day being the one, slowly ebbs. And when nothing happened for several weeks everyone had let down their guard, surmising that somehow God had relented. So when the dreaded morning came without the normal sounds of nature, and the rising sun suddenly became darkened, the fears rushed back. City streets that were normally bustling with pedestrian traffic at that hour became chaotic as hordes of frightened people rushed to seek shelter from whatever it was that the Lord was sending down, never suspecting for a moment that the peril they searched for in the sky was coming up from beneath.

In like manner as the angel of death which swept over the land of Egypt in the days before the Exodus, the demon spirits from below now sweep across the land, unseen, unheard and unhampered, purposefully engulfing everyone in their path like a morning mist coming in from the sea.

Legions of them, now freed from their confinement in the pit, swarmed over their unsuspecting victims looking for receptive lodgings in the hearts of all those who lacked God's protective seal in their hearts and foreheads.

In moments the indwelling was over. The marauding spirits had taken over the lives of their victims and normalcy gave way to utter confusion. Like tortured pacing beasts that suddenly find the doors of their cages open, millions of hapless individuals in the land flee aimlessly trying to escape into solitude.

John was there when the whole thing started. He saw the angel with the key rush to earth, and he watched in awe as the angel touched the ground in front of him. He stared in unbelief as a hole suddenly opened before him and loosed a great column of smoke into the sky. So black was the mushrooming cloud that for a brief period the morning sky was darkened like the night. Then suddenly the cloud dissipated and became a swarm of ugly creatures that quickly descended and spread out over the land. Even while this was going on, John heard a loud voice from heaven issuing a stern warning to the creatures to spare the green grass and trees and plants.

John was startled by the admonition given to the creatures. It aroused his suspicions, causing him to take a closer look at the creatures to see if indeed they were locusts as he had first imagined. He was familiar with the locust as being a type of grasshopper that had often swarmed over the country devouring every leafy plant in their path, but these creatures were something entirely different. They were individually a hideous manifestation that was too impossible to imagine let alone try to describe, yet he managed to put down the best imaginative description of the creatures that he could, but what is described for us is totally unidentifiable with any living creature or inanimate thing, and could only portray an otherwise invisible demon spirit, the manifestation of which was the abject realism of the fifth plague.

As a reminder, these are not the spirits of recently demised unbelievers who have their abode in hell until the day of the great White Throne Judgment. (Rev. 20: 11) These are the relics of a human race that once inhabited our earth in the pre-flood era, whose physical bodies were buried forever under the waters while their souls were confined in the bowels of the earth.

They had characteristically human attributes which were viewed and described by John, such as their human capability of understanding verbal orders about the restrictions that were put upon them. Like humans, they also had a king over them, whose name was 'Destroyer,' which, of course, is a pseudonym for Satan.

These spirits are further identifiable with the ones that Jesus encountered in His ministry on earth. In that particular instance, a legion of them had somehow been able to escape their imprisonment in the 'pit' below, and made their way to the surface of the earth where they sought 'new humans' in which to dwell.

To witness the confrontation between the Lord Jesus and these demons from the pit, we only need to turn to the Gospel of Luke where we find the story of a certain demon-enslaved man whose demeanor and terrible living conditions in hillside-caves will closely approximate the living conditions in Israel during this plague.

Here again is the account of Jesus' meeting with the depraved man and the spirits that dwelled within him. I have included the whole episode of the meeting here, because there are so many features written about the demons in the man that will typify the actions of the demons that sweep over Israel.

Jesus had arrived by boat in the country of the Gadarenes, which is over against Galilee. *(27) And when he went forth to land, there met him out of the city a certain man, which had devils a long time, and wore no clothes, neither abode in any house, but in the tombs.* (caves in the side of the hill) *(28) When he saw Jesus, he cried out, and fell down before him, and with a loud voice said,*

167

What have I to do with thee, Jesus, thou Son of God most high? I
beseech thee, torment me not. (29) (For He had commanded the
unclean spirit to come out of the man. For oftentimes it had caught
him: and he was kept bound with chains and in fetters; and he
brakes the bands, and was driven of the devils into the wilderness.)
(30) And Jesus asked him, saying, What is thy name? And he said
Legion: because many devils were entered into him. (31) And they
besought him that he would not command them to go out into the
deep. (the pit) *(32) And there was there a herd of many swine*
feeding on the mountain; and they besought him that he would
allow them to enter into them. And he allowed them." (33) Then
went the devils out of the man, and entered into the swine: and the
herd ran violently down a steep place into the lake, and was
choked." (Luke 8:26-33)

The legion of demon spirits within the victim recognized Jesus
for who He was, calling Him 'The Son of God most High,' and
caused the beleaguered man to fall down before the Lord, while at the
same time asking for the reason of His coming. These utterances and
actions of the man illustrate the presence of a rational mind that
surfaces when the demons within shrink back in fear at the presence
of the Lord, but when Jesus spoke directly to the spirit within,
inquiring of his name, the answer came back "Legion," that is
"many."

Upon realizing that they had been exposed, and fearing that
they were about to be cast out of the man, the demons pleaded with
Jesus to send them into a herd of nearby swine, rather than sending
them back to the pit where they belonged.

This 'decision making of the spirits' shows some sort of
intelligence and resourcefulness in the demons, however, they
seemed to be either unaware of the Divine restrictions against the
cohabitation of beasts and humans, or they were totally unfamiliar
with the beast. If they were aware of those restrictions and yet chose
to enter into the beasts, they exhibited stupidity in choosing that over
going back to the pit, which is what ultimately happened to them, for
after that unnatural union had been made the maddened animals
sacrificed themselves over a cliff. (Mark 5:13)

168

There are other similarities between the demonic invasion of that lone man in Gadarenes and the present plague of spirits that are deposed in the Jews, which may have been the reason for this earlier confrontation being introduced into the scriptures. At least it gives us a preview of what is going to happen in Israel, beginning with the differences in living conditions between that of the man in the first century and that of the Jews in present day Israel.

It is apparent that the demons within the man had little concern for the three basic necessities of life, food, clothing and shelter, whereas modern man takes these things more or less for granted, even to much higher standards than existed in the first century. But the demons disregarded those physical needs when they prevailed upon the man to go about naked, seek shelter only in a cave, and who knows what he ate. He had obviously been in the wild for many days, evidencing that in some way he did obtain sufficient food and water to sustain life. Beyond that, however, the exhibition of his squalid living conditions, his negligent eating habits and his total depravity illustrates the intrinsic primitive nature of the peoples from which these spirits originally came.

But, then again, it's more than likely that these primal living habits and instincts were exactly what the Lord had in mind when He foisted them into the present victims. With the goal of forcing starvation upon a great number of people in a limited period of time, their imposition would over-ride the normal instincts and quality of life in their modern counterparts. Which in turn would destroy the victim's capability of either locating food or preparing what food they did find. And as a result, many of the victims would eventually succumb to starvation and death, even from such a simple thing as the inability to open a can of beans.

Bear in mind, that in Ezekiel's prophecy, the first punishment specified famine as the means by which a third of the present Jewish population in Israel would have to die, and there was no alternative. (Ezek. 5:12)

With regard to famine being used as a tool for the destruction of the people, it is totally commiserate with, and in many ways preferable to other methods of defeating an enemy. In battles between warring nations or tribes in the past, starvation was actually the preferred means of inducing the enemy to surrender. It wasn't unusual for thousands of people to starve to death during a siege by enemy troops surrounding their city or camp, because it was the accepted strategy in winning a battle without losing your own men. However in today's culture it's the conscience of a modern society that usually prohibits this 'cruel and unusual' punishment to occur without intervention.

And though I wouldn't presume to equate the Lord's use of starvation with the typical 'mass starvation methods' used by the warlords in Somalia, Eritrea and Ethiopia in our last generation, the purpose of bringing the people into submission is the same in both cases. However, the difference is in the selective approach to the problem. The Lord chose to inhibit the individual's ability to obtain and prepare food amidst a plentiful supply, whereas man's approach is to simply remove the food supply. Thus in the present situation, with the obviously plentiful supply of food in the country there was no reason for outsiders to suspect that a famine was in progress, and evidently no need for world intervention. In any event, outside help had been conveniently forestalled by the Lord, by Israel's ostracism from its neighboring countries, because of their eternal hatred against them. As for the rest of the world interfering at this time, they have been just as effectively isolated from assistance by their own tremendous needs after the earth shaking.

As the Lord pointed out, the intrinsic feature of this plague will be the use of demon spirits over all other methods available to accomplish the work of starvation. And that decision stemmed from the unique situation that was before Him, such as the large number (around two million) of the Jews who will have to die, and the present moral and ethical climate in our society which would make such mass starvation efforts extremely difficult to achieve. There is also the relatively short period of five months which has been allotted to accomplish this mass destruction.

But there was another facet of this demise 'by famine and pestilence,' which insisted that the demon spirits could not cause the death of the victim nor could they allow the victim to encourage his or her own death through means other than that of starvation and pestilence, even though the victims themselves might desperately seek it. (Rev.9: 5,6,10)

There was one other command put to the demons that was very unusual. It designated that only those people who did not have the seal of the Lord could be invaded. One of the reasons the Lord selected the use of demons for this undertaking was because He could determine which peoples would be 'off-limits' to the indwelling. They would be the ones who had previously received a 'protective seal' from the Lord, which would allow at least some continuance of normality in the country's governing and administration by sane responsible people. Keep in mind, that except for the selected few, all of the populace will be susceptible to the demons' indwelling, however, only a third of those affected will succumb to death.

Another facet of this demonic plague, which many are not aware of, is its potential for striking a fatal blow to the pride and arrogance of the Jews. The Lord has said of this pride,

"I will destroy it, and you will become disgraced among the nations that are round about you and all that meet you, let what I have done to you be a lesson as to what can happen to you in the execution of my anger and fury. (Ezek. 5:14,15)

We can spiritualize this demon situation all we want to, and the tragedy of it as well as the numbers will still come up the same. The Lord has evidently considered the Jews' obdurate course of rebellion as hopeless, and He has chosen this way to disgrace them before their neighboring nations while diminishing their numbers to a remnant of their present status.

Whatever the extent of the victim's induced torment, whether it's by the sheer number of the demons or through their own inherent wickedness, the spirits' possession of the victim's mind and soul will bring about a wide variation of character changes in the victims, from mild irrationality to ludicrous behavior, and some to extreme lunacy, but whatever the result, the nation became a vast rabble of apathetic people with varying degrees of sensibilities.

Which is exactly the situation that God has intended it to be, because it strikes at the core of a nation that is too proud and self-reliant to repent of their ways and seek the Lord. The only aspect of their circumstances that might be considered fortunate is that the

Lord has kept them as isolated as He has from further indignities, humiliation and scorn.

From the beginning, the mental faculties of the people have become so disrupted that the accomplishment of any work or business ethic is impossible, and even the concept of education in the schools is ludicrous. The essential community services such as policing and fire extinguishing are virtually non-existent and trash and garbage disposal has stopped.

However, their abandonment of industry fails to haunt the victims who are now disposed to aimless wanderings in loneliness. Shunning others in the same circumstances, they converse only with themselves. Seemingly content to let the days slip by in their idle meandering, or prowling as the case may be, when in a desperate search for food. With lips half open and eyes gleaming, and somehow lured by a deceptive instinct to where the food should be, the gnawing of their stomachs becomes more acute and their salvation more assiduous.

The children are as lost in delirium as their parents and spend endless days in hiding, finding solace in a remote corner of the house or under a bed, bewildered and alone, whimpering their presence until that too weakens into silence and death. Here it becomes a struggle to survive, and it is without respite, because everyone is so desperately and ferociously alone, and should there be a helping hand it will be knocked aside in fear. The ultimate result of this pitiless process of disease and starvation is the plummeting of life into its final submission of death amid the squalor and the corpses.

All avenues of escape from the torment of the demons have been blocked, except for the open gates of starvation and pestilence. Though many try to destroy themselves in desperation, as did the afflicted man who also tried to end his life by dashing himself against the stones, the comfort of death will be withheld even as it was then. And though in his case, the demon spirits could give him the strength to break his physical chains, and even the power to shred the ropes that bound him, he was unable to break the bond between his body and the soul. So will it be in the final plague of the demon spirits.

As prophesied, the fifth plague abruptly ends and the spirits depart just as suddenly as they had entered five months earlier. Like a gentle wind that sweeps away the clouds and lets the warm rays of the sun bathe the earth, the sensibilities and reasoning of the victims emerges from their clouded minds and they were again made whole. The torture is ended and the morbidity is replaced with smiles and wonderment. Life becomes precious again, and as each person regains his awareness there is aroused in him an overwhelming joy in the freedom from the torments.

CHAPTER 13

Falling by the Sword

There is no way of dismissing the deaths from the terrible plague of the demons. A third of the population had died and there was a deep mourning among the survivors, whose grief was only worsened by the ignominy of having to bury their dead in a common grave. But there was no other way. The great toll necessitated the expedient disposal of the decaying corpses. The terrible tragedy in Israel has finally been felt in other countries and they have responded benevolently in sending in relief aid as well as heavy machinery to help in the burial and clean-up process.

Meanwhile the quiescent alliance that has existed between Israel and her neighbors has become increasing precarious in the aftermath of the last plague. Some of it has to do with the returning tide of Arab resentment against the Jews because of the 'spilling over' effect of the plague among the Arab and Palestinian residents in Israel. The peace between the Arabs and the Jews had been tenuous at best and these latest developments simply renewed their old commitment against the Jews. And with that purpose in mind, the Arabs began mobilizing troops in the deserts of Iraq.

These military exercises, as they call them, have mushroomed in several locations despite the frantic efforts of the U.N. officials to diffuse the situation. But what the world fails to realize, is that this build-up of the Arab armies has been cultivated by the Lord to bring a war against Israel, a war in which they will serve as His instruments of justice in the coming second round of punishments that had been prophesied by Ezekiel, when he said that:

"a third part shall fall by the sword round about thee."(Ezek. 5:12)

We are reminded that this inexplicable 'bone of contention' or innate hatred that the present day Arabs have for the Jews is not something that has developed since Israel moved into the area and established itself as a nation, or from the 1967 war which followed,

174

wherein the Arab forces were so badly defeated. It had its beginning thousands of years ago in the camp of their common father Abraham, and has only mushroomed to world recognizance in the past century. If we may, let us slip back in time to when this hatred all began.

The Biblical record shows that Abraham had two sons whom he loved with equal fervor, but which love also brought about an innocent sibling rivalry for his attention. As the children grew into their teens their rivalry deepened and created a severe strain within the family. Ishmael was the elder of the two sons and would likely have received the blessing of his father, but at the insistence of his wife Sarah, Abraham had Ishmael and his Egyptian mother Hager sent out of the camp and into virtual exile

God had promised Abraham that he would take care of the lad and that in time he would become a great nation of peoples. The boy grew into manhood in a land that was called the Wilderness of Paran, which was an area that ranged from just below the Dead Sea south to the Gulf of Arabia (Gen.21:20)

In his manhood, Ishmael had eleven sons, who became tribal rulers of their several camps and settlements which were located in the same general area, but beyond this reference, the scriptures speak only of Ishmael's descendents living in hostility toward all of their brothers. These descendents would ultimately become the ancestors of the present Arab nations. (Gen. 25:18)

Meanwhile, Ishmael's younger brother Isaac had two sons, whom he named Esau and Jacob. Esau was the elder of the two and should have received the traditional blessing and birthright of their father, but Jacob maliciously usurped these prized possessions by deceiving his blind father into believing that he was Esau.

Esau naturally became bitter over the incident and would have slain his brother had he been able, but their mother spirited Jacob away to safety to a community in Syria called PaddanAram, where he stayed for many years.

The schism between the two never healed. Meanwhile, Esau had taken wives from among the women of Canaan and had many offspring by them. All of whom later left the land of Canaan and moved south to settle in the land of Seir, which lies immediately south of the Dead Sea. This territory was later called the land of

Edom and is now part of the nation of Jordan.

Living in that same general area were some of the descendents of Ishmael who by then were called Amorites. And through intermarriage between the descendents of both Esau and Ishmael, virtually all tribal lines were erased, but throughout their succeeding generations what continued to rise to the surface was their rebellion against God and their hatred for His Chosen people, the Jews.

In a further determined effort to distance themselves from the Lord and His Chosen people, the unified tribes of Ishmael and Esau gathered in the shadow of Mt Seir, their holy mountain in Edom, and there confirmed their rebellious attitude against 'the God of the Jews' and His Chosen people. And in their rebellion they created their own gods to worship.

Today, the descendents of those generations of people have been bundled into one package and referred to as 'Arabs,' whose ancient kinship with the Jews has all but disappeared, but their rebellion against Jehovah continues through their worship of the man Allah, in place of God's Son, Jesus Christ. This observance of Islam, or the worship of Allah, only serves to further alienate them from the Father's affection.

This then, is the pre-conditioning that exists among the Arab peoples today, and it is something that cannot be smothered by a peace treaty. It will explode to the surface in the coming sixth judgment.

Whether or not this animosity was shared by the Jews is not defined in the scriptures, moreover, in the following verses we find the Lord only stressing the enmity of the Arab peoples against the Jews as it must have existed in the days of Ezekiel and Daniel when the scriptures were written It is readily apparent that Our Lord predicated that this same enmity would continue into modern times and become the basis on which the end-time war is fought.

But it predicts an even greater tragedy will occur among the Arab nation at that time for what the Lord terms "their perpetual hatred of the Jews." He said of this:

"Because you have this perpetual hatred, <u>and have shed the blood of the children of Israel by the force of the sword in the time of their calamity, in the time that their iniquity had an end:</u>

176

(6) **as I live, saith the Lord GOD, I will** <u>prepare thee unto blood,</u> **and blood shall pursue thee: since thou hast not hated blood, even blood shall pursue thee.** (7) **Thus will I make mount Seir most desolate, and cut off from it him that passes out and him that returns.** (8) **And I will fill his mountains with his slain men: in thy hills, and in thy valleys, and in all thy rivers, shall they fall that are slain with the sword.** (Ezek. 35:5-8)

Here we are told that the war will specifically come *'in the end time of their iniquity,'* which refers to the closing period of the Jew's judgment period. *"And because your hatred is so strong that you wish to destroy them so completely,'* promises the Lord, *"I will in turn destroy you in the same manner."*

Unfortunately for the Arabs, this retribution is exactly what will happen in the war of the sixth Trumpet judgment.

To meet the timing requirements of this war, the Lord will have the Arab legions begin their preparations even before the ink is dry on the peace treaty. But at least the covenant will serve to maintain a "status quo" situation between the combatants through the traumatic demonic period. If the Arabs were to make their move during that five-month period when the demonic plague was in process there is no question that the Jews would be completely exterminated.

Being the instigator of this war by His own admission, the Lord would naturally be the one to *"prepare them unto blood,"* as the scripture states. And part of those preparations will be the sending of four angels well ahead of time to ready the Arab forces for what will become the second phase of the prophecy in Ezekiel. The activities of the angels will not be witnessed but the build-up of Arab troops will, and will cause quite a stir in the United Nations.

However the Arabs must also be made aware of the blood bath they will be running into, for the Lord has promised them that, 'because you pursue the blood of war, the blood from war shall pursue you.'

Even so, when the appointed time comes for the judgment to begin, the following command will go forth from the Throne:

"Loose the four angels that are bound in the river Euphrates."

177

Immediately upon that command, the angel with the sixth Trumpet will sound in heaven, which in turn signals the four angels, who will have been holding back any overt action against Israel by the four-nation alliance of Arab forces. Once those restraints have been removed the great armies of the Arab coalition will move forward in their assault. The suddenness of the attack on Israel takes the whole world by surprise, and nothing will be done to stop it.

Might I add, that in this instance, the Arab coalition will be duplicating the invasion tactics that had already been predicated from wars that had been fought between the Syrian and the Egyptian armies over two thousand years ago. In those instances, as we saw in the eleventh chapter of Daniel, the use of overwhelming numbers was preferable to any other strategy in trying to overcome the enemy. And so it will be in this coming war. As long as their numbers continue to outnumber their enemy, the progress of the war goes in the Arabs' favor, but over time the inexorable casualties among their troops mounts so excessively that their advancement becomes mired.

Beyond this initial command to loose the restraints of the angels however, John gives no coverage of the battle. This was not an oversight on his part because the Lord seldom defines battle strategies. We found the same lack of battle details in Daniel's book, except for the last forty days when the Union troops embarked on Israeli soil.

However, John's excuse (if he needed one) for not including such details was the choice he made to amplify on another element of the battle, which was the type of weaponry being used by both sides. This side issue follows a similar pattern of John's, where in the past judgment he left out the effects of the demonic plague on the people, preferring instead to describe the distinguishing characteristics of the demon spirits. His reasoning for going that route was to inform his readers of the Lord's alternative method of using demon spirits as His instruments of punishment, whereas now He is using the Arabs as His instruments.

In both instances, we find that even the basic elements of the punishments have not been touched, in fact, when you look back on the last plague, John's words dealt solely on a description of the spirits with nothing being said about their use in promoting the plague or of their infiltration of the people to bring about the demise of one third of the population. And similarly in this judgment, we are neither told that there was going to be a war or who the combatants would be, but he doesn't fail to point out that one-third of the people would again be expected to die.

Notwithstanding, in both instances it has been this lack of specific information on the make-up of the judgments that has fueled wild speculations about the real purpose and function of the judgments. For instance, some have suggested that the hideous creatures of the last plague depicted present day military 'gun-ship' helicopters, which, in a 'Third World War' scenario of the last days, would sweep their course by the hundreds of thousands over the whole world with the purpose of destroying a third of mankind. Of course this thinking falls right in line with the erred concept of a universal tribulation.

As for the Arab and Israeli war, there are some who still prefer an inoffensive interpretation of this battle. They define the elimination of a third of the population as only being a very stern and severe warning from God. While others, who might have no idea that this is a limited confrontation, see this battle as a depiction of the final stages of the battle of Armageddon, wherein two hundred million warriors from the east and west battle for supremacy in an all out Third World War.

But again, these and other interpretations may very well be the result of the Lord's sealing of the end-time prophecies and visions. In which case the prophetic messages have been left to man's ingenuity to either try and decipher them correctly, or find plausible answers to satisfy their probing minds, which unfortunately, leaves not only these plagues but all of the judgments in ill repute.

Nevertheless, it's interesting to know how the varying theosophical backgrounds of certain expositors brings out such surprisingly different interpretations, which, by the way, are generally derived from four basic schools of thought.

First, there is the *Spiritual Scheme of Interpretation,* whose adherents insist that the purpose of the book of Revelation is not to instruct the Church regarding the future, nor predict certain events, but simply to teach fundamental spiritual principles. This was an ancient concept but surprisingly enough it still finds adherents in some modern evangelical churches.

Then there is the *Preterist Scheme of Interpretation,* which insists that the author was describing only events that took place on earth during the era of the Roman Empire, focusing primarily on the latter years of the first century. This was basically an interpretational devise within the college of the Roman church, to establish a position of justification for pre-set dogmas of the Roman Catholic church, in reaction to vilification by the reformers, who equated chapters 17 and 18 with the Roman church. Mainstream Catholic doctrine continues to follow this line of interpretation.

The *Historical Scheme of Interpretation* is undoubtedly the most prominent of the interpretations. In this conception, the book of Revelation, particularly the prophecies of the seals, the trumpets and the vials, are deemed to set forth notable events that have taken place in the course of world history.

These events in turn are meant to correlate with the welfare and condition of the Church from its beginning until the present time. For instance, events in secular history, such as the invasions of the Goths, or by the Huns under Attila, and the Muslims in more recent times are herein depicted by the various trumpet and vial judgments. The whole scheme of this manner of interpretation is to connote a purification process through which the Church journeys, and how Christianity is strengthened as it passes these various tests down through the ages.

This scheme of interpretation is actually of later derivation than the others and strangely enough has more notable adherents than any one view, but this is chiefly because they haven't been able to establish the correct interpretation, so they settle for that which is least combative with any religious groups. In this way the mysticism of the book is retained but so also is the mystification

Then there is the *Futurist Scheme of Interpretation,* which insists that the visions in Revelation depict literal events and judgments that will take place in the future, and the purpose for the enactment of these judgments is to fulfill God's ancient prophecies about the end-times. The author of this book subscribes to this belief.

While I happen to believe that the demonic plague is an

actuality, another writer may put it in the realm of a "Spiritual scheme of things," in which case the plague would represent "A great outburst of spiritual evil that will aggravate the sorrows of the world and make it learn how bitter is the bondage of Satan." Which is supposed to teach us to feel that even in the midst of enjoyment, that it were better to die than to live in this present evil society.

And when it comes to this sixth judgment of war, the "Historical scheme of interpretation" would determine that "This conflict depicts the terrible destruction that will be brought about by myriads of horsemen in the fearful battle of Armageddon."

Moreover, John's graphic, albeit metaphoric description of the type of weaponry used by the armies has only created more of an enigma to the situation. Whereas in the former judgment we found out that the unique weapons of destruction were famine and pestilence, and the demon spirits were uniquely used to facilitate those weapons, in this judgment we find, much to our amazement, that what the Lord is dealing with are modern infantrymen using standard modern weaponry and vehicles.

As you remember, John first branded the demon spirits as 'locusts,' then he over-rode his own horrendous description by referring to the creatures as "them" and "they," which designated their defunct human materialism. And he further portrayed these creatures as being humans in their former state, and even subjects of a king whose name was Satan. Now we find that, just as he minutely detailed the demon spirits with a particular purpose in mind, he now minutely describes the weapons of war. And in both cases the purpose is for identification.

We must be mindful that the symbolism he uses in describing the weapons. is artfully predicated on his readers' ability to decipher the correlation between the description he gives and the actual weapons, or vehicles, as the case may be, which were being used in the war. In other words, John is singularly directing his message to that particular generation of readers which will come to recognize the type of weaponry being used by his description of them, and thereby recognize the era of the battle as being their own. Thus, when the weapons and war vehicles of a particular era match John's metaphoric description of "futuristic weaponry being used in a futuristic war," the time period becomes identified, and paradoxically, the people living in Israel at that time will be the ones involved in the conflict.

For instance, it was unlikely that John was any more familiar with the exploding magma emitted from a volcano than you or I, yet he selected this 'fire, smoke, and brimstone' emitted by a volcano to illustrate a peculiar missile of death that would be used in the coming war. This missile was obviously not a spear, nor a sword, nor an arrow, which were the common weapons of his day. Thus, before the advent of gunpowder and the musketry of the Middle Ages one could hardy attach the definition of 'fire and brimstone' to any weapon of death.

But it wasn't to be the musket, as might be assumed from a cursory description of the weapon, which spoke of power coming from the rear as well as the mouth or front of the weapon. The musket obviously couldn't fit this type of firearm, although a great deal of smoke does arise from the burning powder on the pan atop the barrel when it is fired. Nor would any of the evolving weaponry since that time fit the description, until the evolution of the common hand-held rocket launcher of our era, which upon firing, produces the snap of rearward flames 'like a striking serpent,' while the missile, or 'hurt' discharges from the front of the tube. (Rev. 9:18,19)

And certainly no less awesome for John to describe, or for readers of a few decades ago to understand, would be the modern field tanks and rocket launching vehicles that he saw rushing across the land like speeding horses and belching cannon fire as they traveled. Here again, this description hardly fits the slow unwieldy and cumbersome tanks of even fifty years ago.

So, it's quite apparent from John's predictive profile of modern weaponry, that his purpose for going that route was to pinpoint the time factor of the battle to the exclusion of any other feature of the war, which incidentally, fits in with God's purpose of locating the time frame of the judgment period, although it circumvents the Lord's sealing of the visions.

Come to think of it, the only feature of the battle that John did mention, was the fact that the war was being fought to kill a third of the population in Israel, and I would assume that at least as many casualties would be experienced by the Arab forces, but beyond that reference John provides no other specifics of the battle.

One bewildering facet of the invading army has been John's reference to its immense size. He mentioned it as being two hundred million men. However, in giving this figure his intention was not to mislead the reader with numbers, but simply to covey the overwhelming enormity of the enemy forces, as he had done earlier in his estimation of the number of demon spirits. There again, in his description of the spirits coming forth from the earth, he likens them to a cloud because of they're enormous numbers, which on his closer inspection was transformed into an 'innumerable horde' of what appeared to be locusts, for want of a better description.

For example, if one stands near the mouth of the Carlsbad Caverns in New Mexico when the bats exit *en masse* in a continuous stream, they appear as a black cloud that extends for miles across the sky, similarly, the awesome numbers of black birds that often sweep over the grain fields of the mid-west seem like dark clouds in the distance. In either case one could not fail to realize that the actual numbering of the individual creatures would seem ridiculous, though we might refer to them as being in the millions, just to emphasize the extent of numbers.

So it was with the legions of troops with their equipment spread over a vast area. John was so awestruck by the sphere of the whole operation of men and vehicles that he arbitrarily chose to define their 'infinity' by the 'finite,' something that he had never experienced before.

Though some might argue that because he wrote of 'hearing the number of them,' that this gives credulity to the count, but the connotation actually gives more credence to a rare phenomenon of the vision. Rather than hearing the sound of someone's voice telling him of the number, what he actually heard was the sound of the battle machines emanating from the vision

With his eyes still transfixed upon the vast array of mobile tanks and troop carriers, he may have been startled to hear the fearful roaring sound of the engines in the vehicles in contrast to the familiar sound of horses' hooves, and so he made note of it. It's also worth considering, that had he been told the actual number of the troops by someone near him, he would have mentioned hearing a voice, as he has done previously.

Again, with respect to the size of the army, the marginal notes in the Geneva Bible aptly terms it as, *"a number most copious, of which a certain number is named for an infinite number,"* in this case "two hundred million." (Rev. 9:16)   In any event, it is a large enough fully equipped army, with all of the latest weaponry and motorized equipment, which the Lord deemed necessary to diminish the Israeli populace.

It's also obvious that John's minute descriptions of the armies' equipment was intentionally done to pass on to the reader the time element of the battle, and if that was so, the key element in establishing the time period justifiably lies in the unfamiliar sound that he heard emanating from the strange vehicles. That noise, coupled with his description of the armored 'horses' that emitted the sound and the peculiar weapons being used, points to only one period in time, that of our own.

When you consider the make-up of the army, with troops that use such weapons as the familiar 'bazooka' anti-tank gun, the mortars, the mobile missile launchers, and the modern troop carriers with their missile firepower, all of which seems to exemplify what John is seeing in the vision. Their counterpart can only be found in contemporary battle firepower, not twenty years ago, and not likely twenty years hence. As a reference, battle weaponry used before the Gulf War in this past decade, would have had no resemblance whatsoever to the weapons John described.

It's also reasonable to assume that John knew that those who would be living in the era in which those particular weapons were used, would know better than he what destruction could come from them, and therefore, there was no need for him to describe the actual battle.

But there is one disturbing element in his journal. That while John was able to maintain the congruity of the judgment without deliberating on the battle itself, he did so at the expense of other germane events, such as the intervention of the European forces that brought an end to the war, and the events surrounding the European President's visit to Israel after the war was ended.

These events may have been omitted to prevent distraction

from the main focus of the judgment, which was to diminish the population of Israel, but when these events are inserted into the picture, the relevancy of the war to further the plans of God becomes quite apparent, such as the interjection of Satan in the next judgment.

Although I hadn't intended to turn this into a Bible study, there is one consideration of this judgment that still remains to be answered, and that has to do with God's allotment of time to accomplish its purpose. As in the plague of demons, for instance, which turned out to be a closely programmed event, watched over by God and pre-determined to end in five months. Though it was not uncommon for God to define the limits of certain events in terms of years, in this case He made that determination based on the required time for the starvation and pestilence to take its toll of a third of the population, which is a lot to accomplish in a hundred and fifty days, and it makes you wonder how it will be done, unless of course, the rapid debilitation of the population was due to use of demon sprits.

In this judgment however, there was no such expediency, yet the time is being closely monitored to *'an hour, and a day, and a month, and a year,* in which to slay the third part of men,'* (Rev. 9:15) which is a considerable portion of the three and one half years, and yet, it too seems such a relatively short time, even in a war, to have well over a million people killed without raising a hue and cry from the world community.

We can only surmise that in both judgments, either the actual numbers of casualties were inconsequential to the division of the population, that is, in 'thirds,' because of the time limitations, or that the numbers were more important than the time schedule, because the Lord knew there would be a vast increase in the population in modern times. Regardless, we can be assured that the 'one third' proportions still stand.

With respect to these specific time limitations, one being five months, and the other thirteen months, they would appear to replicate time periods used in another case. It so happened that there was a siege of Jerusalem by the Chaldeans in 588-586 BC. At the time, Ezekiel the prophet was an exile in Babylon, along with a large number of other captives who were taken in an earlier siege of

Jerusalem, in 597 BC, by King Nebuchadnezzar.

It was Ezekiel's task to record the prophecy of this later siege, when both the city of Jerusalem and its Temple would be destroyed.

In this instance though, the prophet was instructed to dramatize the event in order to emphasize its significance, which seems like an unusual request because this siege was apparently little different from the first, unless of course, we consider that it was meant to be identified with the present plagues against Israel.

The drama was intended to characterize the house of Israel being burdened down by sin and rebellion, and to enact this, Ezekiel was instructed to lay on his left side on the ground for three hundred and ninety days, (13 months) which the Lord said would represent the number of years of their iniquity. And when he had accomplished the three hundred and ninety days, he was told that he must then lie on his right side for another forty days, with each day representing a year, for the sins of the house of Judah. (Ezek.4: 4-6)

The first three hundred and ninety days of the prophecy evidently represented the three hundred and ninety years of idolatrous worship by the ten northern tribes of Israel after the division of the nation in 922 BC, and the extant forty days represented the forty idolatrous years of the tribe of Judah following the death of their great King Josiah.

While this dramatization of Ezekiel was meant to illustrate the length of time that Israel was deigned to suffer for her sins, there is a remarkable similarity between the total siege time then (430 days) and the total span of the fifth and sixth plagues under consideration.

According to historical records, the siege by Nebuchadnezzar's forces lasted from January 15, 588 BC to July 19, 586, for a total of one year, five months, and twenty-nine days. (429 days) And while the five months of the demon invasion is for all purposes separated from the 'year and a month and a day' time period that is determined for the Arab war, the cumulative duration of them both is 431 days.

As for the 'forty days' of Ezekiel's characterization, we see in it a reflection of the forty days between the Anti-Christ's invasion of Israel and closing out of the seventh judgment, with no apparent demarcation evidenced between the two judgments. For indeed, the sixth judgment of war bore the seeds of the seventh judgment, for as the Arab-Israeli conflict dissolved, out of the ashes emerges the man who would deign to be the Messiah, who lives but for a short season, and upon his death, the last judgment, or the third Woe falls, bringing with it the desolation of Israel, three days later. Thus we see the 'forty days' extending from the entrance of the oppressive false Messiah into Israel in the closing days of the sixth judgment unto the dispersion of the Jews from Israel.

In a brief resume of the war, it could be said that it began when the swiftly moving Arab armies crossed the borders into Israel. From the start, the ill-prepared Israelis, who had no opportunity to mount a counter-offense, were forced on the defensive. The invaders come in from Syria over West Bank, from Lebanon south, and from below the Dead Sea, they push north to Jerusalem. Air defenses helped to slow the advance, but the Israeli army was over-run in several locations by the sheer number of Arabs troops, and thousands died in the defense of the cities. There seemed to be no end to the hordes of Arabs pushing over the tortured land, killing and burning everything in their path, and while John might have agonized greatly over the steady extermination of his brethren, he wrote none of it.

The battlefronts shifted back and forth as first one side and then the other gained control of a strategic location, but always, the Jews found themselves sacrificing their lives rather than give ground. For nearly a year, the heroic Jews held out against overwhelming odds before the world community intervened. Diplomatic emissaries were sent to the Arab countries to try and arrange a cease fire, but when that failed, the decision was made to prepare and commit Union forces into the conflict to quell the terrible carnage going on in Israel.

From the book of Daniel we understand that their expeditionary forces descended on the Gaza strip and Egyptian soil. The Egyptian forces were quickly neutralized, while the remaining forces moved north along the Mediterranean coast before heading inland toward Jerusalem. Heavy fighting continued for several days, including a fierce battle for Jerusalem where the greatest resistance was met, but with its capitulation the invasion effort of the Arabs skidded to a halt.

Shortly thereafter the Arabs were brought to a complete surrender and were forced to dispel their remaining troops back across the border. With all fighting ceased, martial law was instituted in Israel and the European President and his staff were allowed to fly into Jerusalem, at which time he took over command of the area. But his command was short lived when his over-bearing attitude brought about his assassination only three weeks later.

Footnote:

In the Greek language, in which the book of Revelation was originally written by John, any quantitative number over 1000 had no designated noun or word to use for that amount. I, e, there were no such terms as "million," or "billion." For quantities over 1000, the number would be "multiplied" or 1000 X, i.e. 1000 X 7, or simply 7,000. This worked well up to 900,000, however more than that quantity was beyond their scope, so there was a word that was used to indicate, really any amount over 10,000, and that was the word "MURIAS," meaning "an infinite number, or innumerable."

Sometimes the plural word "MURIOI" was used, but the meaning of the word is still meant "very many, or innumerable." We have the same situation in Rev.5: 11, where the word murias was translated "ten thousand times ten thousand, and thousands of thousands," when John really only meant that the number of angels in heaven was beyond counting. There are other places where the same word "murias" was used, i.e. Matt.18: 24, Acts 19:19, I Cor. 4: 15. There were similar problems in the Hebrew language, to express large numbers of people, or angels, or what have you, and an equivalent word was used, "rebabah" pronounced "reb-aw-baw,"meaning a "myriad" or a multiple multitude.

In the King James Bible, Gen.24: 60, the word "million" was mistakenly inserted, the only place that it is found in the whole Bible. In other translations the words "thousands of ten thousands" was inserted. When the exodus of the children of Israel took place from Egypt, the scriptures number the multitude of men as 600,000 on foot, besides the children. Had the writer wanted to define the total number of people involved, he would have had no other choice than to use the word rebabah, which would convey a limitless number.

188

CHAPTER 14

The Burden Bearer

John may have purposely rendered his account of the Arab-Israeli war to safe-guard certain information surrounding the entry of the false messiah into the Holy Land, and not because he was ignorant of the details of the battle. For what was coming over the horizon, and about which John had little knowledge, was the concluding stage of this very sophisticated segment of God's plan.

According to Daniel, the sixth judgment war was in the process of winding down, following the landing of the Union troops on the Gaza, and already the complex preparations for Satan's entry into Jerusalem were beginning to fall into place.

As I mentioned earlier, the last forty days of the indignation were designated to begin from the landing of those European troops, who came there on the pretext of returning peace to the area. However, instead of peace, what followed was a period of de-stabilization under the auspices of the President, which ultimately resulted in his assassination by extremists only three days before the indignation period was to close. John would have had no previous knowledge of these circumstances however, other than what he might have picked up by reading Daniel's journal, and without that knowledge he was prevented from making closure on the sixth Trumpet judgment. (Dan. 11:41-45)

Up to now, John has been filling his journal with the details of six of the seven plagues of the Jewish judgment period, with all of the information being derived from the seven sealed book, as told to him by the Lord. But when that information began broaching on the subject of Satan's appearance that would come in the seventh judgment, the Lord called a halt to His disclosure.

You get the impression that He took a time out from releasing further information until He had explained to John some of the necessary details preceding Satan's appearance before actually bringing him on the scene.

189

Until now, any reference to Satan's direct involvement in the tribulation had remained a secret with the Lord, but there came a point in time when that secret had to be shared with John because Satan was due to appear on the last day of the judgment period.

John would also be expecting an explanation for Satan's continued access to heaven after his first rebellion against the Lord's authority, and why there had never been any punishment meted out to him. There was a reason for it all, and John was about to find out.

And there is no doubt that Satan has also been keeping abreast of the situation in Israel, as well as the nurturing of this person who would be taking on the role of the Anti-Christ, but until John's journal was released, there is no reason to believe that he had any inkling of what was in store for him personally in the future.

In the next judgment, or what was called the 'third Woe,' Satan will be sent down to earth with a commission to exact persecution on the Jews and initiate the desolation process of Israel. When that operation is completed, the seventh Trumpet judgment will be closed out and Satan's association with the Jews will be finished. However, that doesn't mean that his mission is over, for there is a second operation, which takes place during the great tribulation, wherein his wrath, and expertise will again be required for a successful completion of that mission. At that time, his role will be expanded considerably. He will be taking on a new role as the leader of the world, an opportunity that has been offered to him by the Lord to make possible the 'world-wide' deliverance of the tribulation saints, which must be accomplished before the Vial judgments can begin.

This is an oversimplification of the complex issues that lie ahead but the sensitive nature of these two programs necessitates an alternative approach to achieving them successfully. All of which John is going to find out when he keeps an appointment with an angel from the Lord, and dutifully records the minutes of that meeting, which is found in Revelation chapter 10.

A NEW COMMISION

Until this moment, the existing method of the transferring the material from the Lord to John had proved satisfactory, but the Lord apparently considered this method inadequate for the transference of the summary details of the seventh judgment, which included the induction of Satan into the world. Or maybe it was because the Lord simply chose to turn the book over to John and let him call forth the remaining judgments. Whatever the reason, the familiar 'predicted descriptive' visionary transfer of information from the Lord to John, wherein he acted as a recording scribe of the events set before him, is about to be changed. And with the ensuing chapters of Revelation, it becomes quite apparent that John's role has been significantly revised from that of a 'scribe' of the events set before him, to that of an authenticator or initiator of the forthcoming events. In other words, from this point on, Jesus will no longer be pronouncing the judgments from the seven-sealed scroll for John to record, but has agreed to turn that job over to him, along with the little book, which seems unorthodox, because we were told in the beginning that only Jesus was qualified to read the book.

However, this change of duty entails John's reading of the next series of judgments in the sealed book and causing them to be brought into realization.

In modern terminology, John's position would be that of a Chief Executive Officer, with the responsibility of programming not only the hitherto secret Gentile judgments, but in a more awesome sense, all of Satan's activities on earth, including his persecution of the Jewish remnant, the expulsion of the Jews into a sanctuary in the desert, and as the "Beast" in the promotion of the resurrection of the tribulation saints which takes place during a two year hiatus immediately following the desolation. Satan is going to be an extremely busy person for the next three and a half years under John's jurisdiction.

Some of these areas that John will be dealing with are extremely sensitive areas, particularly with respect to the summoning of the Devil out of the bottomless pit and depositing him in the body of the Anti-Christ. This event, called the 'incarnation,' must be carried off without a hitch if God's redemption plans for the remnant of Israel and the deliverance of the tribulation saints is to be successful.

The Lord will still set the boundaries of Satan's activities on earth, which are many and varied, but John will be directing his actions to achieve the specific goals set forth. For the Devil, being shunted around as a man and by another man will be an embarrassing and humiliating experience, but to John it's an awesome responsibility. Taking over for God in setting up the program of the great tribulation directly from the scroll had to be some experience but he does an admirable job.

This changeover in authority, which is described in chapter 10, takes place during a discreet meeting between the Lord and John at an isolated spot on the Mediterranean shore. At this time the book of judgments was handed over to John. This is the 'seven-sealed' book that we are talking about, which contained the listings of the judgments on both the Jews and the Gentiles, that prior to this exchange was the sole right of the Lord. (Rev. 5:1) He alone was worthy to open the seals and read the book, and no man was worthy, not even to look upon it, (Rev. 5:4) and although there has been a change of plans, this change by no means detracts from the immutability of God.

As you will notice from Revelation chapter 11, and thereafter, there is a distinct change in the definition and substance of the subject material and in the amount of graphic description that John gives. Chapter twelve, for instance, gives an extensive historical preamble about the Devil, illumining his propensity for wrath, which was a necessary prerequisite for his work on earth. Here also is the tie-in made between the evil king of Daniel and John's Beast in Revelation.

The importance of this meeting between John and the Lord must not be under-estimated, for it catapulted John from recorder to prophet, from being a witness to that of a trusted seer of the greatest secret ever kept by God, so it's no wonder that he recorded the minute details of that moment. (Rev. chapter 10)

As John records in the minutes of the meeting, he found himself standing on the earth, near the shore of the great sea, and looking heaven-ward toward a tall-figured man who was descending through the clouds toward him. He strained to recognize the figure, and looking beyond the clouds that seem to clothe him and the rainbow about his head, he perceived him to be an angel. But as the figure neared, his face was shining so bright that John had to shield his eyes, and turn his head downward towards the feet that were shod with fire.

John followed this 'angel's' descent until he touched the earth whereupon he set his right foot on the sea and his left on the shore, and at that moment he cried out with a loud voice announcing his presence to the earth, and from the clouds overhead the voice of thunders echoed their reply.

Continuing to gaze upon the figure in wonderment, John followed the movements of the man as he raised his arms to the sky, and was heard to say,

"To Him that lives forever and ever, who created the heaven and the things that therein are, and the sea, and the things which are therein, there should be time no longer: but in the days of the voice of the seventh angel, when he shall begin to sound, the Mystery of God should be finished, as He hath declared to His servants the prophets." (Rev. 10: 6-7)

At that moment John is startled by a voice from heaven, telling him to go and take the open book out of the hand of the 'angel,' which he did after much hesitation. And when the angel handed it to him he also issued instructions to read and understand the message within the book. John eagerly did the angel's bidding, and at first he was excited at the prospect of reading the book, but as he continued to read through the pages the realization and the import of the message began to hit home. And when he finally read through and raised his eyes from the pages, the angel said to him,

"You must now write what's in the book, so that all of the world may know what is in their future." (Rev.10: 11)

That concluded the particulars of the meeting, but before the angel left he softened John's consternation about the remaining judgments on the Jews by informing him, in a circumspect way, that their punishments were about to end and the Gentile period was about to commence. This information was given in an allegorical setting;

"And there was given me a reed like unto a rod: and the angel stood, saying, Rise, and measure the temple of God, and the altar, and them that worship therein. (2) But the court which is without the temple leave out, and measure it not; for it is given

unto the Gentiles: and the holy city shall they tread under foot forty and two months." (Rev. 11: 1,2)

Here we see John, figuratively being handed a measuring stick and told to measure the Temple, the altar, and the people worshipping therein. This act of measuring, or inspecting of the finished objects, indicated to John that the full work of the punishments against both the land and the people of Israel has been completed, whereas in verse two, he is made to realize that the "outer court," or "the court of the Gentiles," cannot be measured yet, because the work on this will not be completed for another forty-two months. In short, "The plagues upon the Jews are almost completed, but the Gentiles have another forty-two months of plagues to look forward to."

The use of the term "measure the Temple" in this case was strictly in reference to the location of the punishments being in Israel and should not be stretched to infer that a new Temple will be built in the future anymore than there would be a possibility of John being able to measure it.

Footnote:

Rather than transfer the book to John in the Throne room, Jesus chose this isolated spot on the sea shore to evince the secrecy of the information, but it was the timing of the exchange of this future data that was critical. We have seen that from the opening of the seals on the book through the following six judgments, it has been the strict prerogative of the Lord to reveal its contents. He was the only one found worthy of this honor, and John was a spectator, if you will, of the Lord's actions, but now with the change in plans, John is made privy to the remainder of the judgments before they actually begin. And the occasion for this honor was born out of the necessity to finally reveal the mystery of the Gentile judgments along with the rest of the plans for eternity, and John was chosen to be that revealer. And there just happened to be a small window of opportunity for this exchange before the imminent sounding of the seventh trumpet.

We have probably read the book of Revelation without ever realizing that half of the written pages of the book contain information that only the Godhead knew until the moment that it was revealed to John, which we learn about in chapter 10. And had this meeting not taken place, and had the Lord not chosen to reveal His secret of the Gentile judgments, the second three and one half years would have been quite different, with a scenario of the seven years going something like this:

'The last Trumpet would sound and the Jews would be expelled from the Holy Land, while being pursued by the armies of the beast in their flight. They would remain in exile for the next 3 1/2 years, at the conclusion of which the Messiah would return to earth and set up His Kingdom. Following that, the resurrection of the Jews would occur and the judgment of the nations take place.'

Incidentally, this somewhat abbreviated order of events harmonizes beautifully with all of the Old Testament prophecies and with the writings of Paul, even to including the rapture of the church. (II Thess. 1: 7-10)   The prophet Daniel portrayed this concept in several places, one of which is in Dan. 7: 21 and 22, as seen here,

"I beheld, and the same horn made war with the saints, and prevailed against them; (22) (Until) the Ancient of days came, and judgment was given to the saints of the most High; and the time came that the saints possessed the kingdom."

As you see, these verses promote the concept that the attack made by the evil king on the Jewish saints is the end of the judgments, following which the Messiah returns and destroys the oppressor, leaving the resurrected saints to possess the Kingdom. But what Daniel had little or no knowledge of, was the incarnation of the Devil and the three and one half-year Gentile tribulation that separated those two events.

CHAPTER 15

The Odyssey

The world was rocked with the front-page news of the President's assassination in Israel when only weeks earlier he had been hailed as the savior of the country. Now he is rewarded with an assassin's blade. His body was found early Monday morning in his apartment. He had been stabbed multiple times in the chest and arms and apparently bled to death from the wounds. The story continued:

"Immediately following the discovery of the body in his upstairs apartment, the authorities sealed all the exits from the city and conducted a massive search effort for the killers. Meanwhile preparations are being made for a state memorial service on Thursday in Jerusalem, and dignitaries from around the globe have been invited to attend. A religious confidant of the slain President has been summoned from Brussels to conduct the services. The body will not be embalmed, but can be viewed in the coffin in the rotunda of the legislative building until after the public memorial service. Following the service the body will be transported to Brussels for burial."

As you recall from Daniel's book, this same European leader had sent his military forces into Israel to intervene in the war that had been going on there for nearly a year. Following the intervention by the Union forces, the hostilities were rapidly brought to an end and the remaining Arab armies were expelled from Israel, where martial law was quickly instituted. It was during this interim period that President Ballarius came to Jerusalem and assumed the governing powers from the national leaders. He then proceeded to impose further restrictions on some activities, such as enacting a curfew, closing the heavily damaged synagogues and limiting all access to the Wailing Wall. This effectively shut down all religious worship that was so desperately needed at this time. But while those edicts severely strained the relationship between him and the Jews, it was his blasphemous allegations about God and his brash attempt to inculcate himself as their redeemer that finally turned the Jews against him. And though the idea might seem ludicrous to some, to him it was a valid possibility, even though his dubious character fell far short of his protestations and only helped to alienate himself further. During that short period the relations between him and the people worsened, and efforts were made to get rid of him, but whether he simply refused to leave Israel we will never know, for shortly thereafter he was assassinated. (Dan.7: 25, 9:27)

The President's assassination apparently triggered the next phase in the Lord's plans, which was a cleansing action in heaven, wherein Satan, and all other evidences of sin, including the rebellious angels who followed him, whose seemingly interminable presence God has purposefully endured until this propitious moment, will be removed forcibly from heaven and shunted into the bowels of the earth where they will be confined until the final judgment.

But we can readily assume that there was a great reluctance on the Devil's part to arbitrarily give up his authority and position in heaven, and as John states, this caused a war to break out between the horde of Satan's angels and the dedicated angels of the Lord. But by days' end, Satan and his rebellious angels had been banished from heaven's portals to the inner depths of the earth. (Rev.12: 7-9)

Meanwhile, all was in readiness for the funeral services of the slain President. The large rotunda area of the capitol building had been cordoned off for the event and was near filled to capacity with mourners who were seated around a raised dais that had been hastily built for the occasion and installed in the center of the area.

The coffin, with its upper portion raised for viewing of the corpse, had already been positioned on the platform. The television people who would be documenting the proceedings for the world were strategically located throughout the visitor's section, and on the outer fringes were several of the invited clergy, however there was a noticeable absence of any Jewish Rabbis. Those representatives of the various religious denominations who did attend, were obviously uncomfortable being in the same room with the cultic priest who would be conducting the service, which may have been their reason for hovering close to the exits.

Soon the entry doors were closed and the few latecomers

hastened to sit down and stifle the rustling of chairs. The priest took this as his cue to stand and walk with slow deliberate steps up onto the platform where he stood over and peered into the face of the former President for a few seconds. This action quieted the drone of whispered conversations, and when the audience had stilled sufficiently, the priest turned and moved over to the small podium where he lifted his hands before his face and bowed his head for what appeared to be a time of prayer. This gesture encouraged others in the room to intone what prayers they believed suitable for the occasion in concert with the prayers of the priest, while others simply bowed their heads.

At that 'hallowed' moment however, the solemnity of the occasion was shattered by the shrill cry of a woman who happened to be seated close to the platform. Immediately all heads raised and eyes turned in the direction of the cry and then to where her extended arm and fingers were pointing. And what they beheld was the incarnation moment. Though yet unrealized by the world, Satan had invaded the dead body of the President and caused it to move noticeably.

Almost in unison, everyone in the room stood to their feet with their eyes riveted on the coffin, waiting to catch the next movement of the corpse, but only those closest to it saw the eye lids flicker, and in their excitement tried to communicate to the others around what was happening. Gasps of astonishment arose when the eyelids suddenly popped wide open and the head started jerking from side to side. Then the head deliberately tried to rise from the pillow. The stunned audience watched in amazement as the arms that had been folded over his chest straightened out and his hands slowly raised to where the fingers could grasp the cushioned edges of the coffin. Slowly at first, the figure in the coffin pulled his shoulders upward, bending at the waist until he sat upright. He remained motionless in that position for several seconds while looking over the crowd through glazed eyes. Cries of fright and disbelief broke out from all over the room but every eye remained glued on the spectacle in the coffin.

The priest was as shocked as everyone else and had momentarily stepped back from the coffin, but he quickly overcame this initial reaction and reached forward to assist the figure, who by this time had opened the lower half of the coffin lid and was attempting to swing his feet over the side.   Now with the extended hands of the priest aiding him, the figure slid easily over the side of the coffin until his feet rested on the platform, where again he stood motionless for a few moments while he appeared to be scanning his surroundings. Then waving aside the proffered assistance of the priest, the figure breathed deeply and stepped cautiously forward down the few carpeted steps to the floor of the rotunda.

To everyone who was there the event seemed too incredible to imagine. Although he was fully dressed, his arm movements beneath his clothing gave no indication of anything being wrong with the arm that had been nearly severed. All anyone realized for the moment was that their President had been dead, and now he was alive, and the priest quickly seized on the moment. Without a break in the charged atmosphere, he ran to the man and unabashedly prostrated himself at his feet and proclaimed his deity. Then raising his face and hands skyward he shouted loud enough for everyone to hear,

"Your President lives!   He has conquered death and become the master of life with all the powers of God!   And he is now our god!"

And all who were there were still so much in shock that they echoed the priest's sentiments in a loud crescendo of praise.

Thus began the odyssey of Satan on earth. This was not the picture of an evil king being overwhelmed by an evil spirit, as Daniel had envisioned, nor was he simply a man empowered by the spirit of the source of sin, as Paul had written, but Satan himself, who only days before had been in the pit along with his wicked angels, had now been called forth to dwell in the frame of the dead President.

Standing before that crowd was Lucifer, the father of sin, at the apex of his transmigration from heaven to the body of the slain President, who would now be able to rise and perform a further work for the Lord. But certainly those who attended the ceremony that day, and quite possibly all those who witnessed the transformation on their television screens around the world were unaware of the Lord's purpose for this 'new President' and even less cognizant of God's plans for the future. Nor would they believe that the man who strode in their midst and accepted their adulation was the Devil incarnate.

The scene that has just been portrayed may read like a ghoulish fiction novel, but it could very well duplicate the course of events that take place when Satan does arrive on the earth, though John chose not to incorporate such an introductory salutation in his journal. He knew what had happened all right, but he simply chose to acknowledge his transition and earthly presence with prepositional words.

He said that Satan was first deposited INTO the confines of the earth where only spirits can dwell. And from there he ASCENDED, and was deposited ONTO the earth, and from thence came his persecution of the Jews. (Rev. chapters 12, 13,17) (Rev 17:8)

However, when you consider the magnitude of the operation that was required to extricate the most powerful angel from heaven, together with his great host of angels, and deliver them into the pit in the center of the earth, then immediately turn around and bring him forth from his prison and force him take on what he considered to be the 'ignominy of a human existence,' then certainly the goal of such a stupendous effort must have been extremely important to God. So important in fact, that He had allowed Satan to continue abiding in the heavens for all of these millenniums without repercussions for his prior rebellion, or for his involvement in the death of His Son at Calvary, either of which should have brought him instant expulsion and judgment. But he had been allowed to remain in heaven purposely for this one moment in eternity when he might be used to make ready the miraculous redemption of the remnant of the Jews and the deliverance of the tribulation believers.

The plans of God called for the infusion of Satan into the mainstream of human society, and what better way to accomplish this feat than by incarnating him in the physical frame of a powerful and important human personage. If he had been sent to earth in his celestial body, the prophecies of Daniel, which required the assassination of the evil king, would have been forfeited. The man must die so that Satan can be inculcated into humanity and masquerade behind the face of the Anti-Christ for the next three and a half years, lest the world know his true identity.

It's ironic, that the main reason for Satan's presence on the earth is to help the Lord accomplish those two important objectives, which the Anti-Christ was incapable of before his incarnation. The operation of deliverance requires a prominent earthly political figure with the power and authority of an angelic being, which is accomplished by Satan's incarnation in the frame of the Anti-Christ.

His first objective will be to force the desolation of Israel in the last days of the seventh judgment. This edict falls under the third segment of Ezekiel's prophecy, which stated that the last third of the Jews who remained alive in Israel would be *'scattered to the winds and have a sword drawn after them,'* which means that Satan can use whatever means at his disposal to accomplish the dispersion of the Jews, which he does in a 'pursue and destroy' operation against the fleeing people. (Eze.5: 12)

Evidently, the ulterior motive behind this deployment against the fleeing refugees was to further reduce the remaining third of the Jewish population until only a remnant remained, whereupon this remnant would be delivered into a sanctuary of safety. (Dan.12: 1)

THE SECOND MISSION OF THE DEVIL

But while the deliverance of that remnant will be a major feat in itself, requiring the utmost utilization of Satan's capabilities, the second objective is even greater. It is the centerpiece of God's plans for the tribulation period, which effectively culminates the Harvest program that had begun years earlier.

This operation could be considered as 'catching the gleanings' of the previous Harvest, or the redemption of the "believers of the second chance," which is an operation that is only overshadowed by the Rapture itself. And though not as complex as the harvesting process of the saints which took place years earlier, the necessity of compelling the remnant of believers to expedite their own deliverance through martyrdom requires Satan's unique capabilities. These capabilities are paramount for the success of both missions. No earthly figure could possibly have the authority to dispel the Jews from their land, much less deliver them into an earthly sanctuary, nor could any human authority compel the believers in Christ to stay and suffer death at the hands of their adversary, in order to find eternal life in their heavenly sanctuary.

And with these objectives set before him, John was so convinced within himself of the necessity for the incarnation, that he devoted nearly two full chapters of his book to a biographical sketch of both Satan and the Anti-Christ, so that we, his readers, might fully comprehend what actually takes place when these two figures amalgamate and become an aberration that will henceforth be known only as the "Beast."

In his heavenly spirit form, Satan was known by such names as the "dragon, the serpent, the devil and the accuser of the brethren" as well as the familiar one, 'Satan.' He was also described as the "*dragon* with seven heads and ten horns and seven crowns upon his heads," (12:3) while later on earth he is described as "the *beast* with seven heads and ten horns," which should prove to us that the heavenly spirit-being Satan and the earthly "Beast" are one and the same personage. (Rev.13: 1 and 17:3)

But going back to the memorial-resurrection service that I may have overly elaborated on, we find that John amazingly outlines this transition of Satan in just four short phrases in one verse of scripture: **"And I saw one of his heads** (of the beast) **as it were wounded to death;** (having been killed) **and his deadly wound was healed:** (at the moment of the Lord's touch) **and all the world wondered after the beast."** (after he had been revived) (Rev.13: 3)

As would be expected, the scene of the incarnation, to all who were witnessing it in the great hall as well as those seeing it on the television, brought nothing but awe at this miracle of the resurrection. Without knowing or caring what had transpired before them, they accepted what they saw, and as the scripture says,

"They worshipped the dragon which gave power unto the beast: and they worshipped the beast, saying, Who is like unto the beast? who is able to make war with him?" (Rev. 13: 4)

That ready worship was just what Satan wanted to hear. It must have lifted his spirits to hear that kind of praise, and in a few weeks hence it will give him the impetus to set forth on his quest for the world's admiration, but at the moment he is going to be engrossed in the work of desolating Israel.

If we assume that the whole scenario of the war in heaven with the casting down of Satan, his incarnation in the dead President, and the finally desolation of Israel, have all been precisely programmed according to the Lord's plans, then everything hinged on the President's cooperation in dying on schedule in Jerusalem. Without that the plans would fall apart, but fortunately he did cooperate and the program went into high gear. Three days after his death he was incarnated by Satan and became the newly resurrected President who walked proudly among his admirers and accepted their accolades. But at the same time he was driven by a sense of urgency to get into the business ahead of him, and taking the first opportunity available to him, he left the 'mourning' crowd and returned to his former headquarters from whence he immediately issued orders for the two Witnesses from heaven, who had been incarcerated earlier, to be brought to him.

While waiting, he reflected on the past when he had buffeted them many times in their work for God, and even disputed with the Lord over their presence in heaven without having suffered a physical death. And it angered him to know that they had been proselytizing the Jews these past three and a half years, but now he has the opportunity to end their mission.

His reminiscing was interrupted by riotous sounds emanating from a crowd gathering in front of the building, and he went over to the window where he looked down and saw a mob that had gathered around the military escort of the two Witnesses after leaving the vehicle. But on hearing a series of warning shots fired by the soldiers, he decided to go down to the courtyard to face the crowd. When he exited the building the crowd quieted somewhat and made a passageway for him out to the street where the two Witnesses had already been forced to kneel on the pavement.

The unruly crowd quieted to hear what was going on, but it wasn't difficult hear his voice raging and cursing as he expressed his hate for these two, while snapping his head this way and that at the crowd as though he expected them to wrest the two from him. Then for a few seconds, he too stood silent over the two and glowering while he tried to make up his mind what to do with them. Then turning to the soldiers he shouted; *"Shoot them both."* And watching the crowd for any reaction to his next words, he raised his voice and added;

"Leave them there in the street as a warning to others who will not follow me."

Showing no qualms at having them killed on the spot, and even as the shots were being fired, he was turning on his heel to leave the area in one of the military vehicles that had been conveniently waiting to take him the short distance to the Western Wall, which, after the destruction of the earthquake and the war, was the only Holy Place in Israel that was left intact.

It was already late in the day and the sun was just setting when he arrived in the plaza area before the Wall. The television crews moved hastily to set up their equipment while he tried to curb his impatience at they're not having done this beforehand. But finally he was given the signal to begin his speech, and with as much poise as he could muster, and trying to hold his anger in check at the same time, he blurted forth the words,

" I am your Messiah!"

Following that brusque announcement he added a few conciliatory words espousing his adopted position before cutting loose with a string of highly derogatory statements against the Jews for their recent attack on him, and promising them swift retaliation in exchange. He closed his message by again reiterating his position as being the master of life while at the same time casting aspersions about the God of Israel, which the Jews, even in their worldly minds, considered to be blasphemous. His standing on that spot was in itself a desecration of the Holy Place, but with his added blasphemy of God, it became an intolerable abomination against God. (Rev.13: 5,6)

It was this man's belligerent attitude and defiance of God that made such an impact on Daniel when he was given witness of this very scene in his vision. The experience left him ill for days. And it was this same scene that Jesus recounted centuries later, when He spoke to the Disciples that day on the mountain. He used the same descriptive words and phrases as Daniel in his description of the events, only He added this additional warning for those who would be witnessing that scene for themselves in the coming days. He cautioned:

"When ye shall see the abomination of desolation, spoken of by Daniel the prophet, standing where it ought not, (let him that reads this understand,) then let them that be in Judea flee to the mountains." (Mark 13: 14)

This *'abomination of the desolation,'* is not referring to the Anti-Christ, but to the aberration which resulted from the union of the Devil and the Anti-Christ. He is the Beast.

Caring little for the world's reaction to his recriminations, the Beast quickly issued orders for the immediate expulsion of all Jews from the Holy Land, with little being said of the threat of massacring the evacuees as they departed.

But in their present circumstances the Jews had little choice for refusal. They could leave or be killed, and should they manage to escape they had little hope for survival in the harsh desert with no means of transportation. Anything that couldn't be carried on their backs was left behind in the frantic exodus.

This was a demoralizing experience for a country that had lost over two thirds of its population in the last two plagues. For all those who were too injured and emaciated to flee, it was a death sentence. There would be no prisoners filling the jails, nor hospital space for the infirm, and beyond that, his intentions were made clear that no Jew was to be left alive in Israel. So with no sanctuary in the hostile neighboring nations, and the Union troops on their heels, the mass of refugees fled south into the deserts of the Negev. (Rev 12:15, Matt. 24: 17-20)

In this manner, the third and final requirement of the prophecy of Ezekiel which stated that; *"All those who were left of Israel would be scattered to the winds and a sword would be drawn after them."* was fulfilled. (Eze. 5:12)

But Israel's tragedy will become a miracle of deliverance. They may not have realized it, but from the moment their trek into the wilderness began, they were under the watchful eye of the Redeemer. Their dark flight from death became a lighted path to life, and what they had rued as a tragedy became a joyful redemption to all those whose names were found written in the book of life. (Dan.12: 1)

Their exodus replicates that of their ancestors who were delivered from the cruel oppression of the Egyptian Pharaohs. In their flight into the wilderness, they experienced their every need being supplied by the Lord. And when the oppressors pursued them, they were destroyed by the Lord in a great wall of water. In like manner the pursuing armies of the Beast will be destroyed in a great fissure in the desert that opens before them. (Rev. 12:16)

No better words could be used to describe their present deliverance than this succinct message of John's, when he said of Israel,

"It were as though she were given two wings of a great eagle, that she might fly into the wilderness, into her place, where she will be nourished for a time, and times, and half a time from the face of the serpent," (Rev. 12:14)

Or the words of Jeremiah as he expressed the same sentiments:

"The people, which were left of the sword, found grace in the wilderness; even Israel, when I went to cause him to rest." (Jer. 31:2)

Meanwhile, amid all of this desperation and turmoil in the city, the street in front of the headquarters had remained quarantined by the deteriorating corpses of the two witnesses that still remained crumpled in death. Moreover, for the past three days this bizarre scene of the dead bodies had been shown over and over again on the world's news programs.

However, all those who happened to be watching the news the following Sunday morning saw another miracle happen, when they witnessed the resurrection of the two men. They saw them sit up and slowly stand to their feet. And all around them was a mysterious glow as they stood there motionless for a few moments, then suddenly they were catapulted into the air; and at the same time a voice came out of nowhere that said: **"Come up hither."**

They had no sooner disappeared from view than a severe earthquake shook the city and opened up the ground in the area where the slain witnesses had been. Nearby army barracks, including the headquarters of the Beast were collapsed from the quake, burying over seven thousand soldiers who were inside at the time.

Fortunately, this happened when the majority of the refugees were far removed from the city, but unfortunately, so was the Beast who had already left for Europe and his scheduled meeting with the Council. The army was being left to finish the evacuation process, but after the earthquake their greater efforts were expended in quelling the violence and looting by the remaining Palestinians. (Rev. 11:12,13)

Footnote:
This portrayal of the last few days of Jacob's trouble has been garnered from a number of scattered verses, all of which are within the context of the plan of the Lord that included Satan's banishment to the earth in order to depose the remaining Jews from the ravages of the great tribulation.

While Jesus seems to be placing an inordinate emphasis on the urgency of the situation, it's apparent that His concern was over of the immanency of the great tribulation. He was urging the Jews to swallow their pride and flee rather than stand up to the Beast, but while it was a warning of an impending storm, it was also a plea for them to come to Him for sanctuary. And though many of the fleeing Jews will find sanctuary in martyrdom, they will rise again in the resurrection, and together with the hundred and forty-four thousand Jews selected earlier, become the first fruits of the Kingdom. (Rev. 12:6)

The killing of the two Witnesses, who by this time had completed their mission of testifying for the Lord, was an inevitable act, done to attest the convictions of Satan to the Jewish community. Had they chosen to do so, they could have escaped, but by their sacrifice and wondrous resurrection, they exemplified their unwavering faith to both the souls in Israel and the recalcitrant believers of the coming tribulation, that they must be willing to go through the same experience of death in this present world to gain deliverance for eternity. (Rev. 11:7-12)

Footnote II

The destination of the fleeing remnant of the Jews is believed to be the city of Petra, the "Rose red City," that was carved out of the sandstone rock walls by the Nabatean peoples in 300 BC. The city is located in the Wadi Musa Canyon, some fifty miles south of the Dead Sea in Jordan. There, they will be completely cut-off from the events of the world and sustained by the Lord during the next three and a half years of the great tribulation.

CHAPTER 16

The Deliverance

I have tried to imagine what would have been going through the mind of the Beast as he sat comfortably on that plane heading back to Brussels. Was he thinking with the aptitude of the former President or was that capability all washed out of his system when Lucifer took control? In one respect, as the President he might have been experiencing an exhilarating euphoria in his new found life of power and fortune, but if things were the other way around, and the Devil was uppermost in this new being, his ethereal mind would likely be overburdened with somber brooding and a wrath that was bubbling just below the surface for what he believed was an unjustifiable sentence to a degrading earthly existence. But regardless of who was on the short end of the stick, the Beast knew somehow that his present situation was going to be short lived and he had important things to do before it all came to an end.

He had been summoned back to Brussels to assume the Presidency of the new world Union, whose plans for reorganization had been in progress for several months. Modifications to its charter were necessary to allow for an increase in the number of member nations, to cope with the deteriorating economic conditions in the world and the desperate programs of reconstruction since the earthquake. While the former President was in Israel, the Union had culminated these reorganization efforts, and had also modified the election procedures and term limits of the Presidency.

It was a forgone conclusion that the revived President would be re-elected, particularly since the Lord was guiding the whole situation, and the fact that the man had recently shown some outstanding leadership qualities, which all told made him the leading candidate. In the past week alone he has shown himself to be a very decisive and authoritative figure, who also possessed talents as a negotiator, as was evidenced by his mitigation of the problems within the Council over the recent situations in Israel. They accepted his solemn promise of returning the Jews' to their homeland just as soon as the Arab boundaries were negotiated. The Council also accepted his explanations about the desolation and set aside the refugee situation until after the formalization of the world union and the installation of the new governing Council and President. So it's understandable, that on his swift flight back to Brussels he would also be pondering somewhat about his future.

His angelic sense tells him that he has been shunted to earth for a purpose, but he hasn't been told what it is. His mission is two-fold, first, to administer the evacuation of the remaining Jews from Israel, and secondly, to expedite the remnant of believers around the world into making a demanding commitment for the Lord. He has successfully accomplished the first mission and he is now working on the second mission of extricating the Christians.

But his immediate thoughts were on his new world dominion, and how he would be able to achieve the due submission of its subjects without having his former rare powers and the innumerable angelic host to assist him. Strapped as he was in a mortal shell, and unable to invade the minds of his subjects, he will be forced to depend solely upon earthly minions to carry out his objectives.

With these and other problems before him, he ruminates in self-pity while his anger deepens. So it wasn't any wonder that as his plane began lowering over Brussels, and he could see down below him the many towering cathedral spires and crosses, that a new resolve welled up in him. He was immediately brought back to the reality of his task and a new determination to rid his new kingdom of any semblance of God's presence.

Even as the plane settled onto the tarmac ending the flight, the great tribulation was already beginning as described by John in this brief interposing message of the task set before the Beast;

'The Beast was sorely angered with the Jews over their worship of God, and now his wrath will be spilled over all of the peoples of the earth, (on those) who continue to profess their belief in God.' "And whatever it takes," he determines, "I'm going to rid the earth of those believers in the same way that I have gotten rid of the Jews.* (Rev. 12:17)

But the 'as yet unresolved' factor in ridding the whole world of those Jews and believers, was how it could be done. He knew that without some form of extended authority or power over all the world, his ability to reach into remote areas and persecute the believers would be futile, just as he knew that the likelihood of furthering his ambitions by military intrusion into other sovereignties would be untenable.

To overcome these hurdles, he would need all of the celestial powers that had been stripped from him when he was cast out of heaven. Only with them intact would he be able to transcend borders and cultures and make it possible for him to *'deceive all those that dwell on the earth, and cause all those whose names are not written in the book of life to worship him,'* as John writes. (Rev. 13:7-15)

It's odd, that seven hundred years earlier the prophet Isaiah had foreseen this frustrating moment of Satan, after he had been cast out of heaven, and he penned these taunting words to him,

"O Lucifer, son of the morning, why have you been cast out of heaven to the earth?"   "Is it because you have been overcome with pride in your desire to be like the Most High?"

He further questioned this foolish angel on how he hoped to gain 'equal status with God' by merely building an earthly empire of worshippers.

"What I'm telling you Lucifer," wrote Isaiah, "Is that while you're busy reaching for your goal of homage from everyone on earth, you will be reaping only scorn by those same followers, who will call you the 'destroyer' rather than a creator, but nevertheless, they will still be inexorably drawn to you." (Isaiah 14:12-18)

Notwithstanding Isaiah's faulting words, the Lord did return certain powers to the Beast but with conditional restrictions put on their use. They could only be used to fulfill the Lord's plans for the redemption of the tribulation saints, and everything he does must perpetuate that end. The Beast will soon realize that this was going to be a daunting task. It would be far more difficult to get rid of the myriad of believers through death than bring about the expulsion of the Jewish remnant into the desert.

But you can well imagine that the Beast's top priority will be focused on adding these same converts to his kingdom, rather than driving them away. And he will do whatever it takes to seduce all

211

the people of the world into surrendering their will and soul to him.

Admittedly, some of the methods he uses to achieve that goal are pretty radical. Two proclamations in particular that were handed down from the throne of the Beast, authorized the death penalty for anyone who refused to submit to his demands of ownership and worship. These edicts immediately caught the attention of the Lord and He rebuked the Beast for initiating them, but only because of their deceitful inspiration and not because of their intended purpose. Consequently He didn't try and stop them from being enacted. He made counterclaims of His own and issued them through the voice of angels circling the globe.

If the world doesn't recognize that it's the Devil on the throne in Brussels, it's unlikely that the saints would recognize that it was he that was issuing these mandates. And had not the Lord made these announcements from heaven countermanding the mandates of the Devil, the saints would undoubtedly have misconstrued these edicts as being judgments sent down from God, and that misconception, if only in a few of the believers, would certainly effect their decision making. And when Satan allowed that misconception to continue without retraction or explanation, the Lord rebuked him

The only excuse that Christians today might have for making the same error would be in their misunderstanding of the linkage between the Lord's program of deliverance and the Beast's program for gaining converts. The two are entirely different programs but mutually dependent on the same mandates. One is a mission to prove converts for the Lord and bring about their deliverance to heaven, while the other is the Devil's own missionary effort to bring converts to himself.

The linkage between the two missions can be seen the following scripture which opens with a general announcement that the yearned for salvation and redemption of His saints is nigh at hand, but before the Lord Christ comes, 'the accuser,' (Satan) must make his appearance. Ostensibly, this was to accomplish his first mission of evacuating the Jews from their homeland, whereupon the second verse depicts his secondary mission of 'operation rescue' of the believers.

"I heard a loud voice saying in heaven, <u>Now is come</u>

salvation, and strength, and the kingdom of our God, and the power of his Christ: for the accuser of our brethren is (now being) **cast down,"** **(11) And they** (will) **overcome him by the blood of the Lamb, and by the word of their testimony; and they loved not their lives unto the death."** (Rev.12:10,11)

Here we see that Satan has just been cast down to the earth, and when the saints in heaven hear the good news they ring praises and glory to God for they know that the process of redemption for the remnant of Jewish saints had begun and their patience had been rewarded, while the second verse projects an affirmation of the Lord's program of redemption and deliverance of the world's believers.

Both of the latter mandates appear on the surface to be an inducement to all individuals, whether they were believers or not, to give homage to the Beast, or suffer the consequences, whereas in the earlier mandates, the consequences of refusing honor to the Beast were not life threatening. However they were also ineffective in accomplishing the deliverance. And what has to be brought out to the believers at that time, is the necessity of forfeiting their lives rather giving in to the Beast's demands. This facet was clearly brought out in the announcements given by angels circling the earth.

John also cautions the believers about the Beast's deceitful mandates, but at the same time he leans heavily on the reason for their implementation. In the midst of his text he figuratively waves a red flag in the face of those who might find themselves in this predicament. He says: *"If any man hath an ear let him hear."* (Rev.13: 9) Or to put it more succinctly;

" Reader: please understand why the Beast is doing all this."

This is an attempt on John's part to draw attention to the purpose behind these awful mandates. He's telling us, as well as the clandestine believers of that day, that before them is a tunnel of fire that must be gone through as a test of their faith. He then follows this up with a challenging ultimatum which hopefully will stir the wavering believer into making the right choice.

"He that makes his choice for captivity will assuredly go into captivity, and he that makes his choice to die rather than submit will assuredly be killed. Their choice will prove the faith of the believer."

213

(Rev. 13:10 paraphrased)

The willingness to suffer as Christ suffered and died on the cross, has through the ages been the supreme test of the believer's faith, and literally millions of people in the past came to the point where they had to make a choice between Christ or death, and in most cases they were martyred for choosing Christ. We can thank God that we have never had to make that choice for our salvation and redemption, but it will have to be made by everyone who becomes a believer during the tribulation period, and unfortunately, their physical life will have to be forfeited during that same period in order to achieve their redemption and deliverance. John put this challenge very succinctly when he said:

"They become the ones who will come out of (the) great tribulation, and (they) will have washed their robes and made them white in the blood of the Lamb." (Rev. 6:9-11, 7:14-17, 20:4)

John closes out his exposition on those despotic two years with this mollifying thought, which presupposes that the believer will have made his or her choice to accept death rather than submit to the Devil:

"Blessed are the dead which die in the Lord from henceforth: Yea saith the Spirit, that they may rest from their labors; and their works do follow them." (Rev. 14:13)

But no matter how you cut it, this sacrifice will be an extremely difficult choice to make. To obey the laws of the government and succumb to the urgent needs of the family, or refuse the mark of the Beast and give your life over to starvation or martyrdom. Families are involved here, and in many cases there is the fate of children at stake. The easy choice is to accept the mark of the Beast, after all, what can it hurt to give in, nobody will know the difference, and it can't last forever. But sadly enough, God will know, and it will last forever. How much simpler it would be if a person made that choice for the Savior now instead of waiting until the tribulation

On the other side of the coin, the Beast finds out that things are not progressing the way he had anticipated. World conditions are in a sad state following the earthquake with a floundering economy and

214

reconstruction at a standstill. Since the Rapture, society in general has seen a marked decline in morality and ethics and a dramatic increase in lawlessness. In just such an atmosphere religion gained prominence, and with little interference in their religious activities around the world, people continued to worship in their customary way. But all that was about to change.

The great tribulation period had already begun, the Beast has been given his power over the world, and he is ready to thrust forward in his mission to search and destroy all believers in his newly begotten kingdom. John records this stage in world affairs with these words;

"He was given power over all kindred, and tongues, and nations. (that) All that dwell upon the earth shall worship him, whose names are not written in the book of life of the Lamb slain from the foundation of the world.' (Rev. 13:7,8) *(and) In his wrath he went forth to attack the remnant of her seed, which keep the commandments of God, and have the testimony of Jesus Christ."* (Rev. 12:17)

The first mandates coming forth from the Beast were fairly tolerant with limited sanctions for failure to obey. After all, his intentions were to woo the people of the world into worshipping him in place of the Lord. This seems like an almost impossible task, but remember, the Beast is an extremely manipulative and furtive individual, particularly in dealing with people. With the assistance of his co-conspirator, the False Prophet, he performs some amazingly supernatural feats, such as bringing fire down from heaven, and other dubious miracles in an attempt to convince the world of his deity. Presumably, through these acts and his other powers of persuasion he will achieve a certain amount of success, but apparently he was disappointed in the results, so he went one step further.

The places of godly worship had to be closed because the continued propagation of the Creator within those walls presented stiff competition for the Beast, so he mandated their closing. Here again, there was little response or backlash from the secular masses of society, but there was firm resistance from some of the major Protestant organizations as well as the hierarchy of the Greek

215

Orthodox and Roman Catholic churches, which refused to cooperate with the authorities. But gradually even these were forced to succumb to the pressures of the Beast, and one by one the great cathedrals and Temples, including St. Peters in Rome, unwillingly closed their doors and their priests and preachers scattered along with the congregations. But this action of the Beast only confirmed to the populace that he was indeed the destroyer as Isaiah had said, and the closings only tended to bolster the faith of the people rather than destroy it. Simply depriving the congregations of their places of worship only drove the dedicated believers underground.

But there was one irony in the closing down of the churches, and that had to do with the Vatican, which had been the unofficial seat of Satan's earthly operations for the past 1700 years. It was from there that he had guided the world-wide expansion of his alternative gospel, which deceived and distorted the precious soul-winning Gospel of Christ into a gospel of a salvation that was only available through the Roman church. This destroyed the testimony of what could have otherwise been a great church with a tremendous witness for the Lord, but now he is bent on finishing his own creation.

So far the mandates have had little effect upon the true believers, other than discomfiting them along with the rest of the worshippers. It certainly hasn't drawn any of them to sacrifice their life, and it seems as though the Beast's efforts are directed more to obtaining adherents than promoting the work of the Lord.

At this time, there was also some hope within the predominantly Catholic Union Council, that the Roman Church would canonize their leader, making him more acceptable to the people in the giving of their homage, but he refused any form of compromise, still maintaining that he had been anointed.

Now that he has driven millions of possible worshippers underground and his tenure is slowly running out, his anger and resolve to achieve more control over the world becomes more insidious and life threatening. In a warped attempt to gain homage, he has an amazing lifelike image of himself constructed and set in the middle of St. Peter's Square in the Vatican for the whole world to look upon, and wonder and worship. It becomes a visible icon for all peoples to bow before, and to some degree it has been successful, but only because there was a stipulation in the mandate which said that failure to bow down, could, at the discretion of the Beast, invoke the death penalty.

For some reason he has reverted to the practice of the ancient kings who set up images of themselves for all to bow down to and worship. All of this was not lost on the Lord who has been carefully monitoring the outpouring of the Beast's wrath. To go this far a-field in the seduction of the people gives a strong indication that the policies of the Beast are ill suited to draw homage from the crowd. They will acquiesce but only to save their lives.

John reminds us that the Beast's intentions are to have everyone on earth worship him, (Rev.13: 8) and whether a person does so under duress or voluntarily, is irrelevant. However, if we read behind the lines of the scriptures, we can picture the Beast's frustration at not reaching the numbers of people he desires, and as a result, his wrath increases and his desperation grows.

However, there could be another reason for his building of the image with the accompanying death threat. If we assume that a major portion of the people on the earth will submit to the Beast and yield their allegiance to him, if only outwardly to save their lives, then his death threat could only have been directed toward those holdouts, who up until now have had little or no incentive to voluntarily forfeit their lives. And he is certainly not going to let the believers know that this was to be the first real test of their faith.

A short time later there was an accompanying mandate that required everyone to receive a permanent identification mark, either on their forehead or on their right hand. It was a simple request with any number of laudable economic reasons for receiving it, including the security of employment, the ability to purchase food or clothing, while on the other hand, failure to do so would mean ostracism from the community and the social stigma of not having the mark, though nothing was ever mentioned about the life threatening consequences for anyone who wouldn't take the mark.

Herein lay the ultimate test of the believer's faith, but they had no way of knowing that, and there was no reason to believe that the Christians would recognize the deceitful purpose of these mandates, other than by the faith within them. Moreover, millions of people, including the believers, will have no inkling that it's the Devil sitting on the throne of the world and issuing these insidious mandates. This puts them in a dangerous decision-making situation. Which is why, before the final mandates went into effect, the Lord responded to these ultimatums by fostering on the world His own words of warning as well as encouragement to the believers whose faith is being sorely tried.

He did this by interposing three encyclical messages to the worlds' populace through His intermediating angels, which clearly identified the Lord as being the Creator and one who should be worshipped.

As you recall, this angelic method of communicating the Lord's mercy was done once before during the time of the Trumpet judgments, when He announced the dire warnings about the three 'Woes' to be put upon the Jews. In this situation, the angels broadcast similar warnings to all the world, to better convince them of the reality and seriousness of the decisions they face. Now at least, the believers know what their decisions must be to obtain deliverance and salvation.

The angelic messages were separated because of their content and purpose, with the first being a straight forward statement to gain attention and let the populace know whom they should fear and give their worship to.

"Fear God, and give Glory to Him; for the hour of His Judgment is upon them; worship Him who made heaven, and earth, and the sea, and all life." (Rev. 14:7)

Following that, another angel circled the globe in the same fashion, and gave forth his message. But his was an announcement of the fate of the city of Rome, because she had, until the closing of her doors, served Satan well. That city however, would not be destroyed for another year and a half, but this is a pronouncement to the peoples still within the Roman enclave to reach out and put their trust in God, and not in the church. (Rev.14:8)

Soon after, a third angel followed the other two, circling the world until all had heard his message. His will be the last poignant warning to all those who might otherwise ignore the previous messages, and as such it was a direct warning of what the eternal consequences would be if they took the mark of the Beast.

"If any man shall worship the beast and his image, and receive his mark in his forehead, or in his hand, the same shall drink of the wine of the wrath of God, which is poured out without mixture into the cup of his indignation; and he shall be tormented with fire and brimstone in the presence of the holy angels, and in the presence of the Lamb; and the smoke of their torment will ascend up for ever and ever: and they shall have no rest day nor night, <u>whosoever worships the beast and his image, and takes upon him the mark of his name."</u> (Rev. 14: 9-11)

This was a rather lengthy communication, but it would be the last warning against submission to the Beast. Not only will those who worship the Beast and take the mark of his name, have to suffer God's wrath in the great tribulation, as children of the Devil they will be sentencing themselves to eternal punishment.

The moment of truth has arrived and time is running out. A simple choice must be made between abject slavery or deliverance. And in this challenge will be revealed the tribulation believer's worthiness for salvation, or as the scripture says;

"for herein is revealed the faith of the believer."

And if their choice is for the Lord, their decision is borne out in these words:

"They overcame him (that is the Beast) **by the blood of the Lamb and by the word of their testimony; <u>and they loved not their lives unto the death."</u>**   (Rev. 12:11)

And in so doing they have presented an acceptable offering to God, for *"<u>Blessed</u> are those which die in the Lord from henceforth: Yea, said the Spirit, they may rest from their labors; and their sacrifice will bear them witness"* (Rev. 14:13)

There is no doubt that with the horrendous mandates coming out from the Beast, the times will be disruptive and disparaging for everybody on earth. But as terrible as the conditions in the world may be, the actions taken by the Beast at that time must not be construed as being part of the final series of Vial judgments. They have yet to come down from God. This particular two-year time frame within the great tribulation period has been set aside by God strictly for the purpose of delivering up the tribulation saints <u>before</u> the judgments of the great tribulation rain down.

Also, a word of caution here for those who may find themselves in the predicament of having to decide on whether to live or die. According to the scriptures there is no allowance in the resurrection program for anyone who stays free of worshipping the Beast or taking his mark simply through escapism or isolation. Without their sacrifice they will miss the golden opportunity for resurrection and must suffer through the great tribulation with the rest of the world. Their next opportunity for eternal life will not come for another one thousand years when they stand before the Great White Throne judgment and hear their names called out from the book of life.

In retrospect, we can assume that Satan knew that God would be deliberately using him for His own purposes and that he had no alternative but to go along with it. It undoubtedly filled him with great wrath, but there was one consolation in it for him. Rather than being sent back into the pit for all eternity he could reach for the brass ring and hope that it carried with it at least a taste of power and glory. And in his mind he believes that if he can achieve this glory for one fleeting moment, he will be like God, and he isn't about to pass up that chance.

But strive as he may to try and catch that ring, he finds himself unable to be freed from the obligation of serving the Lord. Which ever tack he makes, or whatever scheme he devises, the work for the Lord follows him like a shadow. When he reaches higher, the number of believers abounds, and when he sinks deeper in depravity the converts to heaven multiplies. For behind every action he makes, there is the underlying decision that believers must make, whether to remain in their present fleeting life and sacrifice their soul to the Beast, or trust in the Lord for deliverance.

Footnote:

Christians today who unwittingly apply the '*Historical Scheme of Interpretation*' to the scriptures, inadvertently 'spiritualize' these scriptures in their connotation that _all_ believers will be required to go through a period of final examination of their faith by putting themselves to the extreme test of "trial by blood." It is assumed that God will conduct this testing through His angels on an individual basis. This life or death testing can be likened to the test that was put upon Abraham when he was instructed to sacrifice his son Isaac on the altar. He passed the test and 'his faith was counted to him for righteousness,' the scripture says. Should any adult or child fail the test, they would be simply thrown back into the sea of unbelievers. This interpretation is in direct violation of Romans 8: 38-39 which stipulates that no power can separate the believer from Christ.

On the other hand, it is believed, should a person's faith be found strong enough, (and it's generally assumed that everyone will fit into this category) they will be deemed worthy of being called out in a "mid-tribulation" Rapture. However, this belief relegates the Trumpet judgments on the Jews to a period of testing on all peoples before the qualified "wrath of God comes upon the world," which here again is a gross adulteration of the scriptures and defrauds the purposes of God, especially when the plan has been so clearly established.

CHAPTER 17

The Anti-Christ

Throughout history there have been many celebrated individuals, both good an evil, whose imprints on society have endured for a season before fading into anonymity, but none can compare with the 'Beast' of Revelation whose mark on mankind will last forever. Though his name might ever remain a mystery to the world, his fame will continue through time as the epitome of all that is evil. Even the mere mention of his name, "The Beast" raises a fear in man that far exceeds any fear of Godly judgment, and his mark of possession stands forth as the eternal talisman of the apocalypse.

When we speak of the Beast of Revelation, we are talking about a fearsome composite being of the celestial Satan and the human Anti-Christ. John gives a fairly liberal biography of the Satanic side of the Beast, but when it comes to the human side, he offers very little, other than the fact that he was born of Jewish stock whose parents had migrated to Europe from the Middle East before the terrible years of the Nazi holocaust. In his academic years, Simon Ballarius was undoubtedly a brilliant scholar in the university, and when he chose to go into politics after his graduation, his personality and aptitude brought him quickly to the forefront in leadership capabilities, but in other aspects he was no different from the multitudes of other unregenerate men who seek the power and prestige of leadership positions.

He was admired by his colleagues for his pragmatic and wise decisions, and his name would frequently come up when important leadership posts needed to be filled. So it came as no surprise to anyone, that when he was selected to be a representative on the Council of the European Union, he would fill the job well. And when he was chosen to be President of that same Council he had reached the pinnacle of his career.

But he had no way of knowing that his rise to political greatness had been predestined by the Lord, and that his Presidency was only one step away from global dominion and authority that would one day rattle the very gates of heaven.

It's more than probable that he would have performed his new Presidential duties diligently and successfully in a world that was still fraught with trade unbalances, economic problems and a situation in the Near East that continued to hang in the balance. Soon after his inauguration, it became his frustrating assignment to try and bring peace in the region where so many others had failed. And to what extent his Jewish background biased his decision making, we'll never know, but he evidently acted in good faith in his dealings with both the participants during those weeks of tedious negotiations. Finally, through much diplomatic maneuvering and a lot of persuasion, he managed to produce a tangible peace agreement for both sides.

Though little news of European events ever reaches America, this peace accord was the exception, and it focused a new recognition on the leadership qualities of the President that would serve him well in the near future.

More importantly than what the world sees in the man though, are the attributes that the Lord saw in him before bringing him into leadership. Those close to him knew that he was a secular Jew and that he occasionally dabbled in satanic rights, but he had no noticeably sinister flaws. Nor did he ever display evidence of being a religious person, or for that matter, show condemnation for the religiosity of others, but the Lord would have us to know that in him lies the same dormant infamy of treachery and deceit as Judas had when he was chosen for the purpose of betraying the Lord.

The Old Testament prophet Daniel was given many visions of this individual, and he probably comes closer in his description of him than others. He verbalized the sinister nature of this 'evil king' as being much like the ancient King Nebuchadnezzar of Babylon. Both of whom had power of life and death over their people. This is seen in this passage describing him after his incarnation.

"(He) **became mighty in power, but not by his own power; and he shall destroy wonderfully, and shall prosper, and practice, and shall destroy the mighty and the holy people. (25) And through his policy** (under his leadership) **also he shall cause craft to prosper in his hand; and he shall magnify himself in his**

223

heart, and by peace shall destroy many: he shall also stand up against the Prince of princes; (Jesus)   (Dan. 8:24-25)

Here is a ruler who might be described as a benevolent despot, capable of doing great things to improve the living standards and prosperity with increased production and trade through out the world, which he may well do, but at the same time he will be arrogant, terribly cruel and barbaric in his treatment of the Jews. And he even has the effrontery to ridicule the Lord, showing a much different attitude from his earlier years when he was deemed to be trustworthy and affable and far less than invincible.

The change in his nature appeared after his intervention into the war between Israel and the Arab states where he was viewed as a commanding, arrogant, and a determined individual, who outwardly displayed no evil traits. Certainly a likely candidate for an Anti-Christ. The following scriptures were intended to describe the invasion scene of his Union troops into Israel, however they give us a rather candid background picture of the man going into that confrontation.

"He shall regard neither the God of his fathers, nor the desire of women, nor any god: for he shall magnify himself above all. (38) But in his estate shall he honor the God of forces: and a god whom his fathers knew not shall he honor with gold, and silver, and with precious stones, and pleasant things. (39) Thus shall he do in the most strong holds with a strange god, whom he shall acknowledge and increase with glory: and he shall cause them to rule over many, and shall divide the land for gain." (Dan. 11:37-39)

Although the Apostle Paul was familiar with Daniel's account of the evil king, he had his own reservations about this person, and he doesn't picture him being dressed in the finery of the land but cloaked about with the spirit of Satan, and fully identifiable with being his son. He depicts this person as being the despised Anti-Christ, but stops short of identifying him as such. And where Daniel possibly was trying to soften his view of the man in light of the actions he took against the his fellow Jews, which in some aspects showed concern for their physical welfare, Paul envisions this same individual as being an adversary of the believers, a man who reaches deep for the souls of the weaker ones who might easily be swept away by his deceptive signs and lying wonders, using words like,

"Even him, whose coming is after the working of Satan," and again, *"that man of sin and the son of perdition."* (Dan. 8:24,25) (II Thess. 2: 9)

Both writers were talking about the same man in the interim period following his inauguration, however, both recognized that there was something more to him than meets the eye. They even surmised that in some way Satan was orchestrating the actions of the man, though neither of them were likely aware of the coming incarnation event.

Whereas the most distinctive characteristic of Satan, while he was still in the spirit form, was his anger, and this he brought down with him. He came down in such a state of rage and bitterness against God for removing him from heaven, that when he was deposited in the frame of a human, and that of a Jew, no less, his wrath increased beyond measure. But the irony of the situation, is the way that God uses that wrath, and even depends on it to underscore the mission that He has for the Beast.

The President's former blase disposition would ill fit the requirements that God needed in a world ruler. Whereas the 'new' President will be a person who is domineering, oppressive and extremely intrusive into private lives, attributes that would allow him to complete the harvest in time. Provided of course, that he is given the help of an eager assistant, a man very much like himself who will take on the administrative responsibilities of the Presidency and be his ambassador to the people. Of this other man's character we are told nothing, except that he is a virtual clone of a master who gives him super-natural powers to assist him in deceiving the world. (Rev. 13: 12,13)

CHAPTER 18

The Vials of Wrath

For two years the Beast has been running roughshod over the earth, pressing his claim for the souls of men while delivering an endless stream of innocents to the gallows. He had an insatiable desire for homage and a determination to expend any effort to achieve it. In the meantime, the world under him has been slipping into chaos. His promised utopian society has been diverted into twenty-four months of hell on earth where thousands upon thousands of precious believers have been slaughtered on the gallows of the Beast, while millions more have been driven into the wilderness under his insane purge. Now however, the fateful moment has arrived when the unregenerate world and the myriads who bear his mark are slated to suffer the consequences of their decisions with no avenue of escape.

But for the martyrs who have been raised to eternal life the promised blessings are just beginning. The testimony of their deliverance is a scene of a jubilant celebration in heaven, where all of the redeemed who have been delivered out of the tribulation have been united with their waiting brethren and gathered before the Throne in a joyous occasion of praise and Glory to God. (Rev. 6:9-11, 15:1-4)

But following the glorious celebration, the Throne room is emptied to the last man so that the preparations for the judgments may begin. There will be no one allowed in the presence of God while He is "filling the vials with His wrath" to be sent down to the earth. Seven angels have been summoned before Him and to each is given a container which is said to be full of the wrath of God, and which they are told to judiciously pour out when they are instructed.

The picture John gives of that awesome and frightening moment when the Temple was suddenly filled with smoke from the Glory of God, makes you feel as though you're right there with him. Though no one is allowed to witness that explosion of anger, John hopes that he can portray for the non-listening world the emotional outburst of the wrath of God that is projected at the Beast and all those who choose to worship him. His outburst might have even included this earlier denunciation given by the angel,

"They shall drink of the wine of the wrath of God, which is poured out without mixture into the cup of His indignation; and they shall be tormented with fire and brimstone in the presence of the holy angels, and in the presence of the Lamb: And their cries of torment shall ascend up for ever and ever: and they shall have no rest day nor night, who worship the beast and his image, and whosoever receives the mark of his name."   (Rev. 14:10,11)

The world is being told that their coming suffering under the Vial judgments is nothing compared to what's waiting for them at the Great White Throne judgment to follow. There, they are told, the wrath of God will be undiluted with mercy or tolerance, and their present grief is but a taste of the torment for eternity for those who reject the Lord and favor the Beast.

John presumably knew beforehand what these Vial plagues consisted of because he has read the little book, but this unscripted development in the Throne room was essential to the initiation of the judgments, and his exclusion from the presence of God at this time was because he was not permitted to look upon the wrathful face of God. Thus he found himself outside of the Temple area like everyone else; patiently waiting for the administering angels to emerge from behind closed doors.

When the doors finally did open, the angels emerged, dressed in their pure white linen robes and each carrying a vial given to them by one of the four beasts that circled the Throne. When the last one had exited the Temple, the doors were immediately shut, sealing the Temple and the Throne room once again from any intrusion until all of the plagues had been administered.

Again, before the administering of the plagues by the angels, there was a brief period of silence throughout heavens, along with a heavy sense of anticipation of the terrible things that lay in store for the earth, when all of sudden a great thundering voice issued from the Temple, saying to the seven Angels,

"Go your ways, and pour out the vials of the wrath of God upon the earth."

And anxiously the angels did His bidding, This was the only verbal directive to commence the tribunal, and had not the angels been told beforehand of their individual responsibilities and directions for distributing the plagues, it's quite possible that all of the seven plagues might have been dumped at once. But as it was;

"The first went, and poured out his vial upon the earth; and there fell a noisome and grievous sore upon the men who had the mark of the beast, and upon them which worshipped his image." (Rev.16: 2)

This first plague of the great tribulation is a pestilence that has never been experienced before, and it comes in such a vast epidemic proportion that only a miniscule number of people will escape it. It's an infectious epidermal disease with sores which will undoubtedly be painful as the word 'noisome' seems to indicate, and though an individual might have many of these grievous swellings on their body they will not prove fatal, even as the pestilence of the demon spirits on the Jews were not fatal in themselves.

Like some epidemics in the past, it will spread rapidly through the schools and work places by physical contact and the handling of contaminated articles. It's very possible that these sores will be similar to the boils experienced in the ancient Egyptian plague, (Exodus 9) or the painful sores that covered the body of Job, but it is more likely that this is a new strain of virus for which there is no ready cure.   Fortunately, modern antibiotics and medicines will help relieve the pain and the sores may appear to heal over but the lesion simply breaks out in another area. The plague however, is unremitting and continues through the remainder of the tribulation period, serving as a humiliating and painful reminder of the power of God. Strangely enough, this hits people where they feel it the most, in their pride and self-assurance.

This plague however, like the former plague of the demon spirits will not arbitrarily blanket all peoples, but will be dispersed only upon those who had accepted the mark of the Beast and worshipped his image. Left out again will be the remnant of the Jews in seclusion in the city of Petra, the 144,000 young Jewish men spread around the world, and by chance, those who have hidden away from the reach of the Beast, and had not taken his mark, nor worshipped his image. In any case, the intention of this plague was to pass an indictment against the pride and obduracy of mankind in accepting Satan over the Lord, however the real punishing judgments have yet to follow.

Incidentally, this pestilence, by its coming first in the line of plagues, sends a signal that God has adopted the same pattern of selective plagues upon the Gentiles that He had laid upon the Jews during their indignation, even though the circumstances under which they are applied differ greatly. In the great tribulation period, the Lord will be dealing with billions of peoples from widely differing cultures and environments, however the types of plagues, namely the pestilence, famine and war will remain the same and their sequence will follow the outline prescribed by the prophet Ezekiel. The first plague being pestilence, will soon be accompanied by global famine with severely restricted fresh water supplies, and lastly, the dreaded plague of war, which in this case is not a global confrontation but a confined single battle, wherein armies from around the world will be combined into a single force and under the command of the Beast, who will then battle against the solitary figure of the Lord of Lords near Jerusalem.

The plagues that were put upon the Jews during their time of indignation were consistent with that pattern, so naturally, the same pattern will be used in the great tribulation, with one slight difference. Where the former plagues were intended as punishments on both the land and the Jewish population, there was an added stipulation in both the fifth and sixth punishments, which required the specific demise of two-thirds of the Jewish population in order to reduce their numbers to a remnant of their former status. In that aspect, the prophecy of Ezekiel was followed precisely, whereas in this round of plagues that stipulation has been waived and there is no definitive mortality requirement. This was not an oversight of the Lord's, but the result of purposeful planning of the punishments, which were designated for retaliatory measures and not for decimating the world population, although there will, without a doubt, be myriads of peoples who will succumb to death in any or all of them. In this respect, some countries of the world will be affected more than others, depending on their primary food sources. Heavily congested urban areas again will be the hardest hit because food supplies in these areas will be generally in short supply due to transportation difficulties that have continued since the destructive earthquakes some three years earlier.

There are three main food sources available to mankind. These are fish from the oceans, cereal grains and fruit, and meat sources, with each of these presently in such a delicate balance of supply that even the slightest variation in the food chain could send shock waves of fear through non-producing communities.

The global extent of the protracted famine, continuing as it does through the remaining eighteen months of the great tribulation, will be a far cry from any localized or even national emergency that we have seen in the past. As you can well imagine, blanketing the earth in famine, even in such a relatively short space of time is a monumental undertaking, especially when you consider the diverse regimes of diets around the world. It would seem that the only way that a universal famine could possibly be accomplished would be through a drastic alteration of the weather patterns around the world. This would be above and beyond the already slowed growth and maturation cycle of the grain crops resulting from the increased rotational speed of the earth.

Global weather patterns will in fact be altered on a scale never before experienced, so that on every continent the critical balance of vital food products, whether they are grains, vegetables, or fruits will be totally destabilized through the disruption of the planting and harvesting cycles, until the world is thrown into chaos and famine. Examples of this type of weather pattern change are readily seen in the worldwide 'El Nino' effect, and to some degree the 'green house' effect that we are now experiencing.

In a brief review of these famine inducing judgments, we find the first one tackling the one primary food source that is not subject to the weather conditions, this being the fish supply from the oceans.

The judgment calls for the daily catch of fish in the oceans to be sharply diminished, thereby initiating the process of starvation upon those nations and peoples whose primary food source is from the sea. The next one exacerbates the hunger situation by eliminating much of the world's potable water supplies as well as the vital irrigation needs. The third in line eradicates the potential moisture from rains and snow for the planted crops, while the last of these four judgments dismisses any hope of a harvesting crops, by bringing on unseasonably freezing temperatures world-wide. This completes the cycle of the plagues on the food crops and meat sources. How effective this pattern of plagues will be in the one or possibly two growing and harvesting cycles is conjectural, but the intention is not to destroy completely but to punish.

The remaining two judgments swing from the 'famine mode' and deal with the third phase of punishments, that of war. Not a war of global proportions, such as a Third World War, as some have speculated, but a selective combat in a predetermined location in Israel where massive numbers of representative troops from around the world will congregate in a small combat area.

The sixth judgment involves the preparations that will be made by the Beast preparatory to this final conflict, with the seventh judgment being the war itself. In this case, the battle will be fought between the solitary figure of the Lord against the amassed forces of the Beast, who, by his time has come to realize that his reign on earth is about over and he must make this last stand to seize control of the earth. This battle culminates the tribulation period.

The cycle of 'universal starvation' begins with the first of four 'famine-inducing punishments' wherein the seas are suddenly devoid of fish, although John expresses it in a somewhat different manner when he says;

"And the second angel poured out his vial upon the sea; and it became as the blood of a dead man; and every living soul died in the sea." (every living thing was gone from the sea.) (Rev 16:3)

Right away the Lord invokes the method that man uses to bring about starvation of an enemy, that of withholding the food supply, and in this case the source is from the oceans. He takes the simple approach for initiating a world famine by severely limiting the daily catch of fish by commercial fishermen.

Many have wondered if this plague wouldn't be man's massive poisoning or pollution of the seas that kills off the fish, but such is

231

not the case. This plague entails a directive from the knowing Creator who charged man in the beginning to obtain a portion of his food supply from the sea, and who now unobtrusively disperses that precious marine food source from man's ability to retrieve it. The daily catch grows less each day and as it does the first tentacles of famine begin enveloping the world.

John uses the idiom **"became as the blood of a dead man,"** in describing the condition of the ocean waters when they become void of its life giving sustenance, just as the draining of blood brings on death. Soon the seas will give forth none of their needed food source, because the Lord will either diminish or scatter it into inaccessible waters, and seemingly overnight, oceans which in the past had furnished upward of a third of the world's food, become barren. The men of the fishing fleets will not understand what is going on, when day after day their nets come up empty, and it's going to be a desperate situation all around.

The Lord demonstrated this power over the catch of fish in the Sea of Galilee one afternoon when His disciples went fishing. When nothing came up in the net which was throne from one side of the boat, He told them to cast their net from the other side, whereupon the net came up so full of fish that they could not drag them into the boat. (John 21:6)

The next phase of the famine process came in a more dramatic way when the third angel followed the command of God and loosed his plague upon the fresh water sources, and they became contaminated.

"And the third angel poured out his vial upon the rivers and fountains of waters; and they became blood. (Rev.16: 4)

The effects from this plague are cataclysmic. The normal flow of water from lakes and rivers and even underground sources is turned into blood, or otherwise contaminated, which seems inconceivable to us. John validates this contamination of the water with the same angel's remark that this was in retaliation for man's destruction of the saints and prophets.

This plague is similar to the one in ancient Egypt, when the Lord turned all of the waters of the Nile, including its tributaries and lakes, and all of the stored water into blood, which forced the people to dig wells to survive. The waters remained contaminated for seven days until the Lord removed the plague. As for this plague, there seems to be no time limit on its application but there is also no indication that precipitations of rain or snow were contaminated, nor that which is stored in reservoirs. But there is no reason to believe that they wouldn't become contaminated by infusion with the running streams of 'water.' How long the stored water reserves will last, or if they become polluted we can only conjecture, but even with severe rationing these stores would be soon depleted. On the other hand, the lack of irrigation water severely limits the planting of food crops, which will be compounded by the next plague that brings a prolonged drought over the whole world.

When the fourth angel directed his plague against the sun, the result was excessively long periods of higher than usual temperatures. The normal cycles of high and low pressure systems in the atmosphere which produce the needed moisture, have been radically altered, so that severe drought conditions exist for weeks at a time pressuring the crops to dry up. Feed crops for farm animals suffer along with the rest, further exacerbating the conditions for world famine.

"And the fourth angel poured out his vial upon the sun; and power was given unto him to scorch men with fire. (9) And men were scorched with great heat, and blasphemed the name of God, which hath power over these plagues: and they repented not to give Him glory." (Rev. 16:8-9)

Not withstanding the primary purpose of this plague, which was to bring on these drought conditions, the punishment aspect of it on the people is equally devastating. If the earth had never experienced excessive heat we would not know how easily a person could be overcome by it, particularly if it's over long periods of time. The heat tolerance level of the human body is relatively high, but only for short periods. For instance, in the mid-western United States, during July of 1995, the temperatures reached 112 degrees Fahrenheit, with high humidity, allowing some dwellings without air-cooling to reach temperatures of 130-135 degrees. Under these conditions over 350 people in the region collapsed and died from heat prostration. A few days later the same temperatures and weather patterns were experienced in Europe, where hundreds more succumbed to the heat.

Through all of this, and knowing full well that God is pouring this upon them, there is no repentance, nor pleading to God for relief. Only blasphemy comes out of the hardened hearts and between the parched lips. The excessive heat wave does not abate even at night, and the shortage of refreshing water becomes more acute than ever.

This situation continues for several weeks before the Lord relents and allows the water sources to turn fresh again and the heat of the sun to cool down. Overnight the streams and rivers once again bring forth the precious life-saving water and people are revived for the moment.

But then, without warning the fifth punishment is cast upon the earth and it becomes shrouded in darkness.

"And the fifth angel poured out his vial upon the seat of the beast; and his kingdom was full of darkness; and they gnawed their tongues for pain, (Rev. 16:10)

God, in His own inimitable way, has darkened the sun in this plague, by shielding the rays from passing through the atmosphere, to warm the earth. Whether He has used the black clouds of rain to surround the earth or placed the moon between the sun and our globe in a continual eclipse, the whole earth remains shaded from the light and warmth of the sun. While for weeks the earth had suffered under its oppressive heat, and the people cried for respite from the searing sun, now its light remains hidden and the atmosphere turns cold, and in their bitterness and suffering they curse God all the more. Finally, the Lord relents and the clouds are rolled away, the darkness is broken, the days and nights become tolerable again, and there is neither excessive heat or freezing cold.

Through the past eighteen months and five terrible plagues, people all over the world have been scourged and punished to the limit with pestilence and famine. Untold millions have died from disease and starvation, which presumably has sufficed to satisfy the Lord's vengeance. As the Lord suffered from being whipped by the Roman soldiers and forced to drag His cross on His tortured body through the streets to Calvary, so now must the living move their tortured bodies that have been wracked with hunger and thirst and bruised with the elements in their slow progression toward the final judgments.

Several months ago, the Beast had begun mobilizing a military force from around the world. He knew that his time was growing short and that there must be a final confrontation with God, but he imagines that this time the Creator will back away from destroying His precious creation. Still, he doesn't know what to expect.

In his last confrontation with God over the dominion of the world, he lost, and the earth was immersed in the flood, except for one family who was true to God. However in this conflict, the Beast knows that it is his life that will be on the line, and if he goes down, everyone goes down with him.

In the past few months, the economic and social conditions around the world have deteriorated rapidly. The famines, the unemployment, poverty and disease have completed the job. Civil strife is rampant in every land with continuous uprisings and killings, and a general contempt for law and order. The social order is near the breaking point. Anarchy prevails in many areas with the strong destroying the weak, and fear and mistrust pervades even through the family structure.

And amidst all of this, the sixth judgment slipped quietly on to the scene. There was nothing spectacular about its entrance, other than the fact that overnight it seems; the primal river of the Mid-East became a dry riverbed from beginning to end. To those living in the region it would have been an awesome experience, but elsewhere it caused little reaction. However to the one individual to whom this miracle was pointed, it was an expectant sign.

"The sixth angel poured out his vial upon the great river Euphrates; and the water thereof was dried up, that the way of the kings of the east might be prepared." (Rev. 16:12)

The Euphrates River was one of the irrigating waters of the Garden of Eden, and continues to flow today, some six thousand years later. It was this same river that many generations ago had been designated to be the eastern boundary of the promised land which was to be given to the descendants of Abraham. (Gen.15: 18) And it was in this same general area that the Arab armies had gathered for a war against Israel, but were restrained by the angels from advancing too soon. (Rev.9: 14)

It has its origin in eastern Turkey and flows through the countries of Syria and Iraq for 1700 miles, much of it un-navigable, before emptying into the Persian Gulf. However it provides no formidable barrier for any advancing armies, as the phrase " *way of the kings of the east might be prepared"* seems to imply, and it's for sure the Lord wouldn't be trying to make their journeying easier by affording them safe passage over a dry riverbed. Nor will He be sending any angels to aid in the mobilization preparations as He did earlier or issue any instructions by heavenly messengers.

In essence, the shutting down of the flow was meant to be a recognizable sign to the Beast, calling for the gathering of his troops for battle. It also sanctioned that only ground troops were to be used because of the vast numbers involved and the type of combat expected.

By this sign, the Beast recognizes that the end is near, and he becomes desperate and filled with wrath, sending out his commands to all the nations to mobilize and bring their armies to the valley of Megiddo in Israel. It's extremely unlikely that the world knows what is coming, or for that matter, anything of the Beast's diabolical plans to battle against God. In the countries of eastern Asia, where the Beast had little success in gaining adherents let alone receiving their worship, there were undoubtedly other inducements given to have them send their troops, but we are only told that he issued forth lies and deceit to get their consent. And the scriptures tell us that despite the emaciating plagues and the terrible conditions in the world at the time, the fidelity of the people to their master continues to draw millions to his side. Though we shouldn't forget that God has had a hand in this doomed situation, for some years back He had put the desire in their hearts to believe and trust in the Beast. (II Thess.2: 11)

THE STAGING AREA

The Beast and the False Prophet were in Israel weeks before the first armies came from Europe, planning the logistics of encampment space for the expected million or more troops to come. He intends to locate the main body of the vast army in the Valley of Megiddo, which is about 80 miles north of Jerusalem. This is the only flat area that is large enough to assemble such a vast army of men and machines, and will serve as the staging area. From here the armies will march south, in three columns, to reassemble for battle in the Kidron Valley, that lays on the east side of Jerusalem between the old city and the Mount of Olives.

As the time of engagement draws closer, the armies begin arriving at the staging area and the Beast moves his headquarters and staff to a location on Mt. Carmel, overlooking the valley from the south.

The following is a proclamation by one of the Old Testament Prophets that projects this future battle of Armageddon,

"Proclaim this among the Gentiles; Prepare war, wake up the mighty men, let all the men of war draw near, and let them come up. (For) **I will also gather all nations, and bring them into the valley of Jehoshaphat.** (Judgment) **Multitudes, multitudes in the valley of decision: for the day of the Lord is near in the valley of decision."** (Joel 3: 9, 14 and 2)

The world has no excuse for not knowing what is coming. This is not a typical war, nor is it just one battle of a many faceted war, as some would imagine. This is the one encounter between God and Satan in which Satan is ready to sacrifice every man in his army, if that is what it takes, to achieve victory over God and stave off his own demise.

It's reasonable to assume that the amassing of so many into one area will create a logistics problem. We can remember from the records of the war called Desert Storm in Iraq, which from the first deployment of the troops in Saudi Arabia until they actually went to the front lines took nearly six months. In this case, the logistical problem of amassing twice as many troops into this relatively small area will be even greater.

We can imagine that the patience of the Beast is growing thinner by the day and the troops are growing more restless. Anxiety runs high among the soldiers as the armies continue to roll in from around the world and compress into the staging area that is already swollen over its capacity, but still the leader waits for the Russian troops to show.

Meanwhile, the Lord above has been witnessing this gathering of the nations against Him, and His anger explodes with the fury of the seventh plague, sending it down in the form of another great earthshaking.

"And the seventh angel poured out his vial into the air; and there came a great voice out of the temple of heaven, from the throne, saying, It is done. (18) And there were voices, and thunders, and lightning; and there was a great earthquake, such as was not since men were upon the earth, so mighty an earthquake, and so great. (19) And the great city (Jerusalem) **was divided into three parts, and the cities of the nations fell; and great Babylon came in remembrance before God, to give unto her the cup of the wine of the fierceness of his wrath. (20) And every island fled away, and the mountains were not found. (21) And there fell upon men a great hail out of heaven, every stone about the weight of a talent: and men blasphemed God because of the plague of the hail; for the plague thereof was exceeding great."** (Rev. 16:17-21)

When the thunderous voice of God spoke the words **"IT IS DONE,"** He wasn't implying that everything about the judgments was finished at that moment, it only intoned the readiness of the situation on earth for the last judgment. It has come down to the last week of the most spellbinding days of the tribulation. Tremendous things are going to happen, beginning with the second great earthshaking. With time running out and so much to be done, the Lord began the countdown to Armageddon by bridling the earth and slowing down its rotation to the previous twenty-four hour day.

Immediately the earth began convulsing and violent storms ripped through the skies. In Megiddo the fury of the storms brought great ice chunks down from the sky, causing bedlam throughout the encampment. Thousands of soldiers were being killed by the missiles of ice, and the Russian troops, some of whom were already within the borders of Israel, were caught in the hill country and all but destroyed in the deluge of rain and great hailstones. (Ezek. 38:27)

Destruction around the world is beyond description and the adjectives "great," and "exceeding great" spoken of by John can hardly describe the convulsions of this great planet as it slows down in rotational speed. With the sudden diminishing of such great centrifugal energy all of the fractures and faults around the world are again moving and twisting. Mountains crumble, and in the oceans great tidal waves rise up and pound against the shores. Volcanoes burst open and throw their voluminous clouds of magma and poisonous gases into the sky while lava descends in torrents down their sides. Tornadoes and hurricanes sweep vast areas where other elements couldn't reach. There was no place to run and no escape from the fury of these disasters. All of the great cities are razed, and typically the mountains under Jerusalem were lifted and the city split asunder.

What a great and terrible tragedy has happened to this once beautiful planet. Continents have been shifted and changed in size, many great salt water basins are formed where former fresh water lakes once existed. The poles of the earth have been shifted slightly, and great islands of polar ice drift silently out to sea.

For three days and nights the sun was turned into darkness, and the moon into blood by the great palls of smoke and ash from the myriad of fires that refused to be extinguished. The world has never experienced such a terrible catastrophe, but even through it all there will be millions who will survive.

This earthshaking was prophesied by several of the Old Testament writers, who correctly ascribed these violent happenings with the coming of the Messiah. One of whom described the earthquake in these words,

"The earth shall quake before them; the heavens shall tremble: the sun and the moon shall be dark, and the stars shall withdraw their shining: (11) ... **for the day of the LORD is great and very terrible; and who can abide it"** (30) **"And I will show wonders in the heavens and in the earth, blood, and fire, and pillars of smoke. (31) The sun shall be turned into darkness, and the moon into blood, before the great and the terrible day of the LORD come."** (Joel 2: 10,11, 30,31)

Jesus quoted these very lines of the Prophet Joel, when he answered the Disciple's questions about the signs of His coming. Reiterating how the sun and the moon will become darkened, and the stars will have their light hidden by the smoke of the fires, He went on to say that these signs would immediately follow "the tribulation of those days," meaning of course, the tribulation on the Gentiles that has just been described (Matt. 24:29).

In the encampment there was heavy damage and a great number of casualties. The combination of the earthquake the deadly hail storms have cost the lives of over a third of the forces, and destroyed a large portion of the mechanized equipment. The dead from the storm have been quickly buried in shallow unmarked graves, while the wounded have been shifted into several large mess tents that have been hastily turned into infirmaries. Except for minor injuries, the Beast and most of his staff have miraculously escaped. However now the incentive for going to battle is beginning to wane in the weary soldiers, and the Beast must decide quickly to move out or the battle plans will be in jeopardy. He passes the message on to the army, that on the morrow at daybreak, the troops will move out.

Footnote:
In the book of Ezekiel in the Old Testament, chapters 38 and 39, we are given a prophetic account of a union of armed forces, under the headship of Russia, (Gog) being drawn down to the land of Israel to take part in the siege against Jerusalem in the last days.

At that particular time, their troops were spread out in long columns that were moving through the hills of Syria and northern Israel at the time of the earthquake. They were caught unexpectedly by the earthquakes in the area, along with the terrible ice storms, and unfortunately the eruption of a volcano in the area. With such terrible forces coming at them from all directions the troops became completely demoralized. Add to that, the fear of the Lord was so great in their hearts at that moment, that many of the wounded soldiers took their own lives, or begged others to kill them. Through it all, only a small number survived to continue on to the rendezvous.

The following is the prophecy of that momentous event, as recorded by the prophet Ezekiel,

"And thou shall come up against my people of Israel, as a cloud to cover the land; it shall be in the LATTER DAYS, and I will

240

bring thee against my land, that the heathen may know me, when I shall be sanctified in thee, O Gog, before their eyes. (18) And it shall come to pass at the same time when Gog shall come against the land of Israel, saith the Lord GOD, that my fury shall come up in my face. (19) For in my jealousy and in the fire of my wrath have I spoken, surely in that day there shall be a great shaking in the land of Israel; (20) So that the fishes of the sea, and the fowls of the heaven, and the beasts of the field, and all creeping things that creep upon the earth, and all the men that are upon the face of the earth, shall shake at my presence, and the mountains shall be thrown down, and the steep places shall fall, and every wall shall fall to the ground. (21) And I will call for a sword against him throughout all my mountains, saith the Lord GOD: every man's sword shall be against his brother. (22) And I will plead against him with pestilence and with blood; and I will rain upon him, and upon his bands, and upon the many people that are with him, an overflowing rain, and great hailstones, fire, and brimstone." (Ezek. 38:16-22)

The prophet also added this little excerpt about the ignominy heaped upon the Northern Alliance because of the destruction of their armies in their passage to Israel

"Thou shall fall upon the mountains of Israel, thou, and all thy bands, and the people that is with thee: I will give thee unto the ravenous birds of every sort, and to the beasts of the field to be devoured. (5) Thou shall fall upon the open field: for I have spoken it, saith the Lord God." (Ezek. 39: 4-5)

And we also have this account by the prophet Joel as he summarized that ill-fated expedition on their way to Jerusalem. The first sentence of which seems to be a warning to the Beast that the Russian forces will not be able to reach the staging area before the deadline.

"But I will remove far off from you the northern army, and will drive him into a land barren and desolate, with his face toward the east sea, and his hinder part toward the utmost sea, and his stink shall come up, and his ill savor shall come up, because he hath done great things." (Joel. 2:20)

241

CHAPTER 19

Mystery- Babylon

Once again the earth has been shaken by the Lord, and there is no sanctuary from the pitching and violence that exuded from the earthquakes and the elements. On the continents, great sections of the mountain ranges settled into the plains, and in the oceans, towering tidal waves swept their course, racing over and devouring island barriers and coastal cities in their path like great whales in a school of herring. But after three days the elements were finally drained of their madness and sank into silence and oblivion, leaving only the legions of fires to pillar their grievance to the skies. And with the undoing of the upheaval, the finery of the long day was allowed to settle anew over the ravaged earth while the glistening sun stripped the darkness away to reveal the devastation of a subdued planet.

Myriads of cities around the world have been stripped of their magnificence and devoid of their affectation, but none has suffered like the one referred to in scripture as the 'great Babylon.' And it was not because of her architectural beauty or the particular sagaciousness of the inhabitants that she was selected for this notoriety, but for the odd distinction of allowing herself to become the earthly stronghold of the enemy of God. Of all the other cities on the earth, John relates, she alone *'came up in God's remembrance, and unto her was given the cup of the wine of the fierceness of His wrath.'* (Rev.16: 19)

Through the scriptures, we become painfully aware that over the centuries this city had succored an obsequious spiritual relationship with Satan, who in the past had made his earthly throne there with the Vatican as his footstool, a situation for which she is now being rewarded. But in her supposedly finest hour, and adorned as she is with the great image of the Beast in the square of St. Peter, she had reached her total degradation.

In his journal, John reveals in poignant figurative language the terrible indictment that God had laid on the city of Rome because of her abominable existence, wherein, he says, she has forever glorified herself within by allowing the "kings" of the earth to dine sumptuously from her fares and array themselves in her finest robes of purple and scarlet, with adornments of precious stones and gold, while nurturing those without with the wine of her adulterous gospel of Christ. In her infidelity, John reiterates, she is being doubly rewarded according to her works, and the cup of her fornication which she has so long been giving forth, has been returned to her double. (Rev. 18:6)

In speaking of the judgment that God has passed upon this city, John tells us that in her heyday she sat as a queen over the peoples of the earth, dispensing the Lord's eternity as her own, and for this she will now receive the judgment of her fornication, with death and devastation as her end. And when she is destroyed, all of the nations of the earth will be plunged into mourning by the smoke of her burning. Her hour of judgment has come, and she has been made desolate. The light of the gospel will no longer shine in her, nor will the voice of the Lord or the sound of the saints be heard in her, for she has been laid waste and her seven hills made barren.

Such are the censures proclaimed by a jealous and vengeful God who has chosen to inculcate the city of Rome with the judgments against the Roman church which it has fostered throughout the centuries.

But how wrong was the Roman church, you might ask, and in what respect did her ministry differ from other religions that have abused the word of God, that He would select that church and its harboring city over all other religions and cities to suffer His damnation in the great earthquake? And by what standard was the city of Rome compared to ancient Babylon in the desert, which He also destroyed from the earth?

The answers to these questions lies in the city's unique situation of embracing Satan's throne and his seat of authority despite the Lord's repeated warnings to her that persisting in that relationship would mean her desolation in the tribulation. Instead of heeding His warning in the beginning, and separating herself from the pagan idolatry, the union between the Devil and the Roman Church forged stronger until finally she acquiesced to becoming the habitation of devils. Moreover, the Lord is not averse to destroying any such

243

habitations. He has deemed that her end would serve as a fitting epitaph for a city that had chosen, as her ancient predecessor did, to become the citadel of the father of sin and the stronghold of his authority. And though many noble cities of the world will crumble in the great earthquake, including the Holy city of Jerusalem, John attests that none will suffer the wrath of God in such total devastation.

When the end of the city does come, no one will be more shocked than John, who was allowed to witness beforehand the incredible demise of that great city and the annihilation of the evil spirit forces that emanated from the throne of Satan. This was done by yet another great and powerful angel whose visible workings of destruction astounded him.

He watched in utter amazement as the angel descended over the city in a brilliant aura that outshone the sun, and in the Glory of his presence every building and habitation trembled and fell to the ground. And when the dust had settled the city was gone from its place, and only the nakedness of her seven hills remained, echoing back the words of the angel:

"Babylon the great is fallen, which was once the habitation of demons, and the stronghold of every foul spirit, and a cage of every unclean and hateful bird. For all nations have drunk of the wine of the wrath of her fornication, and the kings of the earth have committed fornication with her, and the merchants of the earth are waxed rich through the abundance of her delicacies." (Rev.18: 2)

And with these words of condemnation still ringing from his lips, the angel took up a great millstone and cast it far out into the sea, saying as he did:

"Rejoice over her destruction, thou that are in heaven and you holy apostles and prophets; for God hath avenged you on her. Thus with violence shall that great city Babylon be thrown down, and shall be found no more at all." (Rev. 18: 21)

And when he had finished his work, the land and the sea calmed, then out of the stillness came the voice of yet another angel calling to John; *"Come, and I will show you the reason for this judgment of the great city that held such power over the peoples of the world."* (Rev. 17:1)

And with this, the angel carried John away to a place in the wilderness, where he was confronted by a repulsive scene that the angel would use to explain the previous revelation. This time the vision before John was that of a woman who was seated on the back of a hideous looking beast which had seven heads and ten horns. The beast was similar to one that he had seen before, but was made even more grotesque by having seven heads instead of one.

But for the moment it was the woman that riveted his attention because of her diabolical appearance. There she sat, straddled on the back of the hideous beast while being arrayed from head to toe in purple and scarlet robes, and richly adorned with jewelry of gold precious stones and pearls. In one hand she held a golden cup that she had obviously been drinking from, but which still remained full and spilling over of its contents.

When she turned her head toward John, he first saw the words written across her forehead, *"Mystery, Babylon the great, the Mother of Harlots and Abominations of the Earth."* Then his eyes caught her gross inebriety and the cruel grin that came over distorted lips. John could see that the wine of her drunkenness came not from the grape, but from human blood that drooled from her lips onto her clothing and then down to the beast upon which she sat.

John was astonished at the picture in front of him, and seeing his bewilderment the angel quickly responded with;

"The beast that you see is the Deceiver, who had been in the heavens, until he was cast out and sent into the bottomless pit, from where he was brought and allowed his freedom for a short while, to live in the body of the Anti-Christ on earth."(Ref. Rev.17: 8)

And then he went from describing the beast to that of the woman:

"The woman that you see, dressed in all her fine linen of purple and scarlet, and bejeweled with precious stones and gold and pearls; that was the city that you looked upon being destroyed and swept into the sea. The seven heads on the beast before you, are the seven hills whereon the city once rested. And the potion in her cup from which she drinks is the blood of the saints and the martyrs that she has slain upon the earth. And waters beneath her are the myriad of peoples she has seduced to her ways."

245

These words and much more depicted the union between the church, the city, and the Beast, but it was to be the city that would ultimately carry the burden of the punishment for such a union.

During the formative years of the church in Rome, the secular power of the Roman state held sway over the kings of the earth, but over time the power of the state waned while the authority of the church waxed greater. The stranglehold over the kings continued through the powers of 'excommunication from the church,' but still the seat of that power was in Rome.

In earlier times the Christian fellowship had been introduced to pagan worship practices by the new converts, who, over time outnumbered the true believers. This was bad enough, but when the source of that pagan worship stepped into the picture and overshadowed them both by his deceptions and lies, from that moment on the communion between the two blossomed. Eventually his deceptive theology and the church's heresy spread throughout the western world. The angel explained this unholy union to John thusly:

"The city willingly shrouded herself with the power of Satan through the adoption of the evil hellish rites of ancient Babylon, and she perpetuated these deceptions upon great numbers of people in every nation and country, causing them to worship other gods, as the Babylon of old had done before it was destroyed." (Rev.17: 15)

Then he added, as if to explain the ten horns with the ten crowns upon them:

"The ten horns that you see on the beast are the kings of the world who first gave their loyalty to the woman, but in the last days have turned their obeisance and will to the Beast, to the ultimate destruction of the woman."

This and much more the angel spoke of, in describing the vision, revealing to John the multitude of sins for which the fury of God's judgment was deigned to come upon the city of Rome which symbolized the pagan hierarchy whose destiny had been turned over to Satan. God has remembered her iniquities, and has rewarded her with a double portion according to her works, and the city which had been immortalized as the eternal city, is destined to be utterly burned with fire and found no more on the face of the earth. (Rev.18: 8,21)

Naturally there will be a great mourning around the world at the loss of this particular citadel of their worship and devotion, but in heaven there will be rejoicing over the judgment of the 'woman,' who was corrupted through her fornication with the Devil, and espoused that corruption to all the world. (Rev. 19: 1,2)

Rome's future had also been prophesied by Jesus and recorded in His letters to the churches. In them He foretold that Rome would become the center of Babylonian worship, with the great Deceiver having his abode there, where he might overshadow the truths of God with false teachings with the full intention of deceiving the elect into idol worship. And it was early in the first century that Jesus warned the church, that if they would not repent of their deeds, the wrath of God would descend upon the city in the great tribulation. (Rev. 2: 20-24)

But while all of His words were prophetic, the content was kept to generalities because the Revelation was yet in the future. But we can see in this stern warning to the church at Pergamos, that Jesus was picturing the destiny of the church that was heading in the wrong direction,

"I know thy works, and where thou dwellest, even where Satan's seat is.... where Satan dwelleth." (Rev. 2:13)

The scripture in Rev. 2:20 infers that this incursion of the spirit of Satan into the fellowship occurred first in Pergamos and then shifted to the church at Rome upon the death of the king of Pergamos. His leadership over the pagan cult was first offered to the Caesar in Rome, but when he refused the offer it was extended to Damasis, the Bishop of the early Christian Church in Rome, who considered it a great honor to accept the offer. And thus it was, that in the year 378 AD, the pagan cult of the Etruscan Order of Pergamos, with all of its Babylonian gods and deities and idol worship became ensconced in the Christian Church in Rome.

The union took on its deadliest form in the Middle Ages, when the Roman hierarchy further perverted the Gospel of Christ into the 'gospel of the Roman church,' and from then on the salvation of the soul became a prerogative of the Roman church. The Inquisitions followed, first in Europe then in the Americas until late into the eighteenth century, trying to force this distorted Roman gospel and its doctrines throughout the world while destroying millions of souls in the process.

As to why this city is considered to be synonymous with the ancient city of Babylon, it is because its pagan beliefs and practices had their origin in that ancient city, which had it's beginning soon after the flood. Nimrod, the wicked apostate great-grandson of Noah, founded the city and became its first full time minister of Satan on earth. There is folklore about Nimrod being married to a woman named Semerimus who bore him a son whom they named Tammuz, because he was supposed to be God's future savior. (Gen.3: 15) And Nimrod instituted a cult in Babylon which made both her and the son objects of divine worship, thus instituting the mother-child worship which eventually spread in one way or another around the world and continues to this day.

From Babylon the worship of the mother and son subsequently spread to Phoenicia, under the name of Ashteroth and Tammuz. From there the mother and son worship spread to Pergamos, (Rev. 2:3) and finally to Rome, where the mother-son relationship was worshipped as Venus and Cupid.

But there was another facet in the teaching of this pagan cult that pointed in the direction that the Roman church was headed. Because her child was worshipped as the son of God, the mother's position was esteemed as a better way to reach God, and she assumed the title of 'the Queen of Heaven' which is what she had always claimed to be. As such she could administer the sacraments.

Later on, the feast of Ishtar was instituted to celebrate the resurrection of her son who had supposedly been slain on a hunting trip, and was supposed to have been brought back to life forty days later. And as a commemoration of his death and resurrection small cakes were baked and marked with the letter 'T.'

As early as the ninth century BC, the nation of Israel was introduced to this pagan worship by Jezebel, the heathen wife of King Ahab, and the cult was worshipping under the name of Baal. (Ezek. 8:14) (Jer. 7:18,44:25).

And so it was no happenstance that by 64 AD, the cult of ancient Babylonian was firmly entrenched in the Roman culture, and it was in the midst of this pagan environment that Paul introduced the belief in Jesus Christ. And with each new convert from the pagan society the insidious idolatrous practices seeped ever stronger into the congregation until the predominance of the pagan cult overwhelmed the true worship of the Creator, which is why the Apostle Peter, when writing his letter to the other believers was able to preface his epistle with the salutation, *"the Church that is in BABYLON salutes you."* (I Pet. 5:13)

But the frightening part of this whole diabolical scheme of Satan, was the rapid proliferation of the Babylonian gospel beyond the bounds of the Roman Empire by the proliferation of Roman Jesuits and missionary priests. For a thousand years this 'missionary work' of the Roman church continued relentlessly with no scriptures being offered to the lay people and with the true Gospel kept hidden, until God found a man named Martin Luther, who broke out the Good News and nailed it to the church's front door, for all to see.

From the beginning, Satan had chosen to clothe himself in anonymity, as a 'mystery,' if you will, even among the inner circle of the Vatican. For that reason, the Papal church has always shrouded herself in typical mysteries, such as the mystery of "Baptismal Regeneration," the mystery of "miracles and magic," whereby simple memorials of the Lord's supper are changed by the mysterious word "Transubstantiation," from their being simple bread and wine into the literal body and blood of Christ. There are also the mysteries of "holy water," "Lights on the Altar," and "mystery plays," and other superstitious rites and ceremonies which only tends to mystify and lead to confusion, which is the meaning of Babylon, whether it's describing the Vatican today, or the ancient city in the desert which also suffered total annihilation because of its adulterous relationship with Satan.

Though it is not my intention to dwell on the issue of the two Babylons, it bears consideration to understand how the destruction of both cities follows the same remarkable pattern with all traces of the debris being removed from their location, in like manner to our modern methods of demolition by implosion of sizable buildings and the clearing of the area of all its debris.

The ancient city was born in antiquity and became the capital of the kingdom of Babylonia. It once stood on the banks of the Euphrates river near the present day city of Al Hillah, in Iraq. It developed into the religious center of the middle east, such as Mecca is today, with several temples of different cults, the most prominent of which was the Temple of Marduke. The city reached its pinnacle during the reign of Nebuchadnezzar II, BC 605 to 562.

Then followed successive sieges and battling over possession of the empire, wherein the city deteriorated and its population dispersed. Eventually the city was overthrown by the Macedonian King Alexander in the year BC 331, and according to secular records, it continued to be the headquarters of General Selucious who took over the kingdom of Babylonia in BC 323. Disdaining the old city, he had a new capital constructed on the banks of the Tigris river to the east, which he named Selucia, and in the years following, the old city fell into ruin and abandonment to the elements when the few remaining residents moved away.

But the scriptures paint a much different ending to the story.

Some 275 years before its demise the prophet Jeremiah had uttered the following warning about the city's coming destruction, and told his people to flee from its environs lest they suffer destruction with her. "Don't fall prey to her iniquity," he said, " for it is the time of the Lord's vengeance against her, and He will be avenged."

She has been a useful tool in the past to chastise the Jews and serve as a sojourn in their captivity, but now she has enslaved His people and all of the nations round about in her pagan idolatrous worship, and for this she must be destroyed. He informs the people that they may plead for her deliverance, but the schism between the city and God will not be healed, therefore they should forsake her in her time of agony and watch for her judgment from heaven.

"Flee out of the midst of Babylon, and deliver every man his soul: be not cut off in her iniquity; for this is the time of the LORD'S vengeance; he will render unto her recompense. (7) Babylon hath been a golden cup in the LORD'S hand that made all the earth drunken: the nations have drunken of her wine; therefore the nations are mad. (8) Babylon is suddenly fallen and destroyed; howl for her; take balm for her pain, if so be she may

be healed. (9) **We would have healed Babylon, but she is not healed; forsake her, and let us go every one into his own country; for her judgment reaches unto heaven, and is lifted up even to the skies."** (Jer. 51:6-9)

In further scriptures Jeremiah describes the amazing way in which the Lord destroyed and removed all traces of the city for the next twenty three hundred years.

It seems that the water table in the lowland area between the Tigris and the Euphrates, wherein the city was located, had always been rather high, but at one period the land mysteriously sank in the area, allowing a vast shallow lake to form. This 'fluidizing' of the soil beneath the city caused it to sink and disappear, which is a common phenomenon in that area of the world. Eventually the water table lowered, and what the silt hadn't covered of the city the dry drifting sand finally did and the obliteration of the city was complete. And of course, with the disappearance of the city, all traces of the religion of Bel were supposedly gone. The words of Jeremiah described the event in this way:

"... how is (the disappearance of) **Babylon become an astonishment among the nations!** (42) **The sea has come up upon Babylon: she is covered with a multitude of the waves thereof.** (43) **Her cities are** (become) **a desolation, a dry land, and a wilderness, a land wherein no man dwell, neither doth any son of man pass thereby.** (44) **And I will punish Bel in Babylon, and I will bring forth out of his mouth that which he hath swallowed up; and the nations shall not flow together any more unto him; yea, the wall of Babylon shall fall."** (Jer. 51:41-44)

But the destruction of the ancient city was somewhat of an anti-climax because the religions of Bel had already spread to other cities in close proximity to Babylon, and Satan also had moved his headquarters to Pergamos.

In the present situation, the Lord has spent a disproportionate amount of time explaining why it was necessary for Him to destroy the Vatican because it too has spread its false gospel worldwide while keeping the hub of Satan's activities in Rome. It's this dispersion of the Roman gospel that is being depicted in Revelation 18: 11-17, where their missionary Jesuits are being metaphorically described as

251

a 'sales force,' who deceptively purveys their wares to the naive peoples of the world, while portraying them as valuable merchandise for which they are expected to pay with their souls. The merchandise that is being offered is the treasure of salvation and the church rolled into one package. The list in John's journal goes on to mention all of the accoutrements of the Roman church being offered, including its priestly trappings and beautiful buildings. And it is these 'merchants' or far-flung priesthood, whom John describes in the following verses that are the ones in mourning for the loss of the great city and the Vatican.

"And the merchants of the earth shall weep and mourn over the loss of the great city; for their merchandising days are over: (12) Their merchandise of gold, and silver, and precious stones, and of pearls, and fine linen, and purple, and silk, and scarlet, and all thine wood, and all manner vessels of ivory, and all manner vessels of most precious wood, and of brass, and iron, and marble, (13) And cinnamon, and odors, and ointments, and frankincense, and wine, and oil, and fine flour, and wheat, and beasts, and sheep, and horses, and chariots, and slaves, and souls of men."

The writer then describes the reaction of these 'sales people' when they find out that they have been cut off from their source of treasures. Rome has been destroyed, along with the Vatican, and there is a great consternation among the people over its destruction, not over the city per se, but over the loss of the treasure of their salvation. Consider for a moment that 'their treasure of salvation' rested in the survival of the Roman church and now that treasure has suddenly been stripped from them. Rome no longer stands invincible.

(14) And the fruits that thy soul lusted after are departed from thee, and all things which were dainty and goodly are departed from thee, and thou shall find them no more at all. (15) The merchants of these things, which were made rich by her, shall stand afar off for the fear of her torment, weeping and wailing, (16) And saying, Alas, alas, that great city, that was clothed in fine linen, and purple, and scarlet, and decked with gold, and precious stones, and pearls! (17) For in one hour so great riches is come to naught."

The extensive list of 'wares' displayed by these merchants has oft been accepted as literal products derived from 'a new city of

Babylon' which is to be constructed in the future, and which is surmised to be a thriving new metropolis of many exported goods. This would infer that those who mourn the destruction of this new city are the merchandisers of its worldly goods and services. But the scriptures must be taken metaphorically as a description of the many 'dainties' that went along with church affiliation, and which typified the 'abundant life' that the Papal church promised the unwary adherents, but all of this, including their salvation, will be 'as a vapor' and disappear with the destruction of the 'mother' church. (V14) It's no wonder that there will be wailing and bemoaning by all believers in the Roman church at this calamity.

The Beast had taken possession of the Vatican nearly three years earlier, to serve as his headquarters and the prize location for his great image, but the 'monument' of St. Peter's Cathedral still symbolizes the heart of Catholicism to all of its adherents around the world, and the sudden annihilation of that symbol has left them totally distraught and fearful about their own eternal future. And the far-flung priesthood of the church is in dire anguish because they have nothing to offer their parishioners.

In a moment of time, the church, which has been promoted by them as the lost sinner's only way of salvation to eternity has suddenly been obliterated, and they have no place wherein to stand. The priests, who used the gospel of the church to make themselves slaveholders of the souls of men, are themselves now lost. The 'Merchandisers' have indeed sought to secure their own salvation on the bartering of precious lives based on the seduction of the lies and deceitfulness of Satan, and in this relentless pursuit they have inadvertently persuaded millions of people to follow after them and secure their eternal sanctuary in the Roman church. And now, when the end is about to come to the greatest ecclesiastical organism on earth, the Lord's voice rings out;

"Come out of her, my people, that ye be not partakers of her sins, and that ye receive not of her plagues." (Rev. 18: 4)

All heaven rejoices over the judgment of the 'great whore,' which did corrupt the earth with her fornication, and He has avenged the blood of His servants at her hand. Alleluia: (Rev. 19: 2)

CHAPTER 20

Day of the Lord

God's final challenge rings down on the Beast from the ramparts of heaven even as a Great Angel heralds the momentous appearance of our magnificent Lord descending through the clouds to engage in the most decisive battle ever fought over possession of the earth. It is to be a deadly confrontation between the Lord God Almighty and Satan, and the battleground is Jerusalem.

Long before daybreak the endless columns of troop carriers snaked through mountains of Samaria bringing the armies of the Beast to Jerusalem. The light tanks and armored vehicles made their own course over the fields, and all coming together near the old settlement of Shechem, just as the sun swept the shadows out of the valley. Meanwhile, the Beast and his small staff went by helicopter into the airfield north of the city, where they completed the plans for the deployment of the troops that were expected shortly.

Though not a big man, he stood taller than most of those surrounding him and his stature alone seemed to command an inner confidence to those who served under him. While waiting, he strode some dozen yards away from the group before stopping to survey the half circle of the horizon to the south through his field glasses. After a few moments he lowered the glasses, but continued to stare into space, deep in thought and oblivious to the impatience of the officers behind him It seemed as though he was trying to determine the future battle, and what would be its outcome. His face didn't show the fears that were beginning to surface, fears that were common to men going into battle but never before experienced by an angel facing a physical death. His thoughts began to slip back to eternity past when he had relished the peace of heaven, the praises of God, and his power in the universe. Millions of attendant angels did his every bidding, which suffused his pride of notability in creation, but it also became his undoing. His jealousy of the Creator festered into open rebellion, the consummation of which was his being cast out of heaven and bound

254

to the earth, where he is now cursed with the restrictions of a mortal, stripped of his great wisdom and powers, and facing death and ignominy.

Anger swells up within him and he raises a clenched fist to God in one last mocking gesture while cursing Him for the situation he is in. And at that moment, the rising clouds of dust and the noise of the vehicles in the distance brought him back to reality and he spun on his heel and strode defiantly back to the jeep.

Meanwhile, the visions of the destruction of the Roman church were over and John was drawn back in heaven where he heard the overwhelming jubilant sounds of millions of people raising their voices of praise to God over the destruction of the late Babylon. Over and over, the praises of Alleluia, Salvation, and Glory and Honor are made to the Lord our God, while the twenty four elders and the four beasts, knelt before the Throne. And the voice of our Lord responds to the praise, with **"Glorify the Father."**

John scans the great multitude before him, and tears flow down his cheeks as he sees old and dear brothers in the Lord surrounding the Throne, while further out in the crowd are scores of dear Christian friends. And there amongst the crowd are the many prophets and priests and kings and notable women from the past, and all with the same joy in their hearts, and thanksgiving and praise on their lips.

John might have been so overcome with the festivities that he forgot what he was there for, so one of the Elders came over to remind him, and smiling he said,

"Write John." "For these are the blessed which are called unto the marriage supper of the Lamb, and it is for this marriage occasion that we are all here."

John was overwhelmed by the joyous occasion and fell to his knees before the Elder, but the moment he did so, he was cautioned by these words, *"Do not give me your honor, I am your brother and fellow servant. Worship God."*

Through John's eyes we are witnessing the event of that Blessed Hope of all believers, the joy of being in heaven and taking part in the fellowship and reunion of all of the saints at the wedding of the Lamb and His bride.

255

The praises that were ringing out from the multitude of peoples were almost indescribable. John heard what he could only describe as a voice of a great multitude that sounded like the thundering of a great waterfall which roared through the heavens in a chorus of *"Alleluias: for the Lord God omnipotent reigneth."*

And throughout heaven the host of saints and angels gather in the Throne room for the Wedding. The saints are all dressed in fine white clothing and the Bride is adorned in the finest of linen, for *"To her it was granted that she should be arrayed in fine linen, clean and white: for the finest of linen portrays the righteousness of His Bride.* (Rev 19: 6-8)

When the marriage ceremony and the supper had ended, the preparations were made for the departure of the Lord and His Bride to the earth, only instead of a "honeymoon" trip; it will be to the battleground of the enemy. The Day of the Lord has arrived, and though He has often pondered this decisive moment, not with apprehension or fear of its outcome, as the Devil may, but over the warrant of slaying so many people on earth. John pictures Him in His reticence, sitting on a cloud hovering over the earth, and in His right hand He is holding the apocalyptic harvester's sickle, while in the other He holds the scroll of the judgments. On His head there is a golden crown, reminding us of his recent coronation, when He became King of Kings in heaven. (Rev. 14:14)

Now, as He is preparing to go forth and while yet looking down upon the earth, there is that same showing of reluctance at the job set before Him, and the Father sends an angel to hearten and prompt Him in His task. Now another angel is seen who also carries a sickle, and he is waiting to assist in the harvest. And still another comes, one who had been responsible for keeping the fire on the altar in the temple. He came to the angel with the sickle and directed him to go forth to the earth and bring the armies of the Beast to the battleground. (Rev.14:15-17)

Meanwhile, the trumpets have been sounding throughout heaven, not only to declare the Lord's departure to the battle, but to call all of the saints and the host to His side, and when all was in readiness the gates of Heaven were swung open, and the Lord emerges, sitting astride a magnificent white stallion. This was a strange new picture of the Son of God to one who had never seen the Lord on a horse before, but after staring so long, John hurriedly attempts to describe this new warrior before him, from the flaming bright eyes and the many crowns upon His head, to His brilliant red outer cloak over His girded loins where hung a large glistening double-edged sword thrust through a golden sash around His thighs. And on the sash were inscribed the words *King of Kings, and Lord of Lords.*

This vision of the Son of God astride a magnificent white stallion was a far cry from the sight of the humble Son of Man who rode a donkey up that palm-strewn path to Jerusalem. Now He is clothed as the King of all Power and Glory, and it is this grand and glorious personage which the Devil and his armies will see when He draws down to the battlefield facing them.

Following closely behind in the procession came the Bride, all riding white horses, and still dressed in their fine white linen, coming as witnesses, but having no part in the battle ahead. And surrounding the Bride is the host of angels that will take part in the harvest, though not to engage in battle. Such is the assemblage of this glorious appearing; in whose radiance the sun pales in comparison. (Matt 24:27-30) (Joel 3:11-15)

The Day of the Lord is here, and on the earth the drum roll of welcome is proclaimed by thunder and lightning and ominous dark clouds surrounding the earth. Then suddenly the brilliance of the Lord's presence pierces the clouds and bathes the battle ground in light. Those on the battlefield are awestruck with fear as they see the figure descending on the crest of the Mount of Olives before them. And as His feet touch the crest, the mountain gives way beneath, as though shying from His presence. And in the same moment the ground beneath the armies of the Beast shudders as though an earthquake lay below, and fear grew in all. The mountain the Lord stood on began to split in two, from east to west until a new large valley was formed where the mountain once stood. And there in the midst of the valley was the glowing white-robed figure of the Lord slowly walking toward the enemy who by now were in complete

257

disarray and terrified by what they have just seen. There was total bedlam throughout the regiments of soldiers and thousands attempted to flee. The lead columns have been stalled in their tracks because of fear and indecision, and the ones behind are being impelled to go forward by the angel. (Zech 14:4)

"To battle," came the orders of the Beast, "He is the enemy."

And suddenly the mass of soldiers leaps to the command and presses forward, spreading out around the figure before them and firing their weapons at Him.

The Lord waited as they drew closer, standing with His hand on the hilt of the sword as though in hesitation to draw it forth. The Beast saw this hesitation and wrongly translated His inaction as uncertainty on what to do, which in turn encouraged the Beast to impel the troops forward even faster.

But in those moments, the Lord has been searching the hearts of these men racing toward Him, and what He saw was men who had given their souls to the Beast and have become his sons in the process. And being his sons they will reap his inheritance, and with that He raises His massive sword to provide them their estate.

The masses continue to press forward into the valley and surround the lone figure, but like fuel being thrown into a hungry furnace the helpless soldiers are now being slain, row upon row of them, and the heap of falling corpses grows deeper and deeper.

There seems to be no let-up in the mad rush to destruction; no quarter is given on either side. And still the command of the Beast resounds to the troops; *"He must be taken at all cost!"* But the terrible cost is mounting quickly as the Lord strides swiftly through and over the companies of men like a wine presser in a vat of grapes. (Rev.19: 15)

Hours run quickly together, and the day is far spent. And while the Lord continues to traverse the valley the carnage grows and the blood flows freely from streams into pools which overflow down onto the valley floor.

There is no rest or let-up in the ferocity of the battle, and the Lord becomes covered in the blood of the slain. The prophets had foretold of this happening and asked of Him at the time;

"Why have your garments become red like those who tread the grapes?"

And the answer came back from the Lord;

"Because I have trodden the winepress alone; and there was none with me: for I tread them in anger, and trample them in my fury; and their blood is sprinkled upon my garments, and stains my raiment. For it is the day of vengeance and the year of my redeemed. I looked for others, but there was none to help, and I wondered why it was not there, but my fury strengthened me and I continued alone.

And I will tread down the people in mine anger, and destroy them on the earth." (Isaiah 63:3-6 paraphrased)

It would seem as though the Lord was expecting help from some source, maybe from the angels which had accompanied Him to earth, or it may be that He was hoping that some of the enemy might have had a change of heart and stood beside Him. But in that direction, the scriptures point out that this battle is singularly of the Lord's work, and He of course realizes that there is no one to fill the gap so He fights all the harder, that by some chance the fury of His fighting might somehow persuade his enemies to quit the battle.

The one-sided battle has not abated for hours, and will not. The bodies are slowly covering every open spot of ground, and in places are piling deep with the advancing sacrifices. The scene of battle is just as the prophet Isaiah had said it would be:

"For the indignation of the LORD is upon all nations, and his fury upon all their armies: he hath utterly destroyed them, he hath delivered them to the slaughter. (3) Their slain also shall be cast out, and their stink shall come up out of their carcasses, and the mountains shall be melted with their blood. (6) The sword of the LORD is filled with blood, it is made fat with fatness, and with the blood of lambs and goats, with the fat of the kidneys of rams: for the LORD hath a sacrifice in Bozrah, and a great slaughter in the land of Idumea. (8) For it is the day of the Lord's vengeance, and the year of recompenses for the controversy of Zion." (Isaiah.34)

Here the terrible slaughter of the armies is being compared to the slaughter of fatted animals that have been offered up for sacrifice by Satan, and in the following verse the horrendous carnage of the battle is compared to a wine press, wherein grapes are tossed for the extraction of the red juice,

"And the winepress was trodden without the city, and blood came out of the winepress, even unto the horse bridles, by the space of a thousand and six hundred furlongs." (Rev. 14:20)

The daylight hours are now almost gone, but still the troops are being driven into the valley. But the numbers are so great that a new command is sent forth to the host of angels to repulse the remainder of the armies still advancing on Jerusalem. And the angels cause a plague to come over the armies, a plague that causes their flesh to be consumed away, and their eyes to be consumed in their sockets, and their tongues in their mouths. Mutiny against the Beast arises also, and in the tumult, men turn against their fellow soldiers to kill or be killed. (Zech.14: 12,14)

But the day ends, and with the end comes a stillness, the march of death is over, and those who still live fall to their knees in tears. An eerie silence permeates the valley floor and the only sound heard is from the cries of the circling vultures overhead.

The Lord stands alone and silent for several minutes in the last dimming glow of the sun that has already dipped below the horizon. Then He drops the sword at His side and slowly raises His arms to the Father in heaven and gives forth Praise and Glory to God.

"Behold it is come, and it is done, He voiced; **This is the Day, whereof I have spoken."** (Ezek 39: 8)

Epilogue

That such a physical battle could take place between the Lord and mankind is beyond our comprehension. Yet the Bible account couldn't be anymore explicit in its description of the preparations for the battle, the combatants and its specific location. Nor would the Prophets have gone to such great lengths in detailing the Lord's spectacular descent through the clouds to the earth and the splitting of the mountain as He touched it, nor would they have mentioned the blood that covered His clothing if it wasn't to persuade us of the veracity of His second coming.

Sadly, some great expositors of the Bible have managed to stretch their faith to the limit to give credence to such a battle actually taking place, and yet they hedge away from putting their stamp of approval on it. They somehow find it easier to believe that not only this battle but the whole book of Revelation is merely illustrative of a spiritual battle that exists between the forces of good and evil.

One author even describes the conflict as *"a time, when throughout Christendom the spirit of the Anti-Christ will, with the support of the State, make a final stand against a Christianity that has been loyal to the person and teachings of Christ."*

It seems, that to many, this whole episode of the battle of Armageddon has been configured to express the concept that it was the rejection of the Word that brought sin into the world, however, it was also by the Word that salvation was freely offered to men.

It has been said that this battle is not an actual physical confrontation between Satan and the Lord, but a conflict wherein the attributes of sin, anarchy, godlessness, rebellion and the repudiation of the Word of God are on one side, and the Word Himself, the Eternal and the Omnipotent is on the other. This idea perpetrates the concept that the Lord will descend from heaven alright, but only to fulfill the prophecy and destroy the enemies of God with the *'sharp sword that went out of His mouth, that with it He should smite the*

261

nation,' (Rev. 19:15)

And this time He will prove once and for all the authority of the Word through His physical presence, and with the issuance of His words will He remove the presence of sin from the world and eliminate the Anti-Christ and Satan from the earth.

This altruistic approach to the battle may satisfy the hearts of some faint-hearted Christians, but certainly not the souls of those under the Altar or the multitudes who have been martyred. None of the previous plagues have been spiritual punishments, and this last judgment is no less real. If there is no reality in one of the least of these judgments there is reality in none, and therefore no purpose for the tribulation.

Satan and the Anti-Christ have been defeated and are now at the mercy of God, who casts the Anti-Christ and the false Prophet into the lake of fire and brimstone for all eternity, while Satan is bound and returned to the bottomless pit for the next one thousand years. Now begins the cleansing of the land in preparation for the Kingdom and the Lord's judgment of the nations that have weathered the storm of the tribulation. The remnant of the Israelis who have been miraculously kept safe from all harm in the city of Petra, begin their homeward trek to assist the Lord in the cleansing of the land.

May God receive Honor and Glory in your life and soul for the Salvation He has so Graciously given you, and which in turn will bring your Redemption and Deliverance from all of His marvelous works in the coming tribulation. Amen.

THE TRIBULATION PERIOD begins with
the time of INDIGNATION or JACOB'S TROUBLE

Day 1

On **Day One** of the judgment period, the Covenant between the Arabs and Israel is initiated by the President of the European Union. (Dan 9:27)   Within minutes of the covenant's signing the seventh seal is broken in Heaven. But in the few moments between the breaking of the seal and the opening of the scroll, there were tremendous things that happened. Almost immediately, God's two Witnesses were sent down from Heaven into Israel where they would remain for the next 31/2 years to warn the populace of the coming judgments as well as proclaim the everlasting Gospel to them (Rev.11.3) Also, the Believers of the Lord on earth were removed to Heaven in what is referred to as the Rapture of the Believers.   (Rev. 8:1) (I Cor. 15:51-54) (I Thess. 4:16-17)

When the believers were safely ensconced in Heaven, the **First Trumpet judgment sounds in heaven** and the first punishment comes with the eruption of a volcano that covers a major section of Israel in ash, destroying all vegetation in that area.   Several weeks later the **Second Trumpet sounded** and the same volcano erupts again, throwing molten lava over the land of Israel and the sea.   Soon after, the **Third Trumpet also sounded** and a meteor strikes the northern area of Israel where it poisons all of the fresh water supplies. Famine begins to rear its ugly head.

Twelve months went by before the **Fourth Trumpet sounded,** which marked the time when the 24 hour days was made shorter by the Lord. In this action, a world-wide earth-shaking occurred which caused tremendous havoc over all of the earth.

The **Fifth Trumpet sound** introduces the First Woe upon the people of Israel. It is a plague of demonic spirits that indwell all but a selected few in Israel. Their invasion brings about a severe famine and pestilence that destroys one third of the population before it ends five months later. Several months later, the **Sixth Trumpet sounds,** and the Second Woe brings the Arab nations against Israel in a terrible war which lasts for nearly a year. Through this war another one-third of the Jewish population is destroyed before the fighting is finally brought to an end by the incursion of the armies of the European Union.

*The Anti-Christ arrives in Jerusalem at the close of hostilities and sets up his headquarters to ensure the peace. His presence is deeply resented by the Israelis and he is assasssinated

* With the death of the Anti-Christ, the plans of God move quickly forward. Satan is cast out of Heaven and into the bottomless pit from which he is retrieved and sent to the surface of the earth where his soul and spirit immediately incarnates the corpse of the Anti-Christ. In so doing the body is made alive again and the Beast is brought into existence. The **Seventh Trumpet sounds** and the Third Woe, which is the Devil incarnate, is loosed upon Israel in the form of the Beast. His first action after the resurrection is to have the two Witnesses executed. He then desecrates the Holy place and announces his deity to the world as well as a wholesale purge of the Jews from their homeland.

*The remaining Jews in Israel flee from the presence of the Beast in the Third Diaspora.   **Day 1260**

CHART OF THE GREAT TRIBULATION

Day 1261
*The day of Deliverance begins for the faithful new believers.
*The Beast continues his purge of Jews throughout the world after he is selected as the world community ruler. Life on earth deteriorates into chaos under his twenty-four month reign. His jealousy and wrath against God reaches its highest level when he seeks the worship of men, and as proof of their fidelity to him he does the following:
*   He constructs an image of himself for the people to worship and makes preparations to put his mark on the peoples of the world.
*   False prophet demands that the world worship the Beast or face death
*   *First Angel* gives an invitation to the world to believe in God and not the Beast.

* *Second Angel* gives a warning against accepting the mark of the Beast or the worship of him
* *Third Angel* gives a prophetic warning of the destruction of Rome and the eternal punishment for those who worship the Beast.

As the twenty-four month period comes to an end, God prepares to unleash the Vial judgments upon the Gentile nations of the earth.

The Vial Judgments

The **First Vial is poured out** and boils and ulcerated sores appear on the Gentile peoples of the world The **Second Vial is poured out** and the oceans and lakes become mysteriously devoid of edible fish, which initiates a world-wide famine. When the **Third Vial is poured out**, all of the rivers and streams become contaminated and unsuitable either for human use or irrigation purposes, increasing the pressure of starvation. Then the **Fourth Vial is poured out** and the world experiences excessive heat, which coupled with the water shortage further destroys all food sources and increases the famine level on all peoples. The **Fifth Vial** brings about a certain reprieve from the heat, and the water is made pure again, but now the world is plunged into frigid weather conditions and continual darkness, further destroying all food producing crops.

After weeks of darkness and frigid weather the cycle of famine inducing plagues is brought to an end and the sun is again allowed to shine through. The world is now readied for the **Sixth Vial to be poured out,** which signals the Beast to begin preparations for his final war against God. The armies from around the world are gathered in the Valley of Megiddo, and when all is in readiness for the coming battle, the **Seventh Vial is poured out** and the second great earthshaking takes place. The Beast hurriedly brings his troops into position in Jerusalem and readies for the battle of Armageddon which takes place on the last day of the tribulation period. The battle is hard fought between the Lord himself and the vast forces of the Beast, but the Lord single handedly defeats the enemy in one long day called the Day of the Lord.   **Day 2520**

About the Author

Until his retirement in 1996, D. G. Bell had earned a living for his family in the aeronautical engineering field and later on in the home construction business. He has been a Christian believer since 1956 and since that time has been active in the teaching ministry within the Baptist denominational churches that he has attended. This same ministry became an important source of his end-time knowledge, but with it all, the whole story of the Tribulation period eluded him, as it has others, until he was visited by the Holy Spirit whose several sessions provided him with the material for this book.

ISBN 1553695461